D1364151

PLAIN FORMS

Plain forms are used in a number of sentence patterns.

PART OF SPEECH	TENSE		PLAIN FORM
VERB	present	affirmative	書(か)く
		negative	書(か)かない
	past	affirmative	書(か)いた
		negative	書(か)かなかった
-*I* ADJECTIVE	present	affirmative	大(おお)きい
		negative	大(おお)きくない
	past	affirmative	大(おお)きかった
		negative	大(おお)きくなかった
-*NA* ADJECTIVE	present	affirmative	便利(べんり)だ
		negative	便利(べんり)ではない
	past	affirmative	便利(べんり)だった
		negative	便利(べんり)ではなかった
NOUN + です	present	affirmative	本(ほん)だ
		negative	本(ほん)ではない
	past	affirmative	本(ほん)だった
		negative	本(ほん)ではなかった

THE FOUR CONNECTIVE PATTERNS

Present-affirmative *-na* adjectives and nouns + です follow four connective patterns when directly preceding conjunctive and sentence-final expressions.

PATTERN	*-NA* ADJ	NOUN + です	EXPRESSION
BASIC PATTERN	便利(べんり)だ	本(ほん)だ	と言(い)っていました。
			そうです。(hearsay)
			から (reason)
			と (conditional)
なので **PATTERN**	便利(べんり)な	本(ほん)な	んです。
			ので
			のに
NOUN-MODIFYING PATTERN	便利(べんり)な	本(ほん)の	noun
			とき
			よう
			はず
			ため（に）
でしょう **PATTERN**	便利(べんり)	本(ほん)	でしょう。
			だろうと思(おも)います。
			か
			かどうか
			かもしれません。
			なら
			みたい
			らしい

JAPANESE FOR BUSY PEOPLE III

JAPANESE FOR BUSY PEOPLE

Revised 3rd Edition

III

Association for Japanese-Language Teaching
AJALT

KODANSHA INTERNATIONAL
Tokyo • New York • London

The Association for Japanese-Language Teaching (AJALT) was recognized as a nonprofit organization by the Ministry of Education in 1977. It was established to meet the practical needs of people who are not necessarily specialists on Japan but wish to communicate effectively in Japanese. In 1992 AJALT was awarded the Japan Foundation Special Prize. AJALT maintains a website at www.ajalt.org, through which they can be contacted with questions regarding this book or any of their other publications.

Illustrations by Shinsaku Sumi.

CD narration by Yuki Minatsuki, Takako Suzuki, Yuri Haruta, Koji Yoshida, Tatsuo Endo, Sosei Shinbori, and Howard Colefield.

CD recording and editing by the English Language Education Council, Inc.

PHOTO CREDITS: © Sachiyo Yasuda, 2, 47, 231, 244.

Distributed in the United States by Kodansha America, Inc., and in the United Kingdom and continental Europe by Kodansha Europe Ltd.

Published by Kodansha International Ltd., 17–14 Otowa 1-chome, Bunkyo-ku, Tokyo 112–8652, and Kodansha America, Inc.

ISBN 978-4-7700-3011-5

First published 1990
Second edition 1995
Third edition 2007
15 14 13 12 11 10 09 08 07 10 9 8 7 6 5 4 3 2 1

www.kodansha-intl.com

CONTENTS

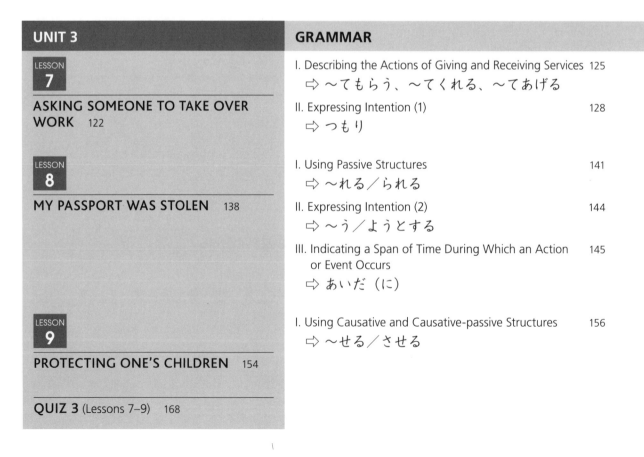

COMMUNICATIVE SKILLS	READING & WRITING

UNIT 4

GRAMMAR

UNIT 5

GRAMMAR

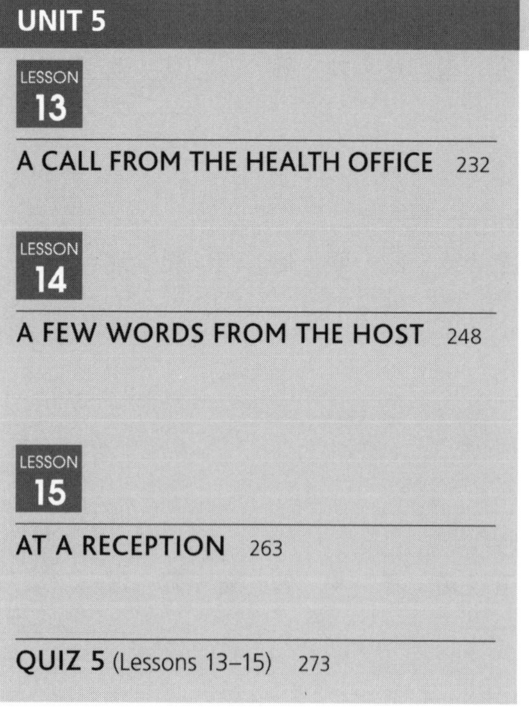

PREFACE TO THE REVISED 3RD EDITION

For busy working adults, progressing to the next step beyond "survival Japanese" is not easy. Books II and III of the *Japanese for Busy People* series were first published in 1990 for learners seeking intermediate to advanced proficiency in Japanese. Yet even with the aid of these volumes, many people still found it difficult to master complicated Japanese syntax and vocabulary in the few hours they had available outside of other commitments. Over the years, we at AJALT have continued to look for new ways to help learners overcome this barrier, and in the process we have developed and implemented numerous improvements to our lesson plans and supplementary teaching materials. Such experience is put to full use in this extensively revised edition of *Japanese for Busy People III*, designed to better enable adult learners to pursue their study of Japanese to the point of intermediate fluency.

Japanese for Busy People III, Revised 3rd Edition incorporates many new ideas developed carefully over time by AJALT instructors. We hope that busy people will find this textbook an enjoyable tool for learning Japanese.

Acknowledgments for *Japanese for Busy People III* (1990)

Four AJALT teachers wrote this textbook. They are Miyako Iwami, Shigeko Miyazaki, Masako Nagai, and Kimiko Yamamoto. They were assisted by two other teachers, Kumiko Endo and Chikako Ogura.

Acknowledgments for *Japanese for Busy People III, Revised Edition* (1995)

We would like to express our gratitude to the following People for Preparing the new editions of Books II and III: Miyako Iwami, Shigeko Miyazaki, Masako Nagai, and Kimiko Yamamoto. They were assisted by Mikiko Ochiai.

Acknowledgments for *Japanese for Busy People III, Revised 3rd Edition*

Japanese for Busy People III, Revised 3rd Edition was written by AJALT instructors Emiko Arai, Yuko Harada, Kaori Hattori, Reiko Sawane, Junko Shinada, and Emiko Yamamoto with assistance from Mariko Mishima, Makiko Nakano, Mikiko Ochiai, Naoko Takatori, Shigeyo Tsutsui, Miyako Utsumi, Yoriko Yoshida, and Tetsunosuke Sakurada.

INTRODUCTION

Aims

Japanese for Busy People III, Revised 3rd Edition is designed to enable learners who worked through Books I and II to complete their mastery of beginning Japanese and progress smoothly into the intermediate level.

Book I covered "survival Japanese" for getting through common everyday situations. Book II taught learners skills for conversing about their present and past lives and other personal topics with people around them at work and elsewhere. Book III will equip learners to talk meaningfully about larger social topics by expressing their own opinions while asking others for theirs. It will also treat language needed for dealing with fairly sophisticated business situations.

Furnished with extensive explanations, CD recordings, exercises, and answers, the book is fit for both instruction in the classroom and self-study.

Major Features of *Japanese for Busy People III, Revised 3rd Edition*

Learners who completed Books I and II should already be able to converse about a significant range of things in Japanese, if not entirely perfectly. In Book III, their goal will be to further improve the naturalness and efficiency of their communication in the language. Toward this end, the book introduces conjunctive and sentence-final expressions for conveying a wide variety of meanings. Also covered are passives, causatives, expressions for the giving and receiving of services, and other constructions distinctive to Japanese. Finally, the book discusses politeness, writing and speech styles, and other things learners will need to know to adjust their language according to situation and audience.

Up through Book II, the lessons were designed so that learners could practice using the language presented immediately in their own speech. Since the dialogues and examples in Book III are considerably longer and more complex than in previous volumes, however, for this book learners should first work toward getting themselves to recognize and understand new expressions whenever they are encountered instead of trying to apply them right away.

Like Book II, Book III is divided into five units consisting of three lessons each. The themes and objectives of the units are as follows.

Unit 1

The theme is "human-animal relationships." Through content dealing with recent pet trends, the future of the pet industry, and other animal-related topics, learners will be introduced to expressions for remarking on things they notice, offering conjectures, reporting information, and making comments. In this way, they will gain the skills to initiate conversations about things or events they come across in daily life. By the end of the unit, learners will also be able to join in on conversations about topics that interest them.

Unit 2

An interview with the owner of an organic farm and passages about global warming form the heart of this unit, focused on the theme "humans and nature." Here learners will encounter expressions for seeking information about facilities, institutions, and people as well as for stating their own opinions about issues. In this way, they will gain the skills to conduct even quite complicated inquiries on their own just as long as they make the right preparations.

Unit 3

This unit takes up episodes involving crime, discussions over childrearing issues, and other content related to the theme "crime and education." Learners will become familiar with expressions for describing the giving and receiving of services, for reporting on the details of damage done to them, and for talking about coercion. In this way, they will gain the skills to efficiently characterize participants' involvement in and attitudes toward the events around them.

Unit 4

Organized around the theme of "conducting business," this unit shows how to carry out formal business exchanges, give and relay messages, and deal with other work-related concerns. Covered will be ways of giving greetings, showing gratitude, making apologies, reporting information, and passing on messages through expressions proper to the circumstances at hand. While the unit does outline the basic characteristics of honorific language, emphasis is placed on familiarizing learners with often-used expressions that can be combined with the *desu/masu* style to produce the appropriate register. At the other end of the scale, the unit also treats casual Japanese used among close friends and family.

Unit 5

This unit provides a comprehensive review of everything covered in beginning-level Japanese, from books I through III.

Lesson 13 gives learners one final practice in listening to spoken Japanese and then summarizing what they were able to understand in their own words.

Lesson 14 takes a final look at formal speech and writing, starting with some basic patterns for delivering a speech in a formal setting. It then turns to writing to explain how to give and respond to invitations to parties and other events. Sample texts range from a highly formal letter exemplifying established protocols to exchanges of e-mail.

Lesson 15 presents some final points about conversational Japanese, drawing on examples of "party talk" to illustrate how to initiate and wrap up social exchanges.

The Structure of the Lessons and How to Approach Each Part

As already mentioned, each of the five units listed above is divided into three lessons. The lessons, in turn, are organized into the following parts:

Target Dialogue
Grammar & Pattern Practice
Practice (1, 2, 3 . . .)
Kanji Practice

Target Dialogue. The Target Dialogues (for some lessons there is a Target Reading instead) in Book III are written to be slightly more difficult than what is usually provided at the beginning level. In Book II, the expectation was that once learners finished a lesson, they would be able to converse at the same level as in the Target Dialogue for that lesson.

By contrast, in Book III the goal set for most learners is to reach the point not where they completely master the Target Dialogue but where they grasp it well enough to be able to answer questions about it after reading or listening to it.

First listen to the dialogue. Although you will probably not get all of it, there are bound to be at least some parts that you can get. Try sorting out what you were or were not able to comprehend. Even native speakers might not always grasp everything that was said if they lack the necessary background information, the speaker did not enunciate clearly, or there was a lot of noise; in such cases, often what they do is to reconstruct the whole by using what they did get to ask questions about and fill in the missing parts. For your first time with the Target Dialogue, it will be sufficient only to make sure that what you think it says is indeed correct. Do not spend time forcing yourself to figure out the parts you did not understand. Simply set them aside for the time being and return to the dialogue after completing the lesson. By then it should begin to make sense.

Grammar & Pattern Practice. This section introduces the lesson's key sentence patterns and offers exercises for trying them out or otherwise internalizing them.

The conjunctive or sentence-final expressions covered in Book III (see Contents for examples) include many with confusingly similar meanings. Where one expression overlaps in function with another discussed earlier, the text duly notes this and sets out the distinctions between them. Pay attention to the expressions as they are used in the Target Dialogue and other examples to see how they fit the explanations given. See also the front endpapers.

Practice. Each lesson comes with several Practice sections made up of Word/Phrase Power and/or Speaking Practice. (Lessons 7, 12, 13, and 14 also have Reading Practice.)

The Word/Phrase Power section groups together words and/or phrases important to talking about the theme for the lesson. Read each item aloud while making sure you understand what it means. Do not try to memorize everything; instead, concentrate on the vocabulary you think might be useful to you, familiarizing yourself with them until you can say them without referring back to the list.

The Speaking Practice section presents several sample dialogues related to the theme of the lesson that are written to be a little less advanced than the Target Dialogue. First listen to each dialogue on the CD, then read and make sure you understand what it says. Refer to the English for any vocabulary you do not recognize. Pick out the new constructions featured in the lesson, paying attention to how they are used within the context of the conversation.

If you have a practice partner, try conducting conversations with that partner using what you learned in the Grammar & Pattern Practice and Practice sections. There is no need to adhere closely to the models provided in the Speaking Practice. If the aim is to talk about recent fashions and trends, for example, then freely express your own opinions and thoughts based on what you have observed in real life out in the streets or through the media.

If you do not have a partner, write down what you might want to say or ask should you have someone to practice with. Take note of anything you cannot figure out how to say. Keep this list and get into the habit of thinking about it whenever you have an opportunity to ask someone or you encounter similar expressions elsewhere in the text.

Kanji Practice. The Kanji Practice for each lesson features ten kanji (150 in total) selected mostly from the Target Dialogue. Weight is given to kanji taken up in level 3 of the Japanese-Language Proficiency Test. Once you master the kanji in Books II and III, you will have covered all the characters needed for this test.

As in Book II, the basic meaning(s) of each kanji are given in English below the character, usage examples and writing instructions to the right of it. The examples are all drawn from vocabulary taken up in Books I through III. Occasionally a word will be given before it appears in the main text, however, and for these you should consult the glossary at the back of the book. Printed below each example are the readings (*furigana*) for the kanji, which in this text are given all in hiragana.

Adjectives and verbs are listed in their dictionary forms with verbal suffixes (*okurigana*) provided in hiragana.

The writing instructions come with numbers to indicate the order of strokes and arrows to indicate direction. Take care to write each kanji exactly in the way that is prescribed.

Note about Kanji

We have provided *furigana* for all kanji appearing the text, regardless of whether their readings have been previously introduced, so as to accommodate learners who choose not to memorize kanji or who wish to learn the characters presented in this text at a more leisurely pace.

Kanji rather than kana are given for all words normally written in kanji once the characters that make up the word in question have been introduced. For example, the characters 最 and 近, which form the word 最近, are both introduced in Lesson 1, so from that lesson onward these kanji, 最 and 近, are used instead of hiragana whenever the word 最近 comes up.

Beyond that, kanji also appear in such elements as titles, proper names, signs, and set phrases used in invitations and other formal writing, regardless of whether the characters that comprise the word or words have been introduced. These kanji are presented for recognition purposes only.

Introducing the Cast

John Mills (35 years old), a Canadian, is a member of ABC Foods' sales department. He is single.

Mike Smith (32 years old), an American, is an attorney for ABC Foods. He is single.

Marie Martin (25 years old) is from Paris, France. A member of ABC Foods' sales department, she used to live in Japan as an exchange student.

Shika Chandra (30 years old) is a member of ABC Foods' systems department. She is from Mumbai, India.

Keiko Sasaki (53 years old), a Japanese, is the manager of ABC Foods' sales department. She is married and has a daughter, Aiko.

Akira Kato (46 years old), a Japanese, is the section chief of ABC Foods' sales department. He is married and has a son, Taro.

Mayumi Nakamura (26 years old), a Japanese, works as a secretary to Ms. Sasaki. She is single.

Daisuke Suzuki (24 years old), a Japanese, is a member of ABC Foods' sales staff. He is single.

Mei Chan (30 years old) is from Hong Kong. She works in ABC Foods' sales department. She is single.

Frank Green (56 years old), an American, is the president of the Tokyo branch of ABC Foods. He lives in Tokyo, with his wife.

Michiyo Kato (45 years old) is Akira Kato's wife. Her hobby is tea ceremony. She loves traditional Japanese art and has a deep interest in environmental issues.

Yoichi Inuyama (42 years old) works in ABC Foods' development department. He is very knowledgeable about animals.

UNIT 1

HUMANS & PETS

Pet businesses are booming in Japan. Some people enjoy pets as part of fashion by dressing them up or by keeping unusual types, while others seek comfort from them by treating them like part of the family. Although this unit focuses on pets and animals, you should not feel yourself limited to talking about this particular aspect of Japanese society. Use the skills covered in Unit 1 to freely describe trends, changes, or anything else you notice or observe at home, at work, or while out about town. Also learn how to develop conversations by sharing information you have gained from other sources or by inviting people to think along with you on questions that concern you.

LESSON 1 A LOST PET

TARGET DIALOGUE

While at home eating dinner, the Katos notice strange sounds coming from their yard.

加藤(かとう)（妻(つま)）：ねえ。にわでへんな音(おと)がする。何(なに)かいるみたい。→p. 10

加藤(かとう)（夫(おっと)）：え？ (*listens*) ほんとだ。何(なん)だろう。→p. 8 ネコじゃない？

加藤(かとう)（妻(つま)）：しっ。ないてる。鳥(とり)みたいな声(こえ)。→p. 10

加藤(かとう)（夫(おっと)）：ネコじゃないね。ちょっと見(み)てくるよ。

加藤(かとう)（妻(つま)）：だいじょうぶ？　気(き)をつけてね。

The next day, the Katos go to show the creature they caught in their yard to Mr. Inuyama, who is knowledgeable about animals.

犬山(いぬやま)：　これはフェネックです。ふつうは北(きた)アフリカのさばくに住(す)んでいます。キツネのいっしゅで、鳥(とり)のような声(こえ)でなきます。→p. 10

加藤(かとう)（妻(つま)）：そうなんですか。でも、どうしてうちのにわにいたんでしょうか。→p. 8

犬山(いぬやま)：　たぶんどこかのおたくからにげたんでしょう。→p. 7

加藤(かとう)（夫(おっと)）：最近(さいきん)めずらしいペットをかう人(ひと)がふえているそうですね。→p. 12

犬山(いぬやま)：　ええ。ところで、どうやってつかまえたんですか。

加藤(かとう)（夫(おっと)）：にわにケージをおいて、中(なか)にキャットフードを入(い)れておい→p. 14

たんです。少(すこ)しして様子(ようす)を見(み)に行(い)ったら、中(なか)に入(はい)って食(た)べていたので、そっとケージをしめました。

加藤(かとう)（妻(つま)）：どうしたらいいでしょうか。

犬山(いぬやま)：　けいさつにれんらくしたほうがいいでしょう。→p. 7 かい主(ぬし)がとどけているかもしれません。

Mrs. Kato: Say, there are strange sounds coming from the yard. Something seems to be there.
Mr. Kato: Oh? (*listens*) You're right. What could it be? Isn't it just a cat?
Mrs. Kato: Shh. It's crying. Sounds like a bird.
Mr. Kato: It's not a cat, is it? I'll go out a bit to see.
Mrs. Kato: Are you going to be all right? Take care.

Inuyama: This is a fennec. It usually lives in the desert in North Africa. It's a type of fox and has a cry like a bird.
Mrs. Kato: Is that so? But why do you suppose it was in our yard?
Inuyama: It probably ran away from someone else's house.
Mr. Kato: From what I hear, the number of people who keep unusual pets has been growing recently, isn't that right?
Inuyama: Yes. By the way, how did you trap it?
Mr. Kato: I placed a cage in the yard and left some cat food inside it. A little later when I went to look at how things were, it had gone inside and was eating, so I closed the cage quietly.
Mrs. Kato: What do you think we should do?
Inuyama: You should probably contact the police. The owner may have reported it missing.

VOCABULARY

ねえ	say . . . , look/listen . . .
音(おと)がする	there is a sound
音(おと)	sound
みたい（な）	seem, be like (see p. 10)
何(なん)だろう	what could it be?
だろう	(plain form of でしょう; see p. 8)
ネコ	cat
じゃない？	isn't it . . . ?
しっ	shh!
なく	cry (of animal)
鳥(とり)	bird
犬山(いぬやま)	Inuyama (surname)
フェネック	fennec
ふつう	usually, normally
北(きた)アフリカ	North Africa
さばく	desert
キツネ	fox
いっしゅ	a kind (of), a type (of)
よう（な）	seem, be like (see p. 10)
でしょうか	(see p. 8)
たぶん	probably
にげる (R2)	run away, escape
めずらしい	rare, unusual
かう	keep (a pet)
そう	from what I hear, from what I understand (see p. 12)
ところで	by the way

つかまえる (R2)	trap, capture
ケージ	cage
キャットフード	cat food
～ておく	(see p. 14)
少(すこ)しして	after a little while
そっと	quietly
けいさつ	police
かい主(ぬし)	owner (of a pet)
とどける (R2)	report

NOTES

1. THE STYLE OF THE CONVERSATION

The two parts of this dialogue are spoken in different styles. The first conversation, between a couple eating dinner at home, is carried out in the plain style, while the second one, between the couple and Mr. Inuyama, is largely in the *desu/masu* style. You will study the differences between these styles in Lesson 12 (p. 215).

2. 音(おと)がする／少(すこ)しする

する, which by itself means "to do," combines with a variety of words to convey various meanings. For some examples of such する combinations grouped according to meaning, see the Usage Note on p. 6.

3. 何(なに)かいるみたい

Normally we would expect to hear です after みたい. However, as noted above, this conversation is carried out in the plain style, so instead of です we ought to hear だ. But Mrs. Kato omits だ. Women tend to omit だ, or use だわ, after nouns and *-na* adjectives in colloquial speech.

4. ネコ／鳥(とり)／フェネック／キツネ

Foreign terms such as フェネック are written using katakana, as you have already learned. In addition to these loan words, plant and animal names are often written in katakana, regardless of origin, to signify that they belong to the scientific realm or because their kanji are difficult to read. Usually in a given text there will be a policy for how plant and animal names are written, i.e., in katakana or in kanji, and the style will be consistent throughout. In this text we use kanji for the animals and plants whose kanji we teach, e.g., 鳥(とり), and katakana for all others.

5. ネコじゃない？

This utterance, spoken with a rising intonation, is a plain-style negative question equivalent to ネコではありませんか or ネコじゃないですか (both meaning roughly the same thing, with the latter being somewhat more colloquial than the former). When forming questions in plain-style speech, you can usually omit the question marker か. In asking the question ネコじゃない？, Mr. Kato, who at first thinks the animal in the yard is a cat, is looking to Mrs. Kato for agreement. His next utterance, ネコじゃないね, is a straightforward negative statement that he makes upon hearing the animal's cries and judging them to be those of a creature other than a cat.

6. ないてる

ないてる is a contraction of ないている (Book II, p. 206). The verb なく means "to cry" and is used of both humans and animals (though with different kanji).

7. どこかのおたく

Translatable as "someone else's house," どこかのおたく is used in situations like this when it is unclear where the house is or who it might belong to.

8. どうしたらいいでしょうか

In Book II (p. 218), we introduced どうすればいいですか as an expression for asking someone how to solve a problem. どうしたらいいですか is a similar expression that we also commonly use. In the example here, Mrs. Kato uses でしょうか instead of ですか to stress the feeling that she is consulting Mr. Inuyama for suggestions on what to do.

9. （～に）とどけている

とどける here is used in the sense of "to report." While the basic meaning of ～にとどける is "to deliver to," the phrase can also be applied to reporting things or submitting documents to government offices and other official bodies.

うちにビールをとどけてください。
Please deliver some beer to my house.

ひろったさいふをこうばんにとどけます。
I will take the wallet that I picked up to the police box.

クレジットカードをなくしたら、すぐこうばんとカード会社(がいしゃ)にとどけたほうがいいです。
If you lose your credit cards, you should report it to the police box and the credit card companies right away.

USAGE NOTE

noun + する

Here is an overview of the different types of noun + する combinations that you often hear in Japanese.

1. things that can be perceived through the senses + する : 音(おと)がする, 味(あじ)がする, and においがする may be translated as "I hear," "it tastes" [lit., "there is a taste"], and "it smells," respectively (see pp. 17–18).

2. period of time + する : indicates passage of an equivalent amount of time

   ３０分(さんじゅっぷん)ぐらいしてから、もう一度(いちど)電話(でんわ)をかけてみました。
   I phoned again after about thirty minutes.

3. things that can be worn on the body + する : to put on accessories, scarves, gloves, and other small items

   ネクタイをしています。 (Book II, p. 36)
   I am wearing a tie.

   さむいので、マフラーと手(て)ぶくろをしたほうがいいです。
   It's cold, so you should put on a muffler and gloves.

4. occupation をする : used in stating one's occupation

   私(わたし)はＡＢＣのべんごしをしています。
   I am a lawyer for ABC.

5. price + する : to cost

   このうでどけいはブランドもので、３００万円(まんえん)しました。
   This watch is a brand item and cost 3 million yen.

GRAMMAR & PATTERN PRACTICE

I Expressing Suppositions & Wondering Aloud

1. Using でしょう／だろう↘ with a falling intonation to express a supposition

たぶん、どこかのおたくからにげたんでしょう。
けいさつにれんらくしたほうがいいでしょう。

でしょう is one of the inflections of です. です expresses an assertion, でしょう the presence of some uncertainty. だろう is the plain-form equivalent of でしょう.

> * Present-affirmative *-na* adjectives and nouns + です follow irregular patterns when coming before expressions such as でしょう that follow plain forms. This text organizes these patterns into four types: 1) the basic pattern, 2) the なので pattern, 3) the noun-modifying pattern, and 4) the でしょう pattern. (See the front endpapers of this book.)

でしょう is used to express a supposition about future, present, or past events.

あしたはさむいでしょう。
Tomorrow will probably be cold.

１００年前(ねんまえ)の東京(とうきょう)は、夜(よる)とてもくらかったでしょう。
Nights in Tokyo a hundred years ago were probably very dark.

If something is sure to happen, you should use です／ます instead of でしょう, even if the event is still in the future.

ミルズさんはあした来(き)ます。
Mr. Mills will come tomorrow.

でしょう statements may be modified by adverbs such as きっと or たぶん to express degrees of certainty.

ミルズさんはあしたきっと／たぶん来(く)るでしょう。
Mr. Mills will definitely/probably come tomorrow.

でしょう in its plain form, だろう, may also be combined with 思(おも)う when it is necessary to clarify that what you are saying is your own speculation.

ミルズさんは休(やす)みに国(くに)に帰(かえ)るだろうと思(おも)います。
I think Mr. Mills will probably go back to his [home] country during the vacation.

VOCABULARY きっと definitely, certainly

でしょう cannot be used when talking about your own actions. In such cases, other expressions need to be used. For example:

私(わたし)は休(やす)みに国(くに)に帰(かえ)ろうと思(おも)っています。
I am thinking of going back to my [home] country during vacation.

私(わたし)は休(やす)みに国(くに)に帰(かえ)るかもしれません。
I may go back to my [home] country during vacation.

2. Using でしょう／だろう⤴ with a rising intonation to ask for confirmation

The following examples appeared in Book II:

あさってから中国(ちゅうごく)しゅっちょうでしょう。(p. 82)
You leave on a business trip to China the day after tomorrow, right?

パリからギリシャに行(い)くとき、ひこうきからとったしゃしんです。きれいなうみでしょう。(p. 139)
This is a photo I took from a plane when I went from Paris to Greece. The ocean is beautiful, isn't it?

In the first sentence, the speaker is trying to confirm something he understands to be true, while in the second he or she is seeking agreement. Both, then, are a request for confirmation and illustrate another use of でしょう.

3. Using でしょう（か）／だろう（か）⤵ with a falling intonation to ask questions of yourself or others, or to raise an issue

何(なん)だろう。
どうしてうちのにわに（フェネックが）いたんでしょうか。

Questions formed with でしょうか／だろうか are used to wonder aloud to oneself about something, or, if there is also a listener present, to simultaneously raise an issue with that person. People often omit the question marker か if the sentence already has a question word in it.

あそこにいるのはミルズさんでしょうか。
Could that be Mr. Mills over there?

会議はなかなか終わりませんね。今日は何時ごろ帰れるでしょう（か）。
The meeting just won't end, will it? When do you suppose we'll be able to go home today?

この車、いくらぐらいだろう。
I wonder how much this car costs, roughly.

何がいいでしょうか (Book II, p. 5), used to ask someone for a suggestion regarding a choice, is another example of this usage of でしょうか.

4. Using でしょうか↘ with a falling intonation to softly pose a question

でしょうか may also be used to put forward a question without sounding too direct, as in どんなふくろでしょうか (Book II, p. 32, where a salesclerk is speaking to a customer), or 課長、今、ちょっとよろしいでしょうか (Book II, p. 150, where an employee is speaking to her boss).

Complete the sentences by connecting the words in parentheses to でしょう (in part 1) or でしょうか (in part 2).

1 Expressing suppositions:

1) ひこうきより新幹線のほうが……(便利です)
2) ほとんどの人がそのニュースを……(しりません)
3) 雨で人が……から、今日ディズニーランドに行きましょう。(少ないです)
4) 新しいプロジェクトにはかなりコストが……(かかります)

2 Posing questions:

1) きょうしつのＣＤプレーヤーをこわしたのは……(だれですか)
2) 一人で旅行するのは……(きけんですか)
3) 中に何が……(入っているんですか)

VOCABULARY

ディズニーランド	Tokyo Disney Resort
かなり	rather, considerably
コスト	cost
きょうしつ	classroom
こわす	break
きけん（な）	dangerous

II Expressing Impressions (1)

1. Using よう／みたい to describe something based on your perception of it

何(なに)かいるみたい。
何(なに)かいるようです。

You use よう／みたい to state your understanding about a situation or state based on what you have actually seen, heard, felt, or otherwise perceived. よう and みたい are nearly identical in meaning and function, with the distinction being that みたい is slightly more colloquial. Both follow plain forms, with よう taking the noun-modifying pattern and みたい the でしょう pattern (see front endpapers). よう／みたい themselves conjugate like *-na* adjectives.

あかちゃんはおなかがすいているようです／すいているみたいです。
The baby seems to be hungry.

これはだれかのわすれもののようです／わすれものみたいです。
Someone seems to have left this behind. [lit., "This seems to be something that someone forgot."]

2. Using よう／みたい to make similes or figurative comparisons

鳥(とり)みたいな声(こえ)。
鳥(とり)のような声(こえ)でなきます。

よう／みたい may also be used to make similes and figurative comparisons.

ミルズさんはスーパーマンのようです。
Mr. Mills is like Superman.

このおちゃ、薬(くすり)みたいな味(あじ)がします。
This tea tastes like medicine.

グリーンさんはプロのようにゴルフが上手(じょうず)です。
Mr. Green is as good at golf as a professional player.

Using the adverb まるで intensifies the figurative feeling.

まるでゆめを見(み)ているようです。
I feel just like I'm in a dream. [lit., "It feels just as though I were seeing a dream."]

VOCABULARY

おなかがすく	get hungry
スーパーマン	Superman
あじ	taste
まるで	just like

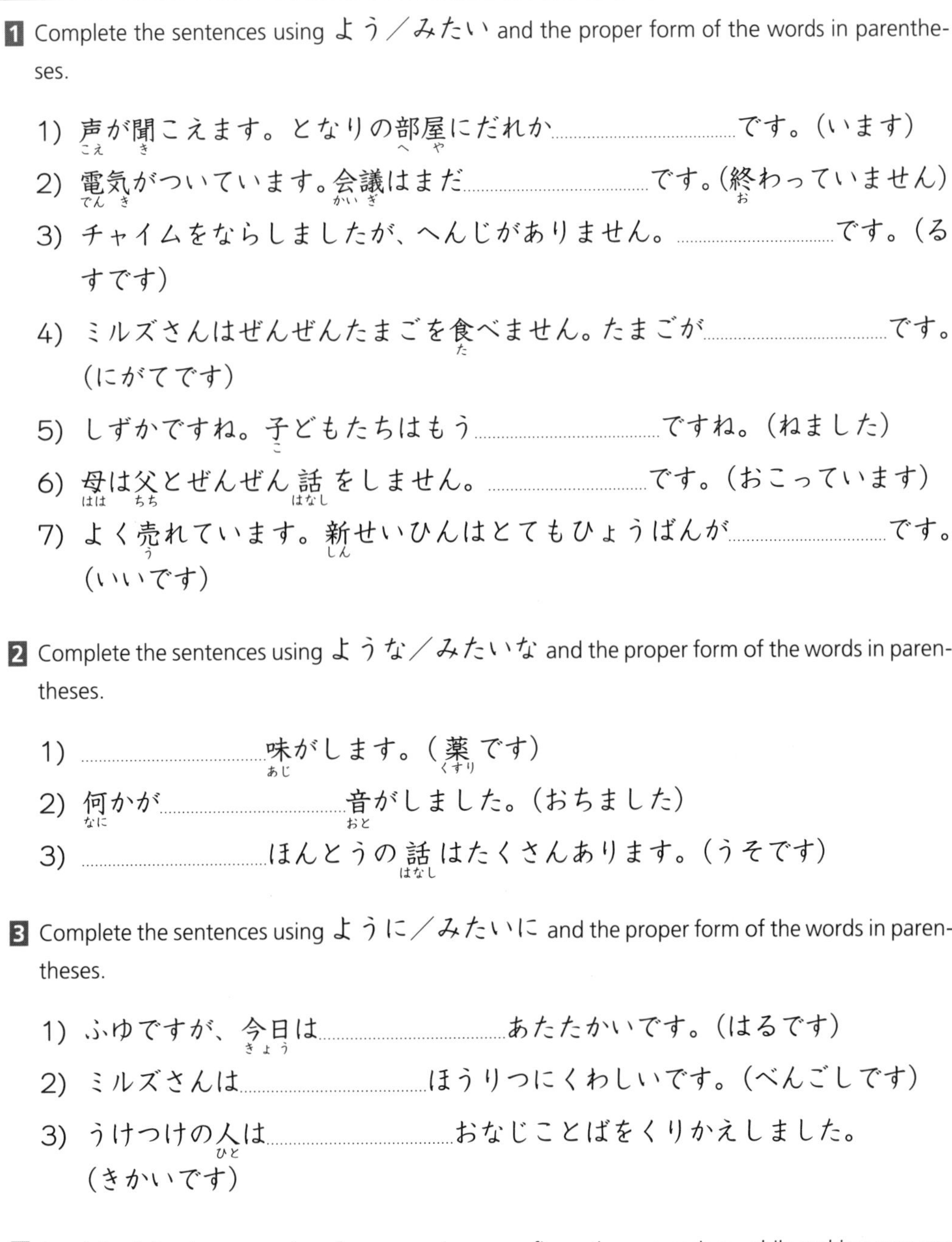

1 Complete the sentences using よう／みたい and the proper form of the words in parentheses.

1) 声(こえ)が聞(き)こえます。となりの部屋(へや)にだれか＿＿＿＿＿＿です。（います）
2) 電気(でんき)がついています。会議(かいぎ)はまだ＿＿＿＿＿＿です。（終(お)わっていません）
3) チャイムをならしましたが、へんじがありません。＿＿＿＿＿＿です。（るすです）
4) ミルズさんはぜんぜんたまごを食(た)べません。たまごが＿＿＿＿＿＿です。（にがてです）
5) しずかですね。子(こ)どもたちはもう＿＿＿＿＿＿ですね。（ねました）
6) 母(はは)は父(ちち)とぜんぜん話(はなし)をしません。＿＿＿＿＿＿です。（おこっています）
7) よく売(う)れています。新(しん)せいひんはとてもひょうばんが＿＿＿＿＿＿です。（いいです）

2 Complete the sentences using ような／みたいな and the proper form of the words in parentheses.

1) ＿＿＿＿＿＿味(あじ)がします。（薬(くすり)です）
2) 何(なに)かが＿＿＿＿＿＿音(おと)がしました。（おちました）
3) ＿＿＿＿＿＿ほんとうの話(はなし)はたくさんあります。（うそです）

3 Complete the sentences using ように／みたいに and the proper form of the words in parentheses.

1) ふゆですが、今日(きょう)は＿＿＿＿＿＿あたたかいです。（はるです）
2) ミルズさんは＿＿＿＿＿＿ほうりつにくわしいです。（べんごしです）
3) うけつけの人(ひと)は＿＿＿＿＿＿おなじことばをくりかえしました。（きかいです）

4 Read the following examples of common Japanese figurative expressions while making sure you understand what they are saying.

1) 仕事(しごと)が山(やま)のようにたくさんあって、たいへんです。
2) 新(あたら)しいコンピューターゲームはとぶように売(う)れました。
3) とてもつかれていたようで、夫(おっと)はしんだようにねていました。

VOCABULARY

チャイム	doorbell	せいひん	product	ことば	word
ならす	ring, sound	ひょうばん	reputation	くりかえす	repeat
にがて（な）	disliked, avoided	うそ	lie, falsehood	きかい	machine
おこる	get angry	～にくわしい	be knowledgeable about ——	コンピューターゲーム	computer game
しんせいひん	new product				

III Conveying Information Gained Elsewhere

めずらしいペットをかう人がふえているそうですね。

そう is used to pass on information that you have gained from some other source. It follows plain forms in the basic pattern (see front endpapers). そう itself conjugates like a *-na* adjective, except that it never appears in past, negative, or adverbial forms. Statements using そう typically reflect the speaker's own summary or rendering of the information being relayed.

ミルズさんは少しおくれるそうです。
From what I hear, Mr. Mills is going to be a little late.

あしたの会議は２時からだそうです。
From what I hear, tomorrow's meeting is from two o'clock.

To specify the source of the information you are relaying, use ～によると or ～の話では.

新聞によると、インドネシアで大きいつなみがあったそうです。
According to the newspaper, there was a large tsunami in Indonesia.

シカさんの話では、インドでは子どものころからすうがくのべんきょうをたくさんするそうです。
To hear Shika tell it, in India people study mathematics a lot from the time they are children.

To straightforwardly quote something you heard or read, use と言っています (Book II, p. 122) or と書いてあります (Book III, p. 71). The former is used especially when stressing the identity of the person who made the statement.

ショコラショコラが１００万ケース売れたら、ボーナスが出ると加藤さんが言っていました。
Mr. Kato said that if a million cases of Chocolat-Chocolat were sold, a bonus would be issued.

The more colloquial って is commonly used when giving hearsay in everyday speech. Women often use it in combination with *desu/masu*.

のぞみデパートの田中さんはしゅっちょう中だって。
I hear that Mr. Tanaka of Nozomi Department Store is on a business trip right now.

ボーナスが出るんですって。
I hear that there is going to be a bonus given out.

VOCABULARY

～によると	according to ——	インド	India
～のはなしでは	to hear —— tell it . . .	しゅっちょうちゅう	on a business trip
インドネシア	Indonesia	って	(colloquial form of the quotation particle と)
つなみ	tsunami		

1 Answer the questions by using そう with the proper form of the words in parentheses.

1) Q：鈴木(すずき)さんは今日(きょう)休(やす)みですか。
   A：ええ。かぜを＿＿＿＿＿＿です。(ひきました)

2) Q：だれか来(く)るんですか。
   A：ええ。ゆうめいなさっかのサイン会(かい)が＿＿＿＿＿＿です。(あります)

3) Q：食事会(しょくじかい)のメニューはやきにくでいいでしょうか。
   A：ええ、いいと思(おも)います。グリーンさんはにくりょうりが＿＿＿＿＿＿ですから。(大(だい)すきです)

4) Q：何(なに)かもんだいがあったんですか。
   A：ええ。フードフェアは＿＿＿＿＿＿です。(ちゅうしです)

5) Q：コピーがつかえないんですか。
   A：ええ。ちょうしが＿＿＿＿＿＿です。(わるいです)

2 Read the following sentences while paying attention to their meanings.

1) 天気(てんき)よほうによると、今夜(こんや)はかぜがつよくなるそうです。
2) 駅(えき)のアナウンスによると、車両(しゃりょう)こしょうで電車(でんしゃ)がとまっているそうです。
3) マリーさんの話(はなし)では、フランスでも日本(にほん)のアニメは人気(にんき)があるそうです。

VOCABULARY

さっか	author	こんや	tonight	しゃりょう	train car
サインかい	autograph session	かぜ	wind	こしょう	breakdown
やきにく	Korean-style barbecue	アナウンス	announcement	アニメ	anime, animation
よほう	forecast	しゃりょうこしょう	train-car breakdown		

IV Describing Actions Done or to Be Done in Preparation for the Future

（ケージの）中(なか)にキャットフードを入(い)れておいたんです。

In its basic sense, the *-te* form of a verb + おく (hereafter 〜ておく) means to perform an action and then to keep the effects of that action going. Depending on the context, it may also mean to prepare for something, to do something in advance, or to maintain some state in readiness for the future.

> 食事会(しょくじかい)のレストランを予約(よやく)しておきます。
> I'll make restaurant reservations in preparation for our dinner party.

> 会議(かいぎ)の時間(じかん)までに、しりょうをコピーしておいてください。
> Please photocopy the documents before the meeting.

In conversation, 〜ておく（でおく） may sometimes be pronounced 〜とく（どく）.

> 今日中(きょうじゅう)にデータをおくっときます。
> I'll send the data [in preparation for you to see] sometime today.

> マニュアルをよく読(よ)んどいて。
> Read through the manual thoroughly beforehand.

Complete the sentences using 〜ておく.

1) こんばん友(とも)だちが来(く)るので、ビールを＿＿＿＿＿＿ます。（ひやす）
2) そろそろ子(こ)どもたちが帰(かえ)ってきます。だんぼうのスイッチを入(い)れて部屋(へや)を＿＿＿＿＿＿ましょう。（あたためる）
3) ネームプレートはうけつけにあいうえおじゅんに＿＿＿＿＿＿ください。（ならべる）
4) けいたいに電話番号(でんわばんごう)を＿＿＿＿＿＿ます。（とうろくする）

VOCABULARY

きょうじゅう	sometime today	あたためる (R2)	warm up	ならべる (R2)	arrange, place
マニュアル	manual	ネームプレート	name plate	とうろくする	register
ひやす	make cold, cool down	あいうえおじゅん	*a-i-u-e-o* order		
だんぼう	heater	〜じゅん	order of ——		

PRACTICE 1 Discussing Things You Do Not Know or Understand

PHRASE POWER

I. Inviting others to join you in thinking about something:

① 何(なん)でしょうか。	What could they be?
② クマでしょうか。	Could they be bears?
③ 何(なに)をしているんでしょうか。	What do you suppose they're doing?
④ どうして立(た)っているんでしょうか。	Why do you suppose they're standing up?

II. Examples of how to respond to the above:

① レッサーパンダですよ。	They're lesser pandas.
② レッサーパンダでしょう。	They're probably lesser pandas.
③ レッサーパンダじゃないですか。	Aren't they lesser pandas?
④ レッサーパンダじゃないですよ。	They're not lesser pandas.
⑤ レッサーパンダのようですけど……。	They seem to be lesser pandas, but . . .
⑥ さあ。	I don't know.

VOCABULARY

クマ	bear
レッサーパンダ	lesser panda

SPEAKING PRACTICE

I. Ms. Martin and Mr. Suzuki see a mysterious box that has been sitting in the office since yesterday.

マルタン：このはこ、何でしょうか。
鈴木：　さあ。きのうからここにあるんです。
マルタン：(*picks it up*) かるいですね。何も入っていないようです。あけてみてもいいでしょうか。
鈴木：　ええ、いいんじゃないですか。
マルタン：やっぱり何も入ってない。すててもいいでしょうか。
鈴木：　さあ、どうでしょうか。

Martin: What could this box be?
Suzuki: I don't know. It's been here since yesterday.
Martin: (*picks it up*) It's light. There doesn't seem to be anything in it. Do you suppose it would be all right to try and open it?
Suzuki: Yes, it should be all right, I imagine.
Martin: Just as I thought, there's nothing in it. Do you suppose it would be all right to throw it away?
Suzuki: Hmm, couldn't say.

II. Dinner at the Katos, Part 1: Ms. Martin sees something in her dish that she does not recognize.

マルタン：　これは何でしょうか。
ミルズ：　レモンじゃないですか。
マルタン：　レモンじゃないですよ。かおりがちがいます。加藤さん、これは何ですか。
加藤（妻）：ゆずですよ。(*shows her a whole one*) ほら、これです。
マルタン：　いいかおり。

Martin: What could this be?
Mills: Isn't it a lemon?
Martin: It can't be a lemon. It smells different. Mrs. Kato, what is this?
Mrs. Kato: It's a *yuzu* citrus. (*shows her a whole one*) See, this.
Martin: What a lovely scent!

VOCABULARY

やっぱり	sure enough, as expected (colloquial form of やはり)
どうでしょうか	I wonder, couldn't say
レモン	lemon
ゆず	*yuzu* citrus (the juice and rind of which are often used in cooking)
ほら	look here

PRACTICE 2 Describing Sounds, Smells, and Tastes

WORD POWER

I. Sounds:

音(おと)

ピアノの音(おと)

ノックの音(おと)

花火(はなび)の音(おと)

雨(あめ)の音(おと)
かみなりの音(おと)

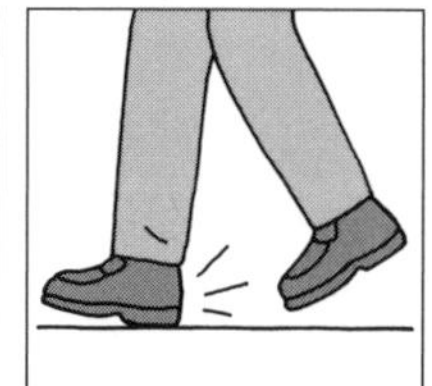

足音(あしおと)

声(こえ)

子(こ)どもの声(こえ)

話(はな)し声(ごえ)

わらい声(ごえ)

あかちゃんの
なき声(ごえ)

ピアノの音(おと)がします。
I hear a piano. [lit., "There is the sound of a piano."]

子(こ)どもの声(こえ)がします。
I hear children's voices. [lit., "There are children's voices."]

II. Smells:

におい

せっけんの
におい

たばこの
におい

いいにおい

ごみのにおい
いやなにおい

何(なに)かがこげて
いるにおい

VOCABULARY

ノック	knock	わらいごえ	sound of laughter	せっけん	soap
かみなり	thunder, lightning	わらう	laugh	いや（な）	unpleasant
あしおと	footstep	なきごえ	sound of crying	こげる (R2)	burn (of food)
はなしごえ	sound of conversation	なく	cry (of person)		

かおり

こうすいの
かおり

コーヒーの
かおり

ハーブの
かおり

花(はな)のかおり

せっけんのにおいがします。
I smell soap.

こうすいのかおりがします。
I smell perfume.

II. Tastes:

味(あじ)

レモンの味(あじ)

にんにくの味(あじ)

しょうがの味(あじ)

あまい

からい

しおからい

すっぱい

にがい

レモンの味(あじ)がします。
It tastes like lemon.

VOCABULARY

ハーブ	herb
にんにく	garlic
しょうが	ginger
しおからい	salty
すっぱい	sour
にがい	bitter

PHRASE POWER

① 大(おお)きな音(おと)がしました。*	There was a loud sound.
② かみなりがおちたような音(おと)がしました。	There was a sound like lightning striking.
③ 夜中(よなか)に外(そと)でひそひそ話(はな)す声(こえ)がしました。	Late at night there were voices outside speaking in whispers.
④ へんなにおいがします。	It smells strange.
⑤ さかながくさったようなにおいがします。	It smells like rotten fish.
⑥ あまい花(はな)のかおりがします。	It smells sweetly of flowers.
⑦ なつかしい味(あじ)がします。	It has a nostalgic taste.
⑧ 薬(くすり)のようににがいです。	It is bitter like medicine.

* 大(おお)きな = 大(おお)きい "big." Although 大(おお)きい and 小(ち)さい are both *-i* adjectives, occasionally the い may be replaced with な when these words modify nouns.

SPEAKING PRACTICE

I. Ms. Chandra notices the smell of cigarettes on entering a meeting room.

チャンドラ：この部屋(へや)、たばこのにおいがしますね。
鈴木(すずき)：　そうですか。
チャンドラ：少(すこ)しまどをあけてもいいですか。
鈴木(すずき)：　ええ。

Chandra: This room smells of cigarettes, doesn't it?
Suzuki: Oh, does it?
Chandra: May I open the windows a little?
Suzuki: Go ahead.

II. Ms. Nakamura notices a good smell while being treated to Ms. Chandra's home cooking.

中村(なかむら)：　いいにおい。カレーですね。
チャンドラ：ええ。さあ、どうぞ。
中村(なかむら)：　いただきます。ん？　なんかふしぎな味(あじ)がしますね。
チャンドラ：母(はは)のレシピで作(つく)りました。特別(とくべつ)なスパイスが入(はい)っているんです。
中村(なかむら)：　インドのかていの味(あじ)ですね。おいしい！

VOCABULARY

おおきな	big	カレー	curry	ふしぎ(な)	mysterious, amazing
よなか	middle of the night	ん？	hmm?	スパイス	spice
ひそひそ	in whispers	なんか	something (colloquial form of なにか)	かてい	home, household
くさる	rot				

Nakamura: What a lovely smell. This is curry, isn't it?
Chandra: Yes. Please, have a taste.
Nakamura: I will. Hmm? It has something of an exotic taste.
Chandra: I made it with my mother's recipe. It has special spices in it.
Nakamura: The taste of Indian home cooking. Delicious!

III. Ms. Nakamura and Mr. Suzuki hear loud noises.

(*crashing sounds*)

鈴木(すずき)： 今(いま)の音(おと)、何(なん)でしょう。
中村(なかむら)： かみなりがおちたような音(おと)でしたね。

(*sirens wailing*)

鈴木(すずき)： あ、サイレン。じこのようですね。ちょっと見(み)てきます。

Suzuki: What was that sound just now?
Nakamura: It sounded like lightning striking, didn't it?
Suzuki: Oh, sirens. There seems to have been an accident. I'll go take a look.

IV. Dinner at the Katos, Part 2: drinking wine

加藤(かとう)（夫(おっと)）：鈴木(すずき)さん、最近(さいきん)ワインのべんきょうをしているそうですね。これ、１９８５年(ねん)のシャトーＡＢＣです。(*pours*) いかがですか。
鈴木(すずき)： んんー、もりの土(つち)のかおりがします。それから……。
マルタン： え？　これ、へんなにおいがしませんか。
加藤(かとう)（夫(おっと)）：(*takes a sip*) ああ、ほんとうだ。(*inspects the cork*) あ、かびだ。すみません。うちはワインセラーがないんです。
マルタン： 鈴木(すずき)さん、まだまだべんきょうが足(た)りないようですね。

Mr. Kato: Mr. Suzuki, I understand that you've recently been studying about wine. This here is a 1985 Chateau ABC. (*pours*) What do you think?
Suzuki: Umm, it has the bouquet of the ground in a forest. And . . .
Martin: Huh? Doesn't this smell strange?
Mr. Kato: (*takes a sip*) Oh, you're right. (*inspects the cork*) Oh, there's mold. I'm sorry. We don't have a wine cellar, you see.
Martin: It looks like you still have a lot to learn, Mr. Suzuki.

VOCABULARY

サイレン	siren	かび	mold
シャトー	chateau	ワインセラー	wine cellar
んんー	(said when smelling wine)		
つち	soil, ground		

PRACTICE 3 Relating or Passing on Information Gained Elsewhere

SPEAKING PRACTICE

TRACK 4

I. While out walking in the park, Ms. Nakamura sees police officers and a large crowd of people.

中村：　何かあったんですか。
男の人：ここでワニを見た人がいるそうですよ。
中村：　えー。ほんとうですか。
女の人：ええ。こわいですね。
中村：　ペットがにげたんでしょうか。
男の人：さあ。かっていた人がすてたのかもしれませんよ。せわがたいへんだからって、ペットをすてる人がけっこういるそうですよ。
女の人：ひどい話ですね。

Nakamura: Has something happened?
man: From what I hear, there's been someone who saw a crocodile here.
Nakamura: What? Really?
woman: Yes. It's frightening, isn't it?
Nakamura: Could it be a pet that got away?
man: I don't know. It may be that the person keeping it abandoned it. I understand that there are quite a lot of people who abandon pets just because they find them too hard to take care of.
woman: What a horrible thing.

II. Mr. Mills calls the office to say that he is stuck in a traffic jam and will arrive late.

ミルズ：ミルズです。少しおくれます。タクシーにのったら、じゅうたいで……。9時10分ごろ着くと思うんですが。すみません。
中村：　わかりました。
………………
中村：　部長、ミルズさんから電話がありました。少しおくれるそうです。
佐々木：そうですか。わかりました。

Mills: This is Mills. I'm going to be a little late. I'm in a taxi, but there's such a traffic jam . . . I think I'll get there around 9:10. I'm sorry.
Nakamura: I understand.
. . . . . .
Nakamura: Manager Sasaki, there was a phone call from Mr. Mills. He said he'd be a little late.
Sasaki: Is that so? I understand.

VOCABULARY

ワニ	crocodile, alligator	けっこう	quite (a lot of)
すてたのかもしれません	it may be that (someone) abandoned (something)	ひどい	horrible
〜のかもしれない	it may be that —— (giving an explanation)		
〜からって	just because —— (colloquial form of 〜からといって)		

III. Mr. Kato relates a story from the office to his wife.

加藤（夫）：サン＝テグジュペリの『星の王子さま』、読んだことある？
加藤（妻）：ええ。むかしね。
加藤（夫）：今日会社で、にわでフェネックをつかまえた話をしたんだ。
加藤（妻）：みんなびっくりしていたでしょう？
加藤（夫）：ああ。マリーさんの話では、『星の王子さま』に出ているキツネはフェネックだそうだよ。
加藤（妻）：へえ、そうなの。そういえば、にわにいたフェネック、みみが長くて、イラストのキツネににてたわね。

Mr. Kato:	Have you ever read Saint-Exupéry's *The Little Prince*?
Mrs. Kato:	Yes, a long time ago.
Mr. Kato:	Today at the office I talked about how I caught a fennec in our yard.
Mrs. Kato:	Everyone must have been surprised.
Mr. Kato:	Yes. To hear Marie tell it, the fox in *The Little Prince* was a fennec.
Mrs. Kato:	Really, is that right? Come to think of it, it did have long ears and looked like the fox in the illustrations.

VOCABULARY

サン＝テグジュペリ	Antoine Saint-Exupéry (French author, 1900–1944)	ああ	yes (used by men)
『ほしのおうじさま』	*The Little Prince* (in Japanese, *The Star Prince*)	そういえば	come to think of it
ほし	star	イラスト	illustration
おうじ	prince	にる (R2)	look like, resemble

PRACTICE 4 Describing Preparations or Advance Steps for Doing Something

SPEAKING PRACTICE

I. Ms. Martin sees a photograph displayed in the Katos' home.

マルタン： この小鳥(ことり)のしゃしん、加藤(かとう)さんがとったんですか。

加藤(かとう)（夫(おっと)）：ええ、鳥(とり)のしゃしんをとるのがすきなんです。

マルタン： どこでとったんですか。

加藤(かとう)（夫(おっと)）：うちのにわですよ。にわにパンをおいておくんです。そして、小鳥(ことり)が来(く)るのをじっと待(ま)っているんです。

Martin: Did you take this photograph of a small bird, Mr. Kato?

Mr. Kato: Yes, I like photographing birds.

Martin: Where did you take it?

Mr. Kato: In our yard. I put some bread out in the yard. Then I wait patiently for birds to come.

II. Dinner at the Katos, Part 3: Ms. Martin is eating the Katos' home-cooked fish.

マルタン： このさかなりょうり、とってもおいしいですね。どうやって作(つく)るんですか。

加藤(かとう)（妻(つま)）：さかなを2、3時間(じかん)みそにつけておきます。それから、やくんですよ。

マルタン： これ、みその味(あじ)ですか。

加藤(かとう)（妻(つま)）：ええ。みそにしょうゆとさとうとさけを少(すこ)しずつ入(い)れて、よくまぜます。そこにさかなのきりみを入(い)れるんです。

マルタン： ふうん。今度(こんど)作(つく)ってみます。

Martin: This fish is incredibly delicious. How do you make it?

Mrs. Kato: You put the fish in miso for two to three hours. Then you broil it.

Martin: So this taste is miso?

Mrs. Kato: Yes. Little by little you put soy sauce, sugar, and sake in with the miso and mix everything up well. Then into this you lay the fish fillets.

Martin: Hmm, I see. I'll try making it myself next time.

VOCABULARY

ことり	small bird	みそ	miso	ふうん	hmm, I see
じっと	patiently, quietly	つける (R2)	marinate		
とっても	very (とても spoken with emotional emphasis)	まぜる (R2)	mix		
		きりみ	fillet		

KANJI PRACTICE

音	音 おと 発音 はつおん
sound	

声	声 こえ 大声 おおごえ
voice	

味	味 あじ 意味 いみ
taste	

鳥	鳥 とり 小鳥 ことり
bird	

住	住む すむ 住所 じゅうしょ
live	

所
place

所（ところ）
名所（めいしょ）
近所（きんじょ）

最
most

最近（さいきん）
最初（さいしょ）
最後（さいご）

近
near
recent

近い（ちかい）
最近（さいきん）
近所（きんじょ）

様
appearance
Mr., Mrs., Miss

〜様（さま）
お母様（おかあさま）
様子（ようす）

主
owner
lord

かい主（かいぬし）
主人（しゅじん）

LESSON **2**

DISAPPEARING COOKIES

TARGET DIALOGUE

Ms. Nakamura notices that the cookies she left on a desk are missing.

中村(なかむら)：　このつくえの上(うえ)にあったクッキー、知(し)りませんか。

マルタン：クッキー？

中村(なかむら)：　ええ、ペット用(よう)のクッキーのサンプルなんです。きのうペット食品開発部(しょくひんかいはつぶ)の人(ひと)がくれたんです。ここにおいたはずなんですけど……。 →p. 31

鈴木(すずき)：　あのう、あのクッキー、ペット用(よう)だったんですか。

マルタン：鈴木(すずき)さん、食(た)べちゃったんですか。

鈴木(すずき)：　ええ。だれかのおみやげだと思(おも)ったんです。だいじょうぶかなあ。

中村(なかむら)：　低(てい)カロリーで、とても体(からだ)にいいらしいですよ。→p. 32 味(あじ)はどうでしたか。

ミルズ：　*(bursts into laughter)*

鈴木(すずき)：　ミルズさん、知(し)っていたんですか。

ミルズ：　鈴木(すずき)さんがおいしそうに食(た)べていたので、→p. 33 言(い)いにくかったんです。

鈴木(すずき)：　それで、すすめたのに、→p. 35 食(た)べなかったんですね。ひどいな。

Nakamura:	Do you know [anything about] the cookies that were on this desk?
Martin:	Cookies?
Nakamura:	Yes, they're samples of cookies for pets. Someone from the pet food development department gave them to me yesterday. I'm sure I put them here . . .
Suzuki:	Um, were those cookies for pets?
Martin:	Did you eat them, Mr. Suzuki?
Suzuki:	Yes. I thought they were souvenirs from someone. I wonder if I'm going to be all right.
Nakamura:	They're supposed to be low in calories and very good for you. How did they taste?
Mills:	(*bursts into laughter*)
Suzuki:	Did you know about this, Mr. Mills?
Mills:	You were munching away like you were enjoying them so much, it was difficult for me to tell you.
Suzuki:	So that's why you didn't eat any even though I offered you some. How mean!

VOCABULARY

ペット食品開発部(しょくひんかいはつぶ)	pet-food development department
食品(しょくひん)	food product
くれる (R2)	give (to me)
はず	ought to, should (see p. 31)
低(てい)カロリー	low in calories
低(てい)〜	low in ——
カロリー	calorie
体(からだ)にいい	good for you [lit., "good for the body"]
〜にいい	good for ——
らしい	supposedly, apparently (see p. 32)
おいしそうに	as if finding something delicious
そう（な）	look, seem (see p. 33)
にくい	difficult (to do)
それで	that's why . . .
すすめる (R2)	offer, urge
のに	even though (see p. 35)
ひどいな	how mean!
〜な	(emotive particle; see Note 6 below)

NOTES

1. くれた

くれた, the *-ta* form (plain, past, affirmative form) of the verb くれる, here means "gave to me." くれる is used when the recipient is the speaker, in which case 私(わたし)に can be omitted. For more on verbs for giving, see the Usage Note on p. 29.

2. このつくえ／あのクッキー

この and あの are both demonstratives. このつくえ refers to a desk there in the office, near Ms. Nakamura. あのクッキー refers to the cookies that Ms. Nakamura is looking for. By saying あの, Mr. Suzuki indicates that he knows what cookies Ms. Nakamura is talking about, even though the cookies are not there at the moment. (See also the Usage Note on p. 30.)

3. だいじょうぶかなあ

You use かなあ, a combination of the question marker か and the emotive particle な, at the end of a question you are asking aloud to yourself. You can lengthen the な to なあ for emphasis. か

なあ connotes wonder, doubt, or hesitation. It usually does not appear together with *desu/masu*. Women sometimes use the equivalent expression かしら.

この本(ほん)おもしろいかな。
Could this book be interesting, I wonder.

買(か)おうかな。
Should I buy it?

どうしようかな。
Should I or shouldn't I?

4. 言(い)いにくかったんです

The *-masu* stem of a verb + にくい (hereafter にくい) means "difficult to do." For the opposite meaning, "easy to do," use *-masu* stem + やすい. In the dialogue, Mr. Mills uses にくい to express his reluctance to tell Mr. Suzuki the cookies were for pets, given how much he was enjoying them. In addition to such difficulties arising from internal abilities or inclinations, にくい／やすい may also be used to state your evaluations of the external qualities or attributes of things around you. にくい／やすい conjugate like *-i* adjectives.

この本(ほん)はじが大(おお)きくて読(よ)みやすいです。
This book has large print and is easy to read.

雪(ゆき)の日(ひ)はみちがすべりやすくて、あるきにくいです。
On snowy days, the roads are slippery [lit., "easy to slip"] and difficult to walk on.

最近(さいきん)のプリンターはこわれにくいです。
Printers nowadays do not break down easily.

5. それで〜んですね

それで means "that's why." Mr. Suzuki uses it with んですね to think back on yesterday's events and to indicate that what he found puzzling then has just now been cleared up.

6. ひどいな

な here is a sentence-final emotive particle. You use it to comment mainly to yourself about your own feelings or opinions. It is the same particle as the one that appeared in Note 3 above, except that here it follows a declarative sentence, not a question. By using な, Mr. Suzuki conveys his feelings of protest against Mr. Mills for failing to tell him about the cookies. な usually comes after plain forms.

USAGE NOTE

Verbs for Giving

In Japanese, different verbs are used to express the action of giving depending on who the receiver is.

GIVER	RECEIVER		
↗	○	(to person of higher status)	さしあげる
○ →	○	(to person of equal status)	あげる
↘	○	(to person of lower status, animals/plants)	やる
○ →	○	(from person of equal/lower status to speaker)	くれる
↘	○	(from person of higher status to speaker)	くださる

The basic meaning of the verb あげる is "to raise." Raising one's hands outward is the typical motion by which one gives something to someone, hence the use of あげる as an expression for giving. When giving something to someone of higher status, the verb さしあげる (the humble equivalent of あげる; see also p. 181), meaning to hold something up high, is used. As part of Japanese culture, however, people will generally avoid referring openly to giving things to those of higher status.

As for やる, the traditional verb for giving something to someone of lower status or to animals or plants, many people today, especially women, tend to favor using あげる, owing perhaps to the condescending nuance of やる. Thus, today あげる is increasingly replacing やる in expressions that should properly use the latter, e.g., 犬(いぬ)にえさをやります, "I will feed [lit., 'give food to'] the dog," 花(はな)に水(みず)をやります, "I will water [lit., 'give water to'] the flowers," or おとうとに本(ほん)をやります "I will give my younger brother the book."

くださる (see also p. 181), historically meaning to bestow to someone of lower status, is the honorific expression for くれる.

USAGE NOTE

Demonstratives

Japanese demonstratives include the following:

これ	それ	あれ	refer to objects
この	その	あの	modify animate and inanimate objects
ここ	そこ	あそこ	refer to places
こちら	そちら	あちら	refer to directions, inanimate objects, people, and places (polite use)
こっち	そっち	あっち	casual forms of こちら, そちら, and あちら
こんな	そんな	あんな	refer to attributes
こう	そう	ああ	refer to situations

To summarize some basic points regarding the demonstratives taken up so far:

1. When the speaker and listener are conversing at some distance from each other, こ-demonstratives are used to specify objects near the speaker, そ-demonstratives to specify those near the listener, and あ-demonstratives to specify those close to neither (Book I, p. 20).

2. When referring to things that are not actually there but only came up in the conversation, speakers generally use そ-demonstratives to specify things that the other person brought up earlier in the discussion (Book I [Kana Version], p. 232; [Romanized Version] p. 233).

3. Again in discourse, あ-demonstratives may be used to specify something either the speaker or listener brought up that the speaker expects both of them to already be familiar with (Book III, p. 27).

GRAMMAR & PATTERN PRACTICE

I Expressing Certainty

ここに（クッキーを）おいたはずなんですけど……。

はず is used after an assertion that you have grounds to believe should be true. Though it is never used without an accompanying modifier, はず is a noun. Thus, words before it take plain forms in the noun-modifying pattern (see front endpapers) just as other noun modifiers do.

1. Making assertions based on reason

はず is used to make an assertion about something you believe should be true based on logic or reason.

きのうたくはいびんでにもつをおくりましたから、今日中(きょうじゅう)にとどくはずです。
I sent the package by courier service yesterday, so it should arrive sometime today.

何度(なんど)もスピーチのれんしゅうをしたので、うまくできるはずです。
I practiced for my speech over and over, so I should be able to do it well.

2. Expressing feelings of suspicion upon encountering circumstances different from what you believe should be true

はず can also be used in cases where you find a situation to be different from how you expected it to be. In such cases, はず connotes feelings of suspicion.

みんな出(で)かけて、部屋(へや)にだれもいないはずですが、声(こえ)が聞(き)こえます。
I hear voices, although everyone has left and there should be no one in the room.

きのう、じむしょのまどを閉(し)めて帰(かえ)ったはずなんですが、けさ来(き)たら開(あ)いていたんです。
I was sure I closed the office windows before I went home yesterday, but when I came in this morning, they were open.

Read the following dialogues while paying attention to the uses of はず.

1

中村(なかむら)：ミルズさんおそいですね。やくそくをわすれたのかもしれませんよ。
鈴木(すずき)：おぼえているはずです。けさ、電話(でんわ)で話(はな)しましたから。
中村(なかむら)：じゃ、ばしょがわからないのかもしれませんね。

VOCABULARY

うまい	good at, skilled
ばしょ	place

鈴木：わかるはずです。前に一度いっしょに来たことがありますから。
中村：じゃあ、どうしたんでしょうね。

2

鈴木：かぎがない。かぎがない。ポケットに入れたはずなんですが……。
中村：よくさがしましたか。ちがうポケットじゃないですか。
鈴木：いいえ。たしかにこのポケットです。あ、あながあいている。

II Expressing Beliefs or Expectations Based on Information Gained Elsewhere

（あのペット用のクッキーは）低カロリーで、とても体にいいらしいですよ。

らしい is used to state something that you guess or suppose to be true based on other information, but oftentimes with the intimation that you either do not wish to be held accountable for or have no significant interest in what you are passing on. らしい comes after plain forms in the でしょう pattern (see front endpapers). らしい itself conjugates like an *-i* adjective, except that it does not appear in negative forms when used in the sense discussed here.

あの会社の今度の新せいひんはすごいらしいですよ。
The new product that company is putting out is supposed to be fantastic.

ミルズさんは学生のころ、人気のホッケーせんしゅだったらしいですよ。
Mr. Mills is supposed to have been a popular hockey player while he was a student.

A second function of らしい is to follow nouns to mean "characteristically like" or "typically like" that noun. Compare this usage with that of よう:

今年のなつはあまりあつくないですが、今日はなつらしいあつい日です。
This summer it is not very hot, but today is a typically hot summer-like day.

まだ4月ですが、今日はなつのようにあつい日です。
Although it's still April, today it is as hot as summer.

The former talks about a hot summer day being the way it should be, while the latter describes a hot day that feels like summer even though it is not.

VOCABULARY

あながあく	a hole opens up	ホッケー	hockey
あな	hole		
にんきの	popular		
にんき	popularity		

Read the following dialogue while paying attention to the uses of そう, らしい, and って.

中村：　加藤さん、たいへんです。今、京都支社から電話があって、支社長の山本さんが6時のレセプションに間に合わないそうです。
加藤：　え、どうかしたんですか。
中村：　支社長ののった新幹線がおくれているそうです。
ミルズ：ああ、名古屋のあたりでじこがあったらしいですよ。
中村：　支社長のあいさつは6時半ごろからなんですが、着くのは7時ごろになるだろうって……。
加藤：　こまりましたね。すぐ部長にもつたえて。
中村：　はい。

III Expressing Impressions (2)

おいしそうに食べていたので、言いにくかったんです。

そう is used to express what the state of a person or object you are observing seems or feels like to you. Typically そう statements concern immediate impressions or feelings, not reasoned or thought-out assessments. Whether what is said is actually true is of no concern. Elements before そう take the following forms:

verbs:	(雨が) ふる	→ ふりそう	(*-masu* stem)
-i adjectives:	おいしい	→ おいしそう	(plain form minus the *-i* ending)
-na adjectives:	べんり (な)	→ べんりそう	(plain form minus the *-na/da* ending)

Since そう expresses a state, it cannot appear with nouns. Be sure not to confuse this use of そう with that introduced earlier for indicating hearsay (p. 12).

このクッキー、おいしそうですね。
These cookies look delicious, don't they?

このシャツ、ミルズさんににあいそうですね。
This shirt seems like it would look good on Mr. Mills, doesn't it?

そう itself conjugates like a *-na* adjective.

おいしそうなクッキーをもらいました。
I received some delicious-looking cookies.

VOCABULARY

ししゃちょう	branch president	つたえる (R2)	inform, tell
レセプション	reception		
どうかしたんですか	is something the matter?		
あいさつ	address, speech		

鈴木(すずき)さんがおいしそうにクッキーを食(た)べていました。
Mr. Suzuki seemed to be enjoying the cookies that he was eating. [lit., "Mr. Suzuki was eating the cookies as if they were delicious."]

When followed by そう, the adjective いい and the negative ない become よさそう and なさそう, respectively.

このレストラン、よさそうですね。ここにしましょう。
This restaurant looks good, doesn't it? Let's go here.

このキムチはあまりからくなさそうですね。
This kimchi doesn't look very hot, does it?

この店(みせ)には安(やす)いものがなさそうです。
This store doesn't look like it has anything inexpensive.

In addition to using なさそう, negative そう statements may also be formed by negating the whole sentence.

このバッグ、あまり便利(べんり)そうではありません。
This bag doesn't look very easy to use.

この仕事(しごと)はむずかしくて、私(わたし)にはできそうに／もありません。
This job is so difficult, I don't think I can do it.

The verbs appearing in the examples above have so far all either been potential verbs or verbs that express states. When the *-masu* stem of a verb besides these combines with そう, then the pattern expresses the idea that something looks likely to occur at any moment or is indeed just about to do so.

雨(あめ)がふりそうです。
It looks like it's going to rain.

たなの本(ほん)がおちそうです。
The books on the shelf look like they're going to fall.

Finally, そう may be used to state what is likely to happen based on what you have seen or heard of a situation or state.

今年(ことし)のふゆはとてもさむいので、雪(ゆき)がたくさんふりそうです。
It is very cold this winter, so it seems like it'll snow a lot.

この仕事(しごと)は今日中(きょうじゅう)に終(お)わりそうです。
I'll probably finish this work today. [lit., "This job is likely to get finished sometime today."]

VOCABULARY

キムチ	kimchi
たな	shelf

Complete the sentences by connecting the words in parentheses to そう, そうな, or そうに, as appropriate.

1) A：すてきなレストランですね。ここにしましょう。
   B：でも、..............................ですよ。だいじょうぶですか。(高(たか)い)

2) ....ＤＶＤですね。これをかります。(おもしろい)

3) サルがおんせんに入(はい)っていますよ。..............................ですね。(きもちがいい)

4) このロープは..............................見(み)えましたが、すぐきれてしまいました。(じょうぶな)

5) かぜでキャンドルの火(ひ)が..............................です。まどを閉(し)めてください。(きえる)

IV Expressing Ideas that Run Contrary to Expectation (1)

それで、すすめたのに、食(た)べなかったんですね。

Earlier in Book II (p. 152), we introduced ので as the conjunctive form of んです. のに is the corresponding adversative conjunction. Before のに comes a description of circumstances or events that have already occurred, are occurring, or are certain to occur in the future, while following it comes a statement that goes contrary to what would normally be expected from the foregoing information. のに connotes feelings of puzzlement, dissatisfaction, or regret. It comes after plain forms in the なので pattern (see front endpapers).

両親(りょうしん)がフランスから来(く)るので、休(やす)みをとりました。
My parents are coming over from France, so I took a holiday.

両親(りょうしん)がフランスから来(く)るのに、いそがしくて休(やす)めません。
My parents are coming over from France, but I'm so busy I can't take time off.

休(やす)みなのに、どこにも行(い)けません。
I have some time off, but I won't be able to go anywhere.

れんしゅうしなかったのに、うまくできました。
I did well even though I didn't practice.

VOCABULARY

サル	monkey
きもちがいい	feel good
ロープ	rope
きれる (R2)	break, snap (of things that are elongated and pliant, such as string)
じょうぶ（な）	sturdy, strong
キャンドル	candle

1 Complete the sentences using のに and the proper form of the words in parentheses.

1) りょうりがたくさん……………………、何も食べられませんでした。(ありました)

2) ダイエットを……………………、やせないんです。(しています)

3) じしょを……………………、ぜんぜんつかっていません。(買いました)

4) ……………………、会社で仕事をしなければなりません。(日曜日です)

5) グリーンさんは日本語が……………………、ぜんぜんつかわないんです。(上手です)

6) しずかな……………………、今はとてもうるさいです。(まちでした)

7) ねつが……………………、会社に行くんですか。(高いです)

2 Read the following dialogue while paying attention to the uses of のに.

Just past 5:00 p.m., at the office:

鈴木：　はあ…。(*sighs*)

ミルズ：どうかしたんですか。

鈴木：　きのう、会うやくそくをしていたのに、かのじょが来なかったんです。2時間待っていたのに、来なかったんです。今日も何度も電話をしているのに、出ないんです。何度もメールを出しているのに、へんじをくれないんです。

ミルズ：何かあったのかもしれませんよ。すぐアパートに行ってみたほうがいいですよ。

PRACTICE 1 Expressing Things that Puzzle or Trouble You

PHRASE POWER

Complaining about common troubles:

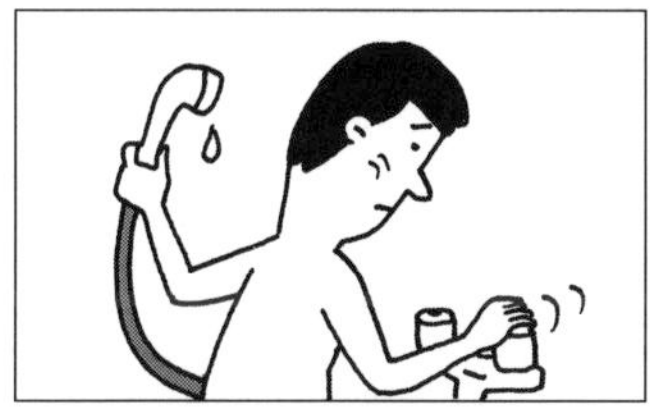

おゆが出(で)ないんです。
There's no hot water.

電気(でんき)がつかないんです。
The lights won't come on.

トイレの水(みず)がながれないんです。
The toilet won't flush.

ふたが開(あ)かないんです。
The lid won't open.

ポケットに入(い)れたはずなのに、きっぷがないんです。
I can't find my ticket even though I'm sure I put it in my pocket.

この電子(でんし)じしょ、でんちをとりかえたのに、つかえないんです。
This electronic dictionary still doesn't work [lit., "I still can't use this electronic dictionary"], even though I changed the batteries

VOCABULARY

ながれる (R2)	flow, flush
でんち	battery
とりかえる (R2)	change, replace

SPEAKING PRACTICE

I. Mr. Kato is looking for a box.

加藤：おかしいな。
中村：どうしたんですか。
加藤：はこがないんです。ここにおいたはずなんですが。だれか、ここにあったはこ、見ませんでしたか。

Kato: This is strange.
Nakamura: What's wrong?
Kato: My box is missing. I'm sure I put it here. Did anyone see the box that was here?

II. Mr. Suzuki is standing in front of the door, muttering.

鈴木：あれ、どうしたんだろう。
中村：どうかしたんですか。
鈴木：あ、ちょうどよかった、中村さん。カードをかざしているのに、ロックがかいじょできないんです。中に入れなくて、こまっていたんです。
中村：え？　へんですね。(*opens the lock with her own card*) 私のはだいじょうぶです。鈴木さんのカードにもんだいがあるようですね。

Suzuki: Huh? What's wrong with this?
Nakamura: Is something the matter?
Suzuki: Oh, Ms. Nakamura, you came at just the right time. The lock won't open, even though I've been holding my card key over it. I was at a loss because I couldn't get in.
Nakamura: Oh? That's strange. (*opens the lock with her own card*) Mine is all right. The problem seems to be with your card key.

III. The Katos are having dinner at a sushi restaurant.

太郎：からい！
加藤（妻）：(*looking at Taro's sushi*) あ、わさびが入ってる。(*to the waiter*) すみません。1人前わさびを入れないでくださいって、おねがいしたはずなんですけど。
店員：もうしわけありません。すぐとりかえます。

Taro: Oh, hot!
Mrs. Kato: (*looking at Taro's sushi*) Oh, there's wasabi in this. (*to the waiter*) Excuse me, I believe I requested that wasabi not be included in one of our orders.
waiter: I'm very sorry. I'll change it right away.

VOCABULARY

かざす	hold (something over something)	いちにんまえ	order (of food) for one person
ロック	lock	もうしわけありません	I'm sorry, I apologize [lit., "I have no excuse"]
かいじょする	release, open		
たろう	Taro (male name)		

PRACTICE 2 Getting Something Cleared Up in Your Mind; Making Excuses

SPEAKING PRACTICE

TRACK 8

I. Mr. Mills and Ms. Nakamura are talking about Mr. Suzuki.

ミルズ： 鈴木(すずき)さん、最近(さいきん)げんきがないですね。何(なに)かあったんでしょうか。
中村(なかむら)： 愛子(あいこ)さんをコンサートにさそおうと思(おも)って、高(たか)いチケットを買(か)ったのに、その日(ひ)、しゅっちょうになってしまったんだそうです。
ミルズ： それで、私(わたし)にチケットをくれたんですね。

Mills: Mr. Suzuki has been down recently, hasn't he? Do you suppose anything has happened?
Nakamura: From what I hear, he bought expensive tickets to a concert, thinking to invite Aiko to it, but ended up having to go on a business trip that day.
Mills: So that's why he gave me those tickets.

II. Mr. Mills and Ms. Nakamura revisit the topic of Mr. Suzuki.

ミルズ： 鈴木(すずき)さん、いつものようにげんきになりましたね。
中村(なかむら)： ええ。しゅっちょう先(さき)で何(なに)かいいことがあったらしいです。
ミルズ： 何(なに)があったんでしょう。そうだ！こんばん飲(の)みにさそって、聞(き)いてみよう。

Mills: Mr. Suzuki has become his usual spirited self again, hasn't he?
Nakamura: Yes. It seems something good happened to him on his business trip.
Mills: I wonder what could have happened. I know! I'll invite him to go out for a drink with me tonight, and I'll ask him.

III. Mr. Mills is looking for something.

鈴木(すずき)： どうかしたんですか。
ミルズ： 佐々木(ささき)さんからあずかったえいごのげんこうがないんです。今日中(きょうじゅう)にチェックしなきゃならないのに。こまったな。
中村(なかむら)： え？　チェック、まだだったんですか。もうできていると思(おも)って、さっき佐々木(ささき)さんにわたしてしまいました。

Suzuki: Is something the matter?
Mills: The English manuscript that I got from Ms. Sasaki is missing. And I have to check it by today. I'm really in a fix!
Nakamura: Oh? You hadn't checked it yet? I thought it had been done, so I handed it to Ms. Sasaki just a while ago.

VOCABULARY

しゅっちょうになる	have a business trip coming up	そうだ！	I know!
いつものように	as usual, like always	のみにさそう	invite (someone) to go out for a drink
しゅっちょうさき	destination of a business trip	げんこう	manuscript
〜さき	destination, receiving end	〜なきゃならない	have to —— (see p. 216)

PRACTICE 3 Describing Appearances and Impressions

PHRASE POWER

おもそうです。
It looks heavy.

かるそうです。
It looks light.

おもしろそうです。
It looks like it'll be fun.

こわそうです。
It looks like it'll be scary.

しあわせそうです。
They look happy.

もんだいがありそうです。
They look like they're having problems.

こっちのレストランのほうがよさそうです。
This restaurant looks better [than that one].

おいしそう！
It looks delicious!

ほんとうにおいしそうなケーキですね。
It really is a delicious-looking cake, isn't it?

うまい！
Delicious!

鈴木(すずき)さん、ほんとうにおいしそうに飲(の)みますね。
You really look like you're enjoying what you're drinking, Mr. Suzuki.

VOCABULARY

しあわせ(な)	happy, blissful
こっちの	this one (colloquial form of こちらの; points to one of two things singled out for comparison)
うまい	delicious (more colloquial than おいしい; used primarily by men)

みんないそがしそうにあるいています。

Everyone is walking along looking busy.

みんなたのしそうにあるいています。

Everyone is walking along looking as if they're enjoying themselves.

おちそうです。

He looks like he's going to fall.

(火が) きえそうです。

(The candle) looks like it's going to go out.

(木が) たおれそうです。

(The tree) looks like it's going to fall over.

(えだが) おれそうです。

(The branch) looks like it's going to snap.

(しょるいの山が) くずれそうです。

(The stack of papers) looks like it's going to fall over.

(ロープが) きれそうです。

(The rope) looks like it's going to snap.

(ボタンが) とれそうです。

(The button) looks like it's going to come off.

(さけが) こぼれそうです。

(The sake) looks like it's going to spill over.

(ボールが) 入りそうです。

(The ball) looks like it's going to go in.

もうすぐ (花が) さきそうです。

(The flowers) look like they're going to bloom.

VOCABULARY

たおれる (R2)	fall down, collapse
えだ	branch
おれる (R2)	break, snap (of things that are elongated and hard, such as branches or bones)
くずれる (R2)	fall apart, crumble
とれる (R2)	come off, become detached
こぼれる (R2)	spill
さく	bloom, flower

SPEAKING PRACTICE

TRACK 9

I. Ms. Nakamura is carrying a heavy-looking load of papers.

ミルズ：おもそうですね。手(て)つだいましょう。
中村(なかむら)：　すみません。おねがいできますか。
………………
中村(なかむら)：　ミルズさん、ありがとう。たすかりました。
ミルズ：いいえ。

Mills: Those look heavy. Let me help you.
Nakamura: Thank you, would you please?
. . . . . .
Nakamura: Thank you, Mr. Mills. It was a big help.
Mills: Not at all.

II. Ms. Nakamura and Ms. Martin are trying to pick out a birthday present for Ms. Chandra.

中村(なかむら)：　このコーヒーカップはどうですか。いろもきれいだし、すてきだと思(おも)います。シカさんのすきそうなデザインですよ。
マルタン：ええ。でも、ちょっともちにくそうですね。
中村(なかむら)：　(*tries holding it*) うーん、たしかにもちにくいですね。

Nakamura: How about this coffee cup? I think it's lovely, and with pretty colors, too. The design looks like something that Shika would like.
Martin: Yes, but it looks a little hard to hold, doesn't it?
Nakamura: (*tries holding it*) Hmm, it certainly is awkward.

VOCABULARY

うーん　hmm, let's see

III. Mr. Kato encounters a neighbor while out walking.

加藤（かとう）：　あたたかくなってきましたね。
近所（きんじょ）の人（ひと）：ええ。３ちょう目（め）のこうえんのさくら、もうすぐさきそうですよ。
加藤（かとう）：　じゃあ、今年（ことし）の花見（はなみ）ははやくなりそうですね。

Kato: It's gotten warm, hasn't it?
neighbor: Yes. The cherry blossoms in the park in 3-chome look like they're about to bloom.
Kato: Then cherry-viewing might be early this year, mightn't it?

IV. Later, Mr. Kato converses with the same neighbor about the outlook for a cherry-viewing party scheduled for that evening.

加藤（かとう）：　今日（きょう）は花見（はなみ）なのに、雨（あめ）ですね。
近所（きんじょ）の人（ひと）：ええ。それに、さむそうですね。
加藤（かとう）：　雨（あめ）はやみそうもないですね。
近所（きんじょ）の人（ひと）：えんきしましょうか。
加藤（かとう）：　そうですね。そうしましょう。

Kato: Today is our day to go cherry-viewing, but it's raining, isn't it.
neighbor: You're right. And it looks like it'll be cold, too.
Kato: The rain seems unlikely to stop.
neighbor: Shall we postpone it?
Kato: Yes, let's.

VOCABULARY

やむ　stop (of rain)
えんきする　postpone

KANJI PRACTICE

知
know

知る(し)
知らせる(し)
知人(ちじん)

品
article
goods

品川(しながわ)
食品(しょくひん)
作品(さくひん)

開
open

開ける(あ)
開く(ひら)
開発(かいはつ)

閉
close

閉める(し)

犬
dog

犬(いぬ)

魚	魚 さかな 魚屋 さかなや
fish	

低	低い ひく 低カロリー てい
low	

体	体 からだ
body	

同	同じ おな 一同 いちどう
same	

服	服 ふく
clothes	

LESSON 3 THE PET INDUSTRY

TARGET READING

２００６年のちょうさによると、日本全国で約３３％の家庭がペットをかっているそうです。→p. 49ペットを家族のようにかんがえる人がふえたため、ペットかんれんの新しいビジネスも生まれました。

ペットといっしょに住めるアパートやマンションがふえています。犬専用のカフェやスパもできました。ペットグッズの専門店もでき、おしゃれな服を着た犬もよく見かけます。動物病院では、動物も人間と同じけんさやちりょうがうけられるようになりました。→p. 50ペットのほけんもあります。

子どものかずがへっている日本では、ペットにお金をつかう人がふえています。→p. 51これからもいろいろなペットビジネスがさかんになっていくでしょう。

According to a 2006 survey, approximately 33 percent of households across Japan keep pets. More and more people are regarding pets as members of the family, resulting in new pet-related businesses coming into existence.

The number of apartments and condominiums where people can live with pets is increasing. Cafes and spas intended exclusively for dogs [and their owners] have been opened. Specialty stores selling pet goods have also opened, and one often comes across dogs wearing fashionable costumes. At veterinary clinics, it has become possible for animals to receive the same exams and medical treatment that people do. There is even pet insurance.

In Japan, where the number of children is decreasing, more and more people are spending money on pets. All kinds of pet businesses are likely to go on thriving in the future.

VOCABULARY

ちょうさ	survey, investigation
全国（ぜんこく）	across the country, nationwide
ため	due to, as a result of (see p. 49)
〜かんれん	relating to ——
グッズ	goods
専門店（せんもんてん）	specialty store
専門（せんもん）	specialty, specialization
〜店（てん）	store selling ——
見（み）かける (R2)	come across, (happen to) see
動物病院（どうぶつびょういん）	veterinary clinic
人間（にんげん）	human
けんさ	(medical) exam
ちりょう	medical treatment
ようになる	become able to, become possible for (see p. 50)
ほけん	insurance
さかん（な）	thriving
〜ていく	continue to ——, go on ——ing (see p. 51)

犬（いぬ）はむかしから人間（にんげん）のよいパートナーでした。右（みぎ）のしゃしんは東京（とうきょう）の渋谷駅前（しぶやえきまえ）のハチ公像（こうぞう）です。このハチ公（こう）という犬（いぬ）は、毎日渋谷駅（まいにちしぶやえき）で、かい主（ぬし）の帰（かえ）りを待（ま）っていました。そして、かい主（ぬし）がなくなってからも、ずっとそこで待（ま）っていました。このエピソードが有名（ゆうめい）になり、この像（ぞう）ができました。今（いま）は待（ま）ち合（あ）わせの場所（ばしょ）として有名（ゆうめい）です。

From time immemorial, dogs have been man's best friend. The photograph to the right is of the statue of Hachiko, which stands in front of Shibuya Station in Tokyo. This dog, Hachiko, used to wait at Shibuya Station every day for his master's return [from work]. Even after his master passed away, he continued to wait for him at the same place. This story became famous, and this statue was built. Now the statue is well known as a meeting place.

VOCABULARY

よい	good (same as いい; used often in writing)
パートナー	partner
ハチ公像（こうぞう）	statue of Hachiko
ハチ公（こう）	Hachiko (name of a famous dog)
〜像（ぞう）	statue of ——
〜という	called ——, named ——
なくなる	die, pass away
エピソード	episode, story
待（ま）ち合（あ）わせ	appointment, arrangement to meet
〜として	as ——, in the capacity of ——

NOTES

1. 専門店(せんもんてん)もでき／有名(ゆうめい)になり

Often in written Japanese, the verb of a clause stating a reason or cause will end in the *-masu* stem instead of being put in the conjunctive *-te* form.

2. 服(ふく)を着(き)た犬(いぬ)

服(ふく)を着(き)た犬(いぬ) is equivalent to 服(ふく)を着(き)ている犬(いぬ). For a verb whose past form expresses ongoing effect, both forms may be used interchangeably.

　めがねをかけた人(ひと)／かけている人(ひと)
　a person wearing glasses

3. そこで待(ま)っていました／このエピソード

このハチ公(こう) and この像(ぞう) both refer to the photograph that is actually there on the page. このエピソード points to the overall content of the story that was previously discussed in the text. In this way, こ-demonstratives may be used to collectively refer to what you stated so far. The antecedent of そこ in そこで is Shibuya Station, mentioned in an earlier sentence.

4. ハチ公(こう)という + noun

ハチ公(こう)という犬(いぬ) informs readers that the dog in the photograph is named Hachiko. The pattern "proper name + という + common noun" functions to introduce the name of a person, place, or thing that you believe your listener does not know, or that you yourself are not entirely familiar with. という is a combination of the quotation particle と and いう, "to say," here meaning "to be called." いう when used with this sense is typically written in hiragana instead of in kanji (言(い)う). という may also be used in the form ～といいます to introduce yourself to someone you do not know, e.g., ＡＢＣフーズのミルズといいます, "I am Mills from ABC Foods."

In addition to when giving names, という may also be used in the pattern "clause + という + common noun" to provide details on the content of that noun.

　ハチ公(こう)はかい主(ぬし)をずっと待(ま)っていたというエピソードがあります。
　There is a story about how Hachiko continued to wait for his master.

　バレリーナになりたいというゆめをもっています。
　I have a dream of becoming a ballerina.

5. 待(ま)ち合(あ)わせの場所(ばしょ)として

として indicates a role or capacity.

　ミルズさんは新(あたら)しいプロジェクトのチーフとして東京(とうきょう)支社(ししゃ)に来(き)ました。
　Mr. Mills came to the Tokyo branch office as the chief of the new project.

GRAMMAR & PATTERN PRACTICE

I Expressing Causes of or Reasons for Situations or Outcomes

ペットを家族(かぞく)のようにかんがえる人(ひと)がふえたため、ペットかんれんの新(あたら)しいビジネスも生(う)まれました。

ため indicates a cause or reason. The cause or reason is stated before ため, the effect(s) or consequence(s) after it. Though it cannot stand alone in a sentence, unmodified by another word, ため is a noun and so follows plain forms in the noun-modifying pattern (see front endpapers). When it is necessary to emphasize the reason, the particle に is used with ため, e.g., ために. A further use of ため, that of indicating a purpose, will be covered in Lesson 5 (p. 90).

サイン会(かい)は作家(さっか)の急病(きゅうびょう)のために、キャンセルになりました。
The autograph session was canceled due to the author's sudden illness.

(*sign on a wall*) 工事中(こうじちゅう)のため、このみちはとおれません。
This road is blocked because it is under construction.

せいで is similarly used to express a cause or reason. It underlines the feeling that the consequences of something were negative and the person or thing that brought them about blameworthy.

雪(ゆき)がたくさんふったせいで、電車(でんしゃ)がとまって、旅行(りょこう)に行(い)けませんでした。
All because it snowed a lot, the trains stopped and I couldn't go on my trip.

おかげで, another related expression, indicates positive results. Both せいで and おかげで follow the noun-modifying pattern, just like ため.

今年(ことし)は雪(ゆき)がたくさんふったおかげで、長(なが)くスキーがたのしめました。
Thanks to it snowing a lot this year, I was able to enjoy skiing for a long time.

ミルズさんのおかげで、仕事(しごと)がはやく終(お)わりました。
Thanks to Mr. Mills, the job got done quickly.

Read the dialogue while paying attention to the usage of ために, おかげで, and せいで.

A：けいたいがふきゅうしたために、せいかつスタイルがずいぶんかわったというきじを読(よ)みました。

B：ほんとうですね。けいたいのおかげで、いつでも仕事(しごと)の様子(ようす)がわかるので、とてもあんしんです。

A：そうですか。私(わたし)はけいたいのせいで、休(やす)み中(ちゅう)も会社(かいしゃ)かられんらくがあるので、うんざりです。

VOCABULARY

きゅうびょう	sudden illness	～のせいで	all because of ——, through the fault of ——	スタイル	style
キャンセル	cancellation			きじ	article
こうじちゅう	under construction	～のおかげで	thanks to ——	あんしん（な）	reassuring, safe
こうじ	construction	ふきゅうする	become widespread	うんざりです	be sick (of), be fed up

II Describing Change (1): Changes Coming into Effect

動物(どうぶつ)も人間(にんげん)と同(おな)じけんさやちりょうがうけられるようになりました。

The pattern "plain form of a present-affirmative potential verb + ようになる" expresses the idea that something that was not possible before has now become so.

1週間(しゅうかん)でひらがなが読(よ)めるようになりました。
In one week I became able to read hiragana.

The verb わかる appears in the dictionary form before ようになる for the reason that it in itself already denotes potentiality.

かんじをべんきょうしたら、みちや駅(えき)のサインがわかるようになりました。
Once I studied kanji, I became able to understand the signs on the roads and at railway stations.

When an ordinary verb in the dictionary form comes before ようになる, then the pattern expresses a change in habit or manner of doing something.

しゅうしょくしてから、毎日(まいにち)けいざい新聞(しんぶん)を読(よ)むようになりました。
Since I got my job, I have gotten into the habit of reading financial newspapers every day.

小学校(しょうがっこう)のじゅぎょうでパソコンをつかうようになりました。
Elementary schools have started using computers in their classes.

For both uses, negative statements are formed with the *-nai* stem of the verb + なくなる.

ふとって、はやくはしれなくなりました。
I grew fat and became unable to run as quickly as I used to.

最近(さいきん)、子(こ)どもがあまり外(そと)であそばなくなりました。
Recently children have begun to not play outside very much.

Use ように and the proper form of the words in parentheses to complete each sentence describing a change in state.

1 Changes in ability:

1) なっとうが……………なりました。(食(た)べられます)
2) 3か月間毎日(げつかんまいにち)リハビリをしたら、……………なりました。(あるけます)
3) 毎日(まいにち)べんきょうしたので、日本語(にほんご)の新聞(しんぶん)が……………なりました。(読(よ)めます)

VOCABULARY

サイン	sign, signboard
ふとる	get fat, gain weight
なっとう	*natto* (sticky fermented soybeans)
リハビリ	rehabilitation

4) パソコンがフリーズして、メールが..................なりました。(おくれません)

5) 最近ふとってきて、気に入っているスカートが..................なりました。(はけません)

2 Changes in habits and ways of doing things, lifestyles, and trends:

1) 最近よくガールフレンドと..................なりました。(けんかをします)

2) 最近の日本人はしょうがつに、着物を..................なりました。(着ません)

3) メールがふきゅうして、みんなあまりてがみを..................なりました。(書きません)

III Describing Change (2): Continuous Changes

これからもいろいろなペットビジネスがさかんになっていくでしょう。

In Book II (p. 202), 〜てくる was introduced as an expression for indicating a process of change.

人口がふえてきました。	The population has increased.
人口がへってきました。	The population has decreased.

The *-te* form of a verb that expresses change + くる indicates a change going on continuously from the past to the present. The *-te* form of the same type of verb + いく, by contrast, indicates a change starting from some point that continues on into the future.

これからは人口がへっていくでしょう。
From now on the population will probably go on decreasing.

新せいひんの売り上げはどんどんのびていくでしょう。
Sales of the new product are likely to go on growing and growing.

Use 〜ていく with the verbs in parentheses to complete each sentence describing a process of change.

1) ネットショッピングをする人はますます..................でしょう。(ふえる)

2) 子どものかずはますます..................でしょう。(へる)

3) 東京のとちのねだんはもっと..................かもしれません。(上がる)

4) 開発がすすむと、まちの様子はどんどん..................ます。(へんかする)

5) 年をとるにつれて、だんだんかんがえ方が..................ます。(かわる)

VOCABULARY

スカート	skirt	ますます	increasingly, more and more
けんかをする	have a fight	とち	land, property
どんどん	rapidly, greatly	ねだん	price
ネットショッピング	Internet shopping	すすむ	progress, proceed
としをとる	become older, age	〜につれて	as (some process takes place)

PRACTICE 1 Discussing Changes in Your Life

PHRASE POWER

① ２４時間買い物ができるようになりました。
It has become possible to shop 24 hours a day.

② ２４時間お金がおろせるようになりました。
It has become possible to withdraw money 24 hours a day.

③ ２４時間ふりこみができるようになりました。
It has become possible to make bank transfers 24 hours a day.

④ いつでも*あたたかいべんとうが食べられるようになりました。
It has become possible to eat warm boxed meals at any time.

⑤ かんたんににもつがおくれるようになりました。
It has become easier to send packages.

⑥ 子どもたちが夜おそく買い物に行くようになりました。
Children have begun to go out shopping late at night.

> * Question word + でも = any-. いつでも means "anytime" (Book II, p. 247), 何でも "anything." Other similar expressions of the pattern "question word + でも" include どこでも (anywhere), だれでも (anyone), and どんな物でも (anything at all).

VOCABULARY ふりこみ deposit (of money into someone else's bank account), transfer (of money)

SPEAKING PRACTICE

TRACK 10

I. Mr. Kato begins a conversation with Ms. Nakamura, who has recently moved to a new apartment.

加藤：　中村さん、新しいマンションはどうですか。
中村：　キッチンがひろくて、とてもいいです。1階にコンビニがあるんです。
加藤：　じゃ、便利でしょう。コンビニで何でも買えるし、いろんなことができますからね。
中村：　ええ。でも、前はよくりょうりを作ったんですが、今はぜんぜん作らなくなってしまいました。毎日コンビニで買った物を食べているんです。
加藤：　ははは。

Kato: How is your new condominium, Ms. Nakamura?
Nakamura: I have a big kitchen, so it's very good. There's a convenience store on the first floor.
Kato: That must be handy then. Nowadays you can buy anything at a convenience store and do a lot of other things there besides.
Nakamura: Yes. But I used to cook a lot and now I don't anymore. Every day I'm just eating things that I bought at the convenience store.
Kato: Ha ha ha.

II. Ms. Nakamura begins a conversation with Mr. Kato, who owns a dog.

中村：　加藤さんのおたくでは犬をかっているそうですね。
加藤：　ええ。
中村：　私もネコをかおうと思っているんです。ひっこしてペットをかえるようになったので。
加藤：　そうですか。動物はいいですよ。うちでは犬をかってから、家族の会話がふえました。それに、朝ばんさんぽに行くようになって、せいかつがきそくただしくなりました。さんぽの後は、ごはんがおいしいし、けんこうにもいいみたいです。

Nakamura: I understand that you keep a dog at your house, Mr. Kato.
Kato: That's right.
Nakamura: I'm thinking of getting a cat. Since I've moved, it's become possible for me to keep pets.
Kato: Is that so? It's good to have animals around. Since we got our dog, our family has started to talk to each other more [lit., "the family's conversation has increased"]. And since I've gotten into the habit of taking it on walks every morning and evening, my life has become more regular. Meals taste more delicious after walks, and all in all it seems to be good for my health, too.

VOCABULARY

キッチン	kitchen
なんでも	anything
いろんな	various, all kinds (of) (colloquial form of いろいろな)
あさばん	morning and evening
きそくただしい	regular, orderly
きそく	rule, regulation
ただしい	correct, orderly

PRACTICE 2 Talking about Trends and Common Sights

PHRASE POWER

I. Common sights in Japan . . .

Out on the town:

① いろいろなじはんきがあります。
There are all kinds of vending machines.

② おしゃれな服(ふく)やドレスを着(き)た犬(いぬ)をよく見(み)かけます。
You often come across dogs wearing fashionable costumes and dresses.

③ 左側(ひだりがわ)つうこうなのに、左(ひだり)ハンドルの車(くるま)がけっこう多(おお)いです。
There are quite a number of cars with left-side steering wheels, even though traffic is to the left.

Inside trains:

① ねている人(ひと)が多(おお)いです。
There are lots of people sleeping.

② まんがを読(よ)んでいるサラリーマンをよく見(み)かけます。
You often come across businessmen reading manga.

③ けしょうをしているわかい女(おんな)の人(ひと)をよく見(み)かけます。
You often come across young women putting on makeup.

④ 夜(よる)おそい時間(じかん)によっぱらったサラリーマンをよく見(み)かけます。
Late at night you often come across drunken businessmen.

VOCABULARY

じはんき	vending machine	ひだりハンドル	left-side steering wheel	よっぱらう	get drunk
ドレス	dress	ハンドル	handle, steering wheel	ゲームソフト	game software
ひだりがわつうこう	to-left traffic	まんが	manga, comic book	はやる	become popular
つうこう	traffic, passage	サラリーマン	businessman		

II. Talking about trends:

① 大人(おとな)もたのしめるゲームソフトがはやっています。
Game software that grownups can also enjoy is popular.

② ６０年(ねん)だいにビートルズがはやっていました。
The Beatles were popular in the 60s.

SPEAKING PRACTICE

TRACK 11

I. Ms. Chandra and Mr. Suzuki remark on vending machines.

チャンドラ：日本(にほん)にはいろいろなじはんきがありますね。この間(あいだ)、花(はな)たばのじはんきを見(み)て、びっくりしました。どんな人(ひと)が買(か)うんでしょう。
鈴木(すずき)：夜中(よなか)に、けっこんきねん日(び)を思(おも)い出(だ)した人(ひと)じゃないですか。
チャンドラ：あはは。でも、たばこやさけのじはんきはいらないと思(おも)います。
鈴木(すずき)：そうですか。私(わたし)は便利(べんり)でいいと思(おも)いますけど。
チャンドラ：子(こ)どもも買(か)えるのはよくないです。

Chandra: In Japan there are all kinds of vending machines, aren't there? The other day I was surprised when I saw a vending machine selling flower bouquets. I wonder what sort of person would buy from such a thing.
Suzuki: Maybe someone who remembered in the middle of the night that it was his wedding anniversary?
Chandra: Ha ha. But I think that vending machines for cigarettes and alcohol are unnecessary.
Suzuki: Do you think so? I think they're good, since they're convenient.
Chandra: It's not good that even children are able to buy from them.

II. Ms. Nakamura and Mr. Suzuki remark on a dog they see wearing a yukata.

中村(なかむら)：見(み)て。かわいい。あの犬(いぬ)、ゆかた着(き)てる！
鈴木(すずき)：かわいいですか。犬(いぬ)にはめいわくだろうと思(おも)いますけど。
中村(なかむら)：そんなことないですよ。犬(いぬ)もうれしいだろうと思(おも)います。ミルズさん、カナダでも服(ふく)を着(き)た犬(いぬ)を見(み)かけますか。
ミルズ：あまり見(み)かけませんねえ。

Nakamura: Look, how cute! That dog's wearing a yukata!
Suzuki: Is it cute? I think it must be annoying for the dog.
Nakamura: Not at all! I think the dog is glad [to be wearing it]. Do you come across dogs wearing clothes in Canada, too, Mr. Mills?
Mills: You don't come across it very often.

VOCABULARY

６０ねんだい	the (19)60s
〜ねんだい	(a certain) era, (a certain) decade
ビートルズ	the Beatles
このあいだ	the other day
おもいだす	remember
いる	need
けど	(used after an opinion or assertion to make it sound less forceful)
めいわく(な)	annoying, inconvenient
そんなことない	that's not so

PRACTICE 3 Referring to Graphs

PHRASE POWER

ＡＢＣフーズ　ペット食品開発部「ペットに関する調査結果」対象１０００人

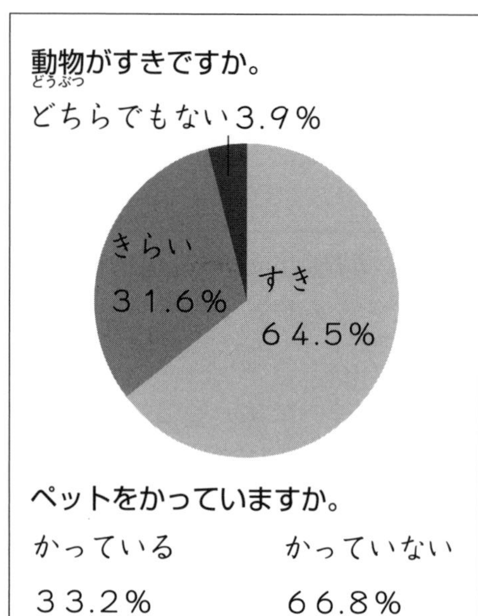

① 動物がすきな人は６４．５％です。
64.5% of the people [questioned] like animals.

② 動物がすきでもきらいでもない人は３．９％です。
Those who neither like nor dislike animals are 3.9%.

③ ペットをかっている人は全体の約３割です。
Those who keep pets are roughly 30% of the whole.

ＡＢＣペット食品
犬用かんづめ「ワンワン」
犬用低カロリーかんづめ
「健康ワンワン」

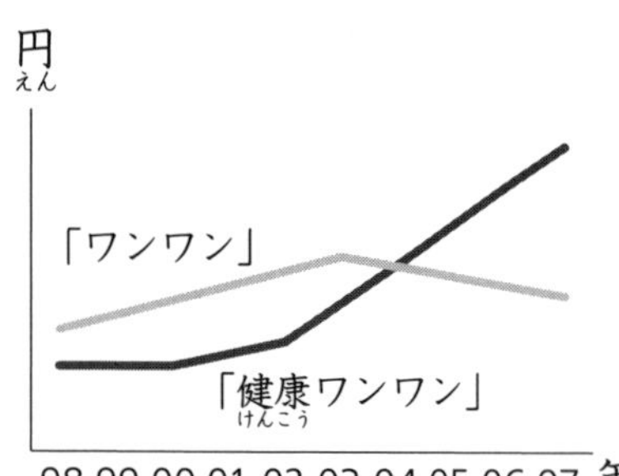

「ワンワン」の売り上げ

④ ２００３年までのびていました。
[Sales] had been growing until 2003.

⑤ ここすう年おちてきています。
For several years now [sales] have been dropping.

「健康ワンワン」の売り上げ

⑥ ２０００年から少しずつのびてきました。
Since 2000 [sales] have grown little by little.

⑦ ２００４年に「ワンワン」をぬきました。
In 2004 [sales] surpassed those of "Wan-Wan."

⑧ これからものびていくでしょう。
[Sales] will probably continue to grow from now on.

VOCABULARY

～にかんする	regarding ——	かんづめ	canned food
けっか	result	ワンワン	Wan-Wan (fictitious canned pet-food product)
たいしょう	subject, respondent	けんこうワンワン	Healthy Wan-Wan
どちらでもない	neither	ここすうねん	these past few years
すきでもきらいでもない	neither like nor dislike	すうねん	number of years
ぜんたい	the whole	ぬく	surpass, exceed
～わり	ten percent		

SPEAKING PRACTICE

TRACK 12

I. Mr. Inuyama is referring to a graph while giving a presentation at a meeting.

犬山（いぬやま）：　では、つぎにこのグラフについてせつめいします。こちらをごらんください。犬（いぬ）をかう人（ひと）のかずは、このようにふえています。特（とく）に、４０だいから５０だいの人（ひと）がふえています。ペットビジネスは、これからどんどんのびていくだろうと思（おも）います。

マルタン：おもしろいデータですね。たしかに、日本（にほん）では犬（いぬ）を子（こ）どものようにかわいがっている人（ひと）をよく見（み）ますね。

Inuyama: Well then, next I'll explain about this graph. Please direct your attention here. The number of people who keep dogs has been increasing, as you can see. There is a rise especially among people in their forties and fifties. I think the pet industry will keep on greatly expanding in the future.

Martin: This data is interesting, isn't it? You certainly do see a lot of people in Japan who treasure their pets as if they were their own children.

II. At the same meeting, Mr. Inuyama discusses the low-calorie cookies for pets that he has just developed while holding up some samples.

犬山（いぬやま）：　最近（さいきん）、ふとりすぎのペットがふえているそうです。

加藤（かとう）：　じつは、うちの犬（いぬ）も最近（さいきん）ふとってきて、こまっているんです。

犬山（いぬやま）：　そうでしょう。ですから、このような低（てい）カロリーのクッキーは、きっと、これから売（う）り上（あ）げがのびていくと思（おも）います。

Inuyama: I hear that the number of overweight pets is growing recently.

Kato: Actually, I've been at a loss because our dog has been getting fatter recently, too.

Inuyama: I'm not surprised. That's why I think that sales of low-calorie cookies like these are certain to grow in the future.

VOCABULARY

グラフ	graph
このように	like this, in this way
４０だいから５０だい	from forties to fifties
～だい	(a certain) generation
かわいがる	love, feel great affection for
ふとりすぎの	too fat
すぎ	too
ですから	that's why, for this/that reason

KANJI PRACTICE

全
全国 ぜんこく
全部 ぜんぶ
安全 あんぜん
whole
all

家
家 いえ
家事 かじ
作家 さっか
家内 かない
house

庭
庭 にわ
家庭 かてい
garden

族
家族 かぞく
tribe
clan

門
門出 かどで
専門 せんもん
gate

物
thing
買い物 (かいもの)
着物 (きもの)
動物 (どうぶつ)

病
sick
ill
病気 (びょうき)
病院 (びょういん)
急病 (きゅうびょう)

院
hall, house
institute
病院 (びょういん)
入院 (にゅういん)

有
have
possess
有名 (ゆうめい)

場
place
scene
場所 (ばしょ)
場合 (ばあい)
会場 (かいじょう)
スキー場 (じょう)

Quiz 1 Unit 1 (Lessons 1–3)

I Fill in the blanks with the appropriate particle.

1) ネコがケージの中（　　）入って、キャットフードを食べています。
2) 花のあまいかおり（　　）します。
3) 魚をみそ（　　）つけておきます。それから、やきます。
4) 『星の王子さま』（　　）いう本を知っていますか。
5) このおちゃ、にがくて薬（　　）ようです。

II Choose the most appropriate word from among the alternatives (1–4) given.

1) あかちゃんがねているので、ドアを（　　）閉めました。
   1. ずっと　2. じっと　3. きっと　4. そっと

2) A：午後7時ごろ、駅でじこがありました。
   B：（　　）、今夜は電車がおくれているんですね。
   1. それが　2. それで　3. それに　4. それは

3) A：今夜パーティーがあるので来ませんか。
   B：友だちと会うやくそくがあるんです。
   A：じゃ、（　　）お友だちも、ごいっしょにどうぞ。
   1. この　2. その　3. あの　4. どの

4) A：売り上げは少しずつですが、のびてきています。
   B：ほんとうですね。たしかに（　　）上がってきていますね。
   1. だんだん　2. どんどん　3. ますます　4. ぜんぜん

5) 去年まではかずがふえていましたが、（　　）へっていくでしょう。
   1. これからは　2. それからは　3. これからも　4. それからも

III Change the form of the word given in parentheses to complete the sentence in a way that makes sense.

1) ひしょの話では、部長は今日（　　）そうです。（休みです）
2) 会議はまだ（　　）ようです。（終わっていません）
3) カロリーの（　　）そうなケーキは食べません。（高いです）
4) ひどい（　　）のに、会社に行かなければなりません。（かぜです）

5) 毎日べんきょうしているので、かんじが（　　　　　）ようになりました。
（読めます）

IV Choose the most appropriate word or phrase from among the alternatives (1–4) given.

1) タクシーの中はたばこの（　　　）がしました。
1. 音　2. 声　3. におい　4. 味

2) A：着物がにあいますね。
B：ありがとうございます。はたちのたんじょう日に両親が（　　　）んです。
1. あげた　2. もらった　3. くれた　4. やった

3) 雨が（　　　）ら、出かけましょう。
1. きれた　2. やんだ　3. きえた　4. とまった

4) たからくじで3おく円あたりました。まるで（　　　）です。
1. ゆめのはず　2. ゆめらしい　3. ゆめだそう　4. ゆめのよう

5) いつ雨がふるかわからないので、いつもかばんにかさを（　　　）。
1. 入れておきます　2. 入れてみます
3. 入れてしまいます　4. 入れるでしょう

V Fill in the blanks with the correct reading of each kanji.

1) 家族みんなでペットを動物病院につれて行きました。
（　　　）（　　　）

2) カロリーが低くて、体にいい食品を開発します。
（　　　）（　　　）（　　　）（　　　）

3) 最近、住所がかわりました。
（　　　）（　　　）

4) 庭に様子を見に行きます。
（　　　）（　　　）

UNIT 2

HUMANS & NATURE

Topics surrounding human beings and nature are sure to become only more relevant not just in Japan but all over the world. No doubt everyone has their own thoughts and points of view on this topic. Use this unit to gain the necessary vocabulary and skills to thoroughly understand others' opinions as well as to state your own on such environmental issues as food, health, and global warming. Also covered will be ways of conducting and participating in simple interviews and of confirming information as you make your way through a complicated conversation.

LESSON 4 A VISIT TO MR. NAKANO'S FARM, PART 1

TARGET DIALOGUE

ABC Foods plans to develop a new product for health-conscious consumers that uses ingredients safely grown without pesticides. Ms. Martin is visiting an organic farm to do research.

Arriving at the farm, Ms. Martin calls out to the man sitting inside the office.

マルタン：こんにちは。先日(せんじつ)お電話(でんわ)したＡＢＣフーズのマルタンです。

中野(なかの)：　マルタンさんですね。中野(なかの)です。

マルタン：今日(きょう)はおせわになります。

中野(なかの)：　こちらこそ。

マルタン：安全(あんぜん)な野菜(やさい)を作(つく)ることは、たいせつなことだと思(おも)います。→p. 69

今日(きょう)はぜひいろいろ教(おし)えてください。

中野(なかの)：　わかりました。何(なん)でもご質問(しつもん)ください。

マルタン：ありがとうございます。さっそくですが、こちらの野菜(やさい)は全(ぜん)部無農薬(ぶむのうやく)ですか。

中野(なかの)：　ええ、そうです。農薬(のうやく)をまったく使(つか)わないで作(つく)っています。→p. 70

では、はたけにごあんないします。どうぞ。

Out in the fields:

中野(なかの)：　そこに農場(のうじょう)のあんないばんがあります。どのはたけで何(なに)を作(つく)っているか書(か)いてあります。→p. 71 (*approaches the guide map and points*)

ここが今(いま)いるところです。

マルタン：広(ひろ)いですねえ。あ、りんごえんもあるんですね。りんごは無(む)農薬(のうやく)で作(つく)るのがむずかしいと聞(き)きましたが。

中野(なかの)：　そのとおりです。りんごは少(すこ)し農薬(のうやく)を使(つか)っています。できるだけ使(つか)わないようにしていますが。

マルタン：じつは、安全(あんぜん)なりんごを使(つか)って→p. 70新(しん)しょうひんを開発(かいはつ)したいんです。無農薬(むのうやく)でりんごを作(つく)るのはむりなんでしょうか。

中野(なかの)：　いいえ、そんなことはありません。おいしくて安全(あんぜん)なりんごがせいさんできるように→p. 72、ずっとけんきゅうしています。来年(らいねん)は無農薬(むのうやく)でせいさんできそうです。

マルタン：すばらしいですね。どうやって作(つく)るんですか。

中野(なかの)：　それはきぎょうひみつです。ははは。

Martin: Hello. I'm Martin from ABC Foods, the one who called you the other day.
Nakano: Ms. Martin. I'm Nakano.
Martin: Thank you for your time today.
Nakano: Please, I should be thanking you.
Martin: I think that growing safe vegetables is an important thing to do. Please, by all means, teach me about all kinds of things today.
Nakano: All right. Feel free to ask me about anything.
Martin: Thank you. To begin right away, are all the vegetables here pesticide-free?
Nakano: Yes, that's right. I grow them without using any pesticides at all. Well then, I'll show you to my fields. Please come this way.

. . . . . .

Nakano: That is a guide map to my farm. It has written on it what is being grown in which field. (*approaches the guide map and points*) Here is where we are now.
Martin: This farm is certainly big. Oh, there's an apple orchard too, isn't there? I heard that it's difficult to grow apples without using pesticides.
Nakano: That's correct. I do use pesticides a little on my apples. I try not to as much as possible, though.

Martin: Actually, we want to develop a new product using safely grown apples. Is it impossible to make apples without using pesticides?

Nakano: No, not at all. For a long time I've been doing research so I can produce apples that taste good and are safe to eat. Next year it looks like I'll be able to produce some without using any pesticides.

Martin: How wonderful! How will you grow them?

Nakano: That's a trade secret. Ha ha ha.

VOCABULARY

中野（なかの）	Nakano (surname)
おせわになります	thank you for your time/assistance [lit., "I'll be receiving your assistance"]
こちらこそ	I'm the one (see Note 4 below)
こと	(see p. 69)
ご質問（しつもん）ください	please ask
質問（しつもん）する	ask a question
さっそくですが	to begin right away, without further ado
さっそく	right away
無農薬（むのうやく）の	without pesticides, pesticide-free
無（む）〜	without ——, -free
農薬（のうやく）	pesticide
まったく	at all, entirely
〜ないで	(see p. 70)
農場（のうじょう）	farm
〜てある	(see p. 71)
りんごえん	apple orchard
そのとおり	that's correct, exactly so
できるだけ	as much as possible
せいさんする	produce
けんきゅうする	research
きぎょうひみつ	trade secret
ひみつ	secret

NOTES

1. こんにちは

こんにちは can often be used not only as a greeting but also to call out to others to let them know that you are there.

2. 先日（せんじつ）

先日（せんじつ）, meaning "a day in the not-so-distant past," is often used in formal situations. In casual speech, この間（あいだ） is commonly used.

3. おせわになります

せわになる, meaning "to receive someone's assistance," is often used as a form of business greeting. It also frequently shows up in telephone conversations. Different tenses are used depending on the state of the relationship between the speaker and listener. They can be summed up as follows.

おせわになります:
used when initiating a business relationship and also while the relationship is going on

おせわになりました:
used when thanking someone at the conclusion of a business relationship

おせわになっています：
used when greeting someone during the course of a business relationship

The above expressions are also commonly used outside of business, in greeting someone who has dealings with members of your own family.

(to a teacher of one's child at school) 子(こ)どもがおせわになっています。
My child has been receiving your assistance.

(to a colleague of one's husband) 主人(しゅじん)がおせわになっています。
My husband has been receiving your assistance.

4. こちらこそ

こちらこそ is used in polite conversation to reciprocate a greeting, expression of gratitude, etc. It is roughly translatable as "the same goes for me."

5. ご質問(しつもん)ください

ご質問(しつもん)ください is a politer way of saying 質問(しつもん)してください, "please ask." The pattern "ご + noun + ください" can be used with any number of nouns to convey similar polite requests and recommendations.

ごれんらくください。
Please contact me.

The pattern "お + *-masu* stem + ください" also conveys a polite request.

お使(つか)いください。
Please use it.

お休(やす)みください。
Please take a rest.

6. さっそくですが

さっそくですが is a set phrase commonly used in business transactions to enter into the main topic of discussion. Although さっそく is similar to すぐ in that it means "right away," unlike すぐ it applies only to carrying out actions planned or expected beforehand. Thus it cannot be used in unforeseen situations, such as when calling a doctor "right away" to attend to an emergency patient.

7. どのはたけで何(なに)を作(つく)っているか

The pattern "plain-form clause + か" can be used to form noun phrases. While particles may appear after such phrases, they are usually omitted.

店(みせ)が何時(なんじ)に開(あ)くか（を）教(おし)えてください。
Please tell me what time the store will open.

会議でだれが何をせつめいするか（を）きめましょう。
Let's decide who will explain what at the meeting.

8. ここが今いるところです

This sentence offers the new information ここ, "here," as an answer to the question どこが今いるところですか (Where [on this guide map] are we now?). While Ms. Martin did not explicitly ask such a question, Mr. Nakano still talks to her in this way because he infers from her looking at the guide map that she must be wondering where on it they are.

9. そのとおりです

そのとおり, "exactly that way," effectively means "what you said now is correct." As can be seen from this example, とおり, aside from its basic meanings of "passage" (as of traffic) and "flow" (as of air), can also mean "same in content." In this sense, it may be used in the following ways.

聞いたとおりに話してください。
Please tell me everything exactly as you heard it.

見たとおりにかいてください。
Please draw things exactly as you saw them.

10. できるだけ

できるだけ carries the connotation of doing as much as can be done without unduly emphasizing the things that fall outside this boundary. だけ is a particle used to delineate range or limits.

11. そんなことはありません

そんなことはありません is a set phrase commonly used when negating something the other person has said or when brushing off a compliment. そんなこと, "such a thing," is a demonstrative used to refer to a part of what someone said or something you otherwise heard. Whereas そのこと points to a specific piece of information itself, そんなこと either refers more generally to things like that information or connotes that the information is surprising or should be denied.

12. 来年は無農薬でせいさんできそうです

As in 雨がふりそうです ("It looks like it's going to rain"; p. 34), the pattern "*-masu* stem of a verb + そうです" indicates your impression of what something seems or feels like to you. Using it to talk about the prospects of your own work, as Mr. Nakano does here, conveys the nuance that you are just about to succeed in accomplishing something.

GRAMMAR & PATTERN PRACTICE

I Nominalizing Sentences

安全な野菜を作ることは、たいせつなことだと思います。

Adding こと after a plain-form verb, adjective, or sentence conceptualizes the content and turns it into a noun phrase. For example, 大きい + こと results in a generalized noun phrase meaning "the fact that something is big." As such, 大きいこと is to be distinguished from 大きさ, a nominalization of 大きい that simply means "size" [lit., "largeness"].

安全な野菜を作ること
growing safe vegetables

安全な野菜を作ることは、たいせつなことだと思います。
I think growing safe vegetables is an important thing to do.

In Book II (p. 136), の was also introduced as a nominalizer. But compare the following:

わからないことは、何でも聞いてください。
Ask me anything that you don't understand.

わからないのは、どのもんだいですか。
Which problem is it that you don't understand?

サルがおんせんに入ることを知っていますか。
Do you know that monkeys take baths in hot springs?

サルがおんせんに入っているのを見ました。
I saw a monkey taking a bath in a hot spring.

わからないこと and サルがおんせんに入ること both refer to abstract generalizations, i.e., "things that are not understood" and "the fact that monkeys take baths in hot springs." By contrast, わからないの refers to a particular problem that is not understood and サルがおんせんに入るの to a particular scene of monkeys taking a bath in a hot spring, or in other words to specific phenomena. In this way, こと is used to explain or describe things in general terms. Thus in a sentence such as the following about a general topic, こと, not の, must be used.

私のしゅみは、しゃしんをとることです。
My hobby is taking photographs.

When こと follows a noun, then it means "things having to do with" that noun, e.g., 日本のこと, "things having to do with Japan," or 仕事のこと, "things having to do with work."

Fill in each blank with either こと or の, as appropriate.

1) すみません。少(すこ)し話(はな)したい（　　　）があるんですが。
2) 私(わたし)のゆめはがいこうかんになる（　　　）です。
3) 仕事(しごと)が終(お)わる（　　　）は7時(じ)ごろです。
4) 何(なに)かたのしい（　　　）をしましょう。
5) 友(とも)だちが来(く)る（　　　）を待(ま)っているんです。

II Indicating Means or Attendant Circumstances

農薬(のうやく)を使(つか)って野菜(やさい)を作(つく)ります。
農薬(のうやく)を使(つか)わないで野菜(やさい)を作(つく)ります。

Two or more clauses strung together in their *-te* forms indicate several different possible kinds of relationships (see also Book II, p. 168).

きのうの午後(ごご)、そうじをして、せんたくをしました。(order of actions)
Yesterday afternoon I cleaned house and then did the laundry.

仕事(しごと)があって、パーティーに行(い)けませんでした。(cause)
I couldn't go to the party because I had work to do.

銀行(ぎんこう)からお金(かね)をかりて、家(いえ)を買(か)いました。(means)
I bought a house by acquiring a loan from the bank.

新(あたら)しいジャケットを着(き)て、会社(かいしゃ)に行(い)きました。(attendant circumstances)
I went to the office wearing a new jacket.

The particular relationship expressed by a series of clauses will depend on the context. Whatever their relationship, though, the clauses will always occur in order of temporal occurrence. The latter two usages of "means" and "attendant circumstances" are discussed here for the first time, but bear in mind that you can usually indicate how or under what kind of circumstances events happen just by describing them in the order they occur.

友(とも)だちに会(あ)って、食事(しょくじ)をします (order of action + attendant circumstances)
I will meet my friend and go out to eat with her.

Care needs to be exercised in forming negatives, since negatives of *-te* forms vary depending on whether they indicate cause or means/attendant circumstances. 〜なくて (e.g., 食(た)べなくて) is used for cause, while 〜ないで (e.g., 食(た)べないで) is used for means or attendant circumstances.

VOCABULARY　ジャケット　jacket

〜ずに after the *-nai* stem (e.g., 食べずに) may sometimes be used in place of 〜ないで . For the verb する, the forms are しないで and せずに, respectively.

子どもが朝ごはんを食べなくて、こまっています。(cause)
My child doesn't eat breakfast, so I'm feeling put out.

朝ごはんを食べないで、会社に行きます。(means/attendant circumstances)

朝ごはんを食べずに、会社に行きます。
I will go to the office without eating breakfast.

> Complete the sentences by changing the verbs in parentheses to the proper form(s) for expressing means or attendant circumstances.
>
> 1) いつもミルクを............コーヒーを飲みます。(入れます)
> 2) ミルクもさとうも............コーヒーを飲みます。(入れません)
> 3) ３時間............コンサートのチケットを買いました。(ならびます)
> 4) かぜをひきましたが、薬を............なおしました。(飲みません)
> 5) とても気に入ったので、だれにも............この家を買いました。(そうだんしません)

III Describing Deliberate Effects

どのはたけで何を作っているか書いてあります。

In Book II (p. 36) 〜ている (the *-te* form of a verb + いる) was introduced as an expression for indicating an ongoing action or a state in effect. 〜ている used with a transitive verb typically indicates ongoing action. The *-te* form of a transitive verb + ある (hereafter 〜てある), meanwhile, expresses the effects of an action while also indicating that the action was performed intentionally, for some purpose.

（私は）今名前を書いています。
I am writing my name [on it] right now. (i.e., am in the midst of writing)

名前が書いてあります。
My name is written [on it]. (i.e., so people know who it belongs to)

The following dialogue shows the distinction in meaning between 〜ている, used to express a state in effect, versus 〜てある.

A：まどが開いていますよ。
B：これからそうじをするので、開けてあるんです。
A: The windows are open.
B: The windows have been left open because I'm going to start cleaning the room now.

まどが開いています is a straightforward report made upon observing that the windows are open. 開けてある, meanwhile, indicates that B (or someone else) intentionally opened the windows in preparation for cleaning the room. B could also have said 開けておいた (p. 14), in which case the focus of the sentence would be on who opened the windows, not on the fact that they are open.

Complete the sentences using てある by changing the forms of the verbs in parentheses.

1) 部屋にしょくぶつがたくさん……………………あります。(おく)
2) グラスがきれいに……………………あります。(あらう)
3) いまに大きいえが……………………あります。(かける)
4) 入口にお知らせが……………………あります。(はる)
5) 子ども用のステーキは小さく……………………あります。(きる)

IV Expressing Purpose (1)

よう is a noun that cannot stand by itself but is combined with other modifiers to mean "situation" or "state." In Lesson 1 (p. 10), よう was covered as an expression for stating perceptions and for likening one thing to another. In Lesson 3 (p. 50), it appeared in the expression ようになる, meaning to change to a certain state. In this section, you will learn how to use ように after a description of some desired state to mean "so as to" in a sentence about your efforts toward realizing that state. ように follows desired states, not specific goals, and so is typically used in speaking of something you are working to bring about or prevent but that you ultimately have no direct control over.

日本語が上手になるように、毎日べんきょうしています。
I am studying every day so I will become better at Japanese.

よくねむれるように、ねる前に少しおさけを飲みました。
I drank a little alcohol before going to bed so I would be able to sleep well.

じこにあわないように、気をつけてください。
Please look out for yourself so you don't get into an accident.

ようにする and ようにしている both mean to strive toward a certain state.

毎日、野菜を食べるようにしています。
I try to eat vegetables every day.

VOCABULARY

しょくぶつ	plant	はる	post, put up
いま	living room	あう	meet (here used in the sense of "encounter a negative event," as an accident or earthquake)
かける (R2)	hang	きをつける	take care, look out
おしらせ	notice		

Read the sentences while paying attention to the uses of ように.

1) どろぼうが入(はい)らないように、ぼうはんライトをつけました。
2) スタイルがよくなるように、ダンスのれんしゅうを始(はじ)めました。
3) スタッフがゆっくり休(やす)めるように、しずかなきゅうけいしつを作(つく)りました。
4) 会議(かいぎ)におくれないように、はやくうちを出(で)ました。
5) よく見(み)えるように、大(おお)きいじで書(か)きました。
6) 車(くるま)がたくさんとめられるように、大(おお)きいちゅうしゃ場(じょう)を作(つく)りました。

PRACTICE 1 Asking For and Giving Opinions

PHRASE POWER

I. Common phrases using こと:

① おねがいしたいことがあるんですが。
There's something I'd like to ask you to do.

② 聞(き)きたいことがあるんですが。
There's something I'd like to ask you about.

③ うかがいたいことがあるのですが。
There's something I would like to inquire of you. (polite for ②)

④ 仕事(しごと)のことでそうだんがあるんですが。
I'd like to consult you about work.

⑤ どんなことでしょうか。
What is it?

⑥ 大学(だいがく)ではどんなことをけんきゅうしているんですか。
What kinds of things are you researching at university?

VOCABULARY

スタッフ	staff	うかがう	ask (humble for たずねる, p. 80)
きゅうけいしつ	lounge	しごとのことで	about work
じ	handwriting, character, print		
うかがいたいこと	something I want to ask		

II. Questions, requests, and opinions:

① ～ことにかんしんがありますか。
Are you interested in . . .

② ～ことにきょうみがありますか。
Are you interested in . . .

③ ～ことを知(し)っていますか。
Do you know about . . .

④ ～ことについて、どう思(おも)いますか。
What do you think about . . .

⑤ ～ことについて、ご意見(いけん)をおねがいします。
Please give me your opinion on . . .

⑥ いいことだと思(おも)います。
I think it's a good thing.

⑦ いいことじゃないでしょうか。
It's a good thing, don't you think?

⑧ ひどいことだと思(おも)います。
I think it's a horrible thing.

⑨ たいせつなことだと思(おも)います。
I think it's important.

⑩ どちらとも言(い)えません。
I can't say one way or the other.

⑪ むずかしいもんだいだと思(おも)います。
I think it's a difficult issue.

⑫ 何(なに)もお話(はな)しすることはありません。
I have nothing to say to you.

⑬ ノーコメントです。
I have no comment.

VOCABULARY

かんしんがある	have an interest (in), be concerned (about)	ノーコメント	no comment
(ご)いけん	opinion		
どちらともいえない	cannot say one way or the other		

SPEAKING PRACTICE

I. Mr. Kato approaches Ms. Martin at the office to ask a favor of her.

加藤(かとう)：　マリーさん、今日(きょう)はいそがしいですか。おねがいしたいことがあるんですが。

マルタン：あのう、どんなことでしょうか。今日(きょう)はしなければならないことがたくさんあるんですが。

加藤(かとう)：　そうですか。じゃ、むりですね。ちょっと時間(じかん)がかかりそうなことなんです。

マルタン：すみません。

Kato: Marie, are you busy today? There's something I'd like to ask you to do.
Martin: What might that be? I have a lot of things I have to do today.
Kato: Is that so? You probably won't be able to take it on, then. It's something that looks like it'll take some time.
Martin: I'm sorry.

II. Mr. Suzuki strikes up a conversation with Ms. Martin at the office during their lunch break.

鈴木(すずき)：　きのう、おもしろいことを聞(き)きました。

マルタン：おもしろいことって、どんなことですか。

鈴木(すずき)：　せかい中(じゅう)からチョコレートしょくにんがあつまって、コンテストをするそうです。

マルタン：へえ。おもしろいですね。どこでそんなことを聞(き)いたんですか。

鈴木(すずき)：　中村(なかむら)さんからです。インターネットのブログで読(よ)んだそうです。

Suzuki: I heard something interesting yesterday.
Martin: Something interesting? What is it?
Suzuki: From what I heard, chocolatiers from all over the world are going to gather to hold a contest.
Martin: Oh? How interesting. Where did you hear such a thing?
Suzuki: From Ms. Nakamura. She said she read about it on a blog on the Internet.

VOCABULARY

しょくにん	craftsperson
コンテスト	contest

III. Mr. Suzuki strikes up a conversation with Ms. Martin at the office shortly after New Year's.

鈴木：　マリーさん。今年のもくひょうは何ですか。
マルタン：おいしくて体にいい食品を開発することです。
鈴木：　そうですか。じつは、ぼくも同じことをかんがえていたんです。これからは、けんこうしこうがますます高まるんじゃないでしょうか。
マルタン：そう思います。じゃ、いっしょにがんばりましょう。

Suzuki: Marie, what is your resolution for this year?
Martin: To develop a food product that tastes good and is good for you.
Suzuki: Is that so? Actually, I was thinking the same thing, too. Don't you agree that from now on people are going to become more and more conscious about their health?
Martin: I do. Well then, let's work hard together [to achieve our goal].

IV. Mr. Kato strikes up a conversation with Mr. Mills at the office during their lunch break.

加藤：　小学生が毎日じゅくに行くことについてどう思いますか。
ミルズ：毎日ですか。私はあまりよくないことだと思います。子どもにはあそぶこともたいせつなんじゃないでしょうか。加藤さんのお子さんのことですか。
加藤：　そうなんです。私ははんたいなんですが、妻はじゅくがひつようだと言うんです。
ミルズ：お子さんはどうなんですか。行きたいと言っているんですか。
加藤：　本人はどっちでもいいようなんです。

Kato: What do you think about elementary school children going to cram school every day?
Mills: Every day? I don't think it's a very good idea. Wouldn't you say that it's important for children to play, too? Is this about your own child?
Kato: Yes, it is. I'm against it, but my wife says that he needs cram school.
Mills: What about your child? Is he saying he wants to go?
Kato: He himself doesn't seem to care one way or the other.

VOCABULARY

もくひょう	goal, resolution	はんたい	opposition
けんこうしこう	health-consciousness	ほんにん	the person himself/herself
たかまる	rise, intensify	どっちでもいい	don't care one way or the other
しょうがくせい	elementary school kid		

PRACTICE 2 Talking about Ways of Doing Things

SPEAKING PRACTICE

TRACK 15

I. Mr. Suzuki starts talking to Ms. Martin while drinking coffee together during their break.

鈴木(すずき)：　マリーさんは、いつもコーヒーに何(なに)も入(い)れないで飲(の)むんですか。
マルタン：ええ。いつもブラックです。鈴木(すずき)さんは？
鈴木(すずき)：　ぼくはミルクとさとうをたっぷり入(い)れて飲(の)みます。
マルタン：ふふふ。子(こ)どもみたいですね。

Suzuki: Do you always drink coffee without putting anything in it, Marie?
Martin: Yes, I always have my coffee black. What about you, Mr. Suzuki?
Suzuki: I drink it after adding plenty of milk and sugar.
Martin: (*laughs*) That sounds just like a child.

II. During their lunch break, Mr. Mills approaches Ms. Nakamura, who is looking through a hotel brochure.

ミルズ：　ホテルさがしですか。なつ休(やす)みに行(い)くんですか。
中村(なかむら)：　(*looking through a hotel brochure*) ええ。
ミルズ：　中村(なかむら)さんは、旅行(りょこう)に行(い)く前(まえ)に全部(ぜんぶ)予約(よやく)して行(い)くんですか。
中村(なかむら)：　ええ、ひこうきもホテルもレンタカーもレストランも、全部(ぜんぶ)予約(よやく)して行(い)きます。
ミルズ：　へえ。私(わたし)とはんたいですね。私(わたし)は何(なに)も予約(よやく)しないで行(い)くのがすきです。着(つ)いてから、まちをあるいて、気(き)に入(い)ったホテルをさがすんです。

Mills: Looking for a hotel, I take it. Are you going [somewhere] for summer vacation?
Nakamura: (*looking through a hotel brochure*) Yes.
Mills: Do you go on trips after reserving everything beforehand, Ms. Nakamura?
Nakamura: Yes, I go after reserving everything, from plane tickets to hotels to rental cars to restaurants.
Mills: Really. That's the opposite of me. I like to go without reserving anything. After I get someplace, I walk around town and look for a hotel I like.

VOCABULARY

ブラック	black
たっぷり	plenty (of), a lot (of)
ふふふ	(onomatopoeia expressing the sound of soft laughter)

III. Mrs. Kato comes over to her husband while he is surfing the Internet.

加藤(かとう)（妻(つま)）：何(なに)してるの？
加藤(かとう)（夫(おっと)）：新(あたら)しいシャツとネクタイを買(か)おうと思(おも)って、えらんでいるんだよ。
加藤(かとう)（妻(つま)）：インターネットで？
加藤(かとう)（夫(おっと)）：うん。このシャツに合(あ)いそうなネクタイをえらんで、がめん上(じょう)でくみあわせて、見(み)られるんだ。ほら、どう？
加藤(かとう)（妻(つま)）：あら、それ、いいわね。
加藤(かとう)（夫(おっと)）：じゃ、これ、ちゅうもんしよう。

Mrs. Kato: What are you doing?
Mr. Kato: I thought I'd buy a new shirt and tie, so I'm choosing.
Mrs. Kato: Over the Internet?
Mr. Kato: That's right. You can choose a tie that seems to fit this shirt, and match them on-screen to see how they look. See, what do you think?
Mrs. Kato: Oh, that looks nice.
Mr. Kato: I'll order these, then.

IV. Mr. Kato comes over to Ms. Martin during their lunch break after trying the dessert she brought into the office.

加藤(かとう)：　このやきりんご、おいしいですね。どうやって作(つく)ったんですか。
マルタン：このレシピを見(み)て、書(か)いてあるとおりに作(つく)ったんです。
加藤(かとう)：　ええと「りんごをよくあらって、かわをむかないでオーブンに入(い)れる。１８０度(ど)Ｃで２０分(にじゅっぷん)やく。やけたら、きってはちみつをかける」これだけでいいんですか。
マルタン：ええ。かんたんでしょう。でも、いいりんごを使(つか)うことがたいせつだそうです。

Kato: These baked apples are delicious. How did you make them?
Martin: I looked at this recipe and made them exactly as it was written here.
Kato: Let me see . . . "Rinse the apples well and put them in the oven without peeling. Bake for 20 minutes at 180°C. When done, slice and pour honey on them." Is this all you need to do?
Martin: Yes. Simple, isn't it? But I understand it's important to use good-quality apples.

VOCABULARY

あう	fit, go well with	ちゅうもんする	order	オーブン	oven
がめんじょうで	on-screen	やきりんご	baked apple	～どC	degrees Celsius
くみあわせる (R2)	put together, combine, match	かわ	peel (n.)	はちみつ	honey
あら	oh (used by women)	むく	peel (v.)	かける (R2)	pour

PRACTICE 3 Explaining How to Use Facilities

WORD POWER

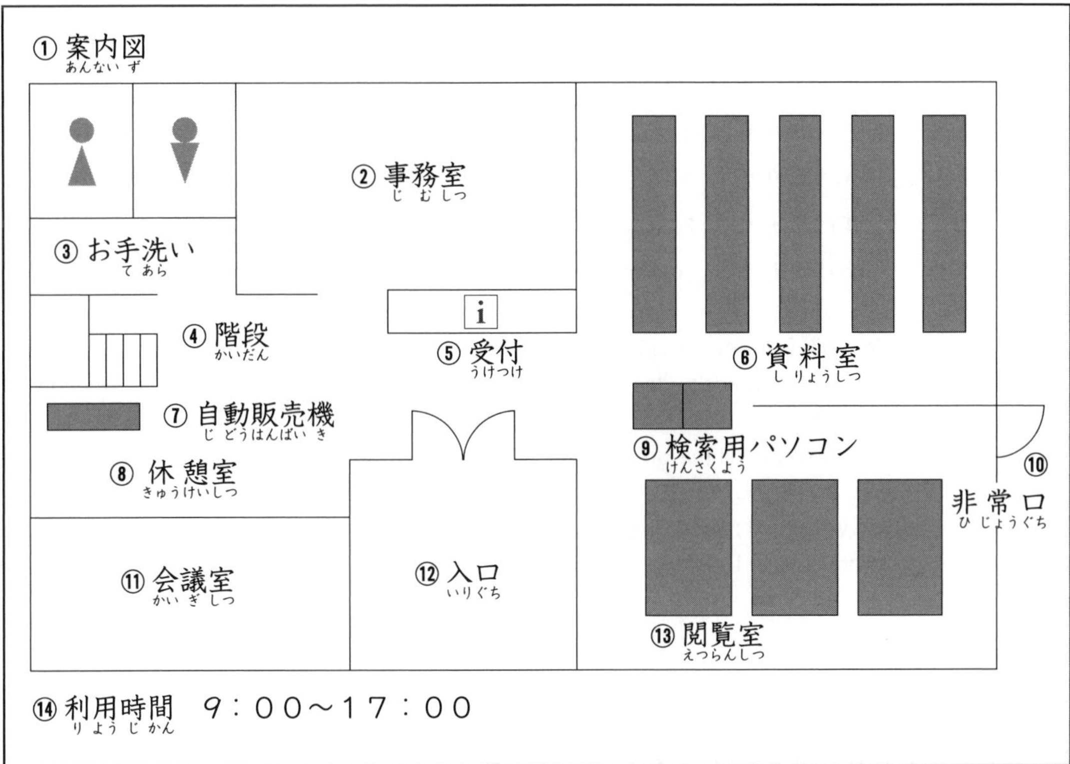

① 案内図（あんないず）	guide map
② 事務室（じむしつ）	office
③ お手洗い（てあらい）	restroom
④ 階段（かいだん）	stairs
⑤ 受付（うけつけ）	reception desk
⑥ 資料室（しりょうしつ）	reference room
⑦ 自動販売機（じどうはんばいき）	vending machine
⑧ 休憩室（きゅうけいしつ）	lounge
⑨ 検索用パソコン（けんさくようパソコン）	computer catalog
⑩ 非常口（ひじょうぐち）	emergency exit
⑪ 会議室（かいぎしつ）	meeting room
⑫ 入口（いりぐち）	entrance
⑬ 閲覧室（えつらんしつ）	reading room
⑭ 利用時間（りようじかん）	service hours

登録（とうろく）	registration
貸し出し（かしだし）	circulation
返却（へんきゃく）	return
公開（こうかい）	open access
非公開（ひこうかい）	restricted access

SPEAKING PRACTICE

TRACK 16

I. Mr. Mills is at a food research institute to view some reference materials.

ミルズ：ＡＢＣフーズのミルズです。しりょうのえつらんに来(き)ました。

係(かかり)の人(ひと)：しりょうのえつらんですね。このカードに名前(なまえ)としょぞく先(さき)とれんらく先(さき)をごきにゅうください。

ミルズ：はい。(*writes*) これでよろしいですか。

係(かかり)の人(ひと)：はい。ありがとうございます。あそこにあんないずがあります。どこにどのしりょうがあるか書(か)いてありますので、ごらんください。

ミルズ：わかりました。ありがとうございました。

Mills: I'm Mills from ABC foods. I've come to view your reference materials.
staff: Perusal of materials. Please write in your name, affiliation, and contact information on this card.
Mills: Yes. (*writes*) Will this be all right?
staff: Yes, thank you. You'll find a guide map over there. It has written on it what materials are where, so please take a look.
Mills: I understand. Thank you.

II. The staff member explains to Mr. Mills how to search for reference materials.

ミルズ：しりょうをけんさくすることができますか。

係(かかり)の人(ひと)：はい。そこにけんさく用(よう)のパソコンがあります。このカードを入(い)れて使(つか)ってください。カードを入(い)れると、とうろくがめんが出(で)ますから、名前(なまえ)としょぞく先(さき)をにゅうりょくしてください。どなたが使(つか)ったかわかるように、使(つか)う方(かた)にとうろくをおねがいしています。

ミルズ：わかりました。

係(かかり)の人(ひと)：何(なに)かわからないことがありましたら、おたずねください。

Mills: Is it possible for me to search for reference materials?
staff: Yes. There you'll find a computer catalog. Please insert this card to use it. Once you insert the card, the registration screen will come up, so please enter your name and affiliation. We ask users to register so we know who used the catalog.
Mills: I understand.
staff: If there is anything you don't understand, please feel free to ask.

VOCABULARY

えつらん	viewing, perusal	きにゅうする	write in, write down
かかりのひと	staff member, person in charge	けんさくする	search for
かかり	duty, responsibility	ことができる (R2)	can, be able to
しょぞくさき	affiliation	おたずねください	please ask (politer way of saying たずねてください)
ごきにゅうください	please write in (politer way of saying かいてください)	たずねる (R2)	ask

III. The staff member calls out to Mr. Mills as he comes out of the reference room.

係の人（かかりのひと）：おさがしのしりょうは見（み）つかりましたか。
ミルズ：ええ、見（み）つかりました。ところで、ここはかんようしょくぶつがたくさんおいてあるんですね。
係の人（かかりのひと）：ええ。目（め）にいいので、あちこちにおいてあるんです。それから、小（ちい）さいじが読（よ）みやすいように、あかるいライトを使（つか）っているんですよ。
ミルズ：そうなんですか。たしかに読（よ）みやすかったです。

staff: Were you able to find the materials that you were looking for?
Mills: Yes, I found them. By the way, you have a lot of potted plants placed here, don't you?
staff: Yes. They've been placed here and there because they're good for the eyes. In addition, we use bright lighting so it'll be easier for people to read small print.
Mills: Is that so? The [print] certainly was easy to read.

VOCABULARY

おさがしの	that you are/were looking for (politer way of saying さがしている／さがしていた)
かんようしょくぶつ	plants appreciated primarily for their leaves
あちこち	here and there, all throughout

KANJI PRACTICE

野

中野 (なかの)
野菜 (やさい)

field
wild

菜

野菜 (やさい)

vegetable

教

教える (おし)

educate

質

質問 (しつもん)

quality
question

問

質問 (しつもん)

inquire
question

無

無農薬 (むのうやく)

no, non-, un-, -free
dis-

農

農薬 (のうやく)
農場 (のうじょう)

farming
agriculture

使

使う (つか)
使用中 (しようちゅう)
大使館 (たいしかん)

use

広

広い (ひろ)

wide
spacious

業

農業 (のうぎょう)

job
business

LESSON 5 A VISIT TO MR. NAKANO'S FARM, PART II

TARGET DIALOGUE

Ms. Martin interviews Mr. Nakano to find out how he came to start his farm.

マルタン：中野さんはなぜこの農場を始めたんですか。

中野：じつは、１０年前まではレストランをけいえいしていたんです。→p. 87

マルタン：そうだったんですか。

中野：ええ。カロリーの高いものばかり食べていたら、体を悪くしてしまったんです。→p. 89 それで、けんこうをとりもどすために、→p. 90 ベジタリアンになりました。

マルタン：へえ。ベジタリアンに。

中野：ええ。ベジタリアンになってから、全国をまわって、安全でおいしい野菜をさがしました。見つけた野菜で作った料理をレストランで出したら、ひょうばんがよくて、毎晩店が予約でいっぱいになりました。

マルタン：それはすごいですね。

中野：おきゃくさんがふえて、野菜がたくさんひつようになりました。それで、自分で農場を始めようと思ったんです。レストランは妻にまかせて、私は野菜を作る勉強を始めました。

マルタン：勉強はどちらで？

中野(なかの)：　しぜん農法(のうほう)の農場(のうじょう)を手(て)つだいながら、勉強(べんきょう)しました。あちこちの農場(のうじょう)で勉強(べんきょう)したんですが、しぜん農法(のうほう)にはいろいろな方法(ほうほう)があることがわかりました。
→p. 91

マルタン：いろいろな方法(ほうほう)があるんですか。

中野(なかの)：　ええ。ちがう野菜(やさい)をくみあわせてうえるとか、むしや鳥(とり)の力(ちから)をかりるとか。その土地(とち)と野菜(やさい)に合(あ)う方法(ほうほう)を見(み)つけることが大切(たいせつ)なんです。

マルタン：なるほど。それで、お体(からだ)の方(ほう)は？

中野(なかの)：　１年(ねん)ですっかりけんこうになりました。

マルタン：そうですか。食(た)べるものってほんとうに大切(たいせつ)なんですねえ。

Martin: Why did you start this farm, Mr. Nakano?

Nakano: Actually, until ten years ago I used to operate a restaurant.

Martin: Was that so?

Nakano: Yes. I was eating nothing but foods high in calories, and ended up making myself unwell. So to regain my health, I became a vegetarian.

Martin: Really, a vegetarian?

Nakano: Yes. After becoming a vegetarian, I went around the entire country looking for vegetables that were safe and good to eat. When I offered the dishes I made with the vegetables that I found back at my restaurant, they proved very popular, so that eventually, every night my restaurant was filled with reservations.

Martin: That's impressive.

Nakano: Because I had more customers, I started needing a lot of vegetables. So I thought of starting a farm on my own. I left the restaurant to my wife and started studying how to grow vegetables.

Martin: Where did you study?

Nakano: I studied while helping out at organic farms. I studied at farms all over the place, and found out that there are many different methods of organic agriculture.

Martin: Are there really so many different methods?

Nakano: Yes. Like combining different kinds of vegetables to plant together, or drawing upon the power of insects and birds. It's important to find the method that fits the soil and vegetable.

Martin: I see. And what about your health?

Nakano: I became entirely healthy in one year.

Martin: Is that so? What you eat really does matter, doesn't it?

VOCABULARY

なぜ	why	悪(わる)くする	damage, hurt
けいえいする	operate, manage	〜くする	make —— (see p. 89)
ばかり	nothing but, only	ために	to, in order to (see p. 90)

ベジタリアン	vegetarian
いっぱい	full
まかせる (R2)	entrust, leave up to
しぜん農法(のうほう)	organic agriculture
ながら	while (see p. 91)
方法(ほうほう)	method
うえる (R2)	plant
力(ちから)	power, ability
見(み)つける (R2)	find
なるほど	I see, I understand
すっかり	entirely, completely
って	(colloquial particle that emphatically identifies the topic of the sentence)

NOTES

1. なぜ

なぜ means the same as どうして, with the distinction being that どうして is used more often in everyday speech. なぜ is frequently employed for questions embedded in a longer statement, e.g., なぜ来(こ)なかったのかよくわからない, "I don't understand very well why he didn't come."

2. そうだったんですか

そうだったんですか is one common way of responding to an explanation of the reasons or circumstances behind something. It often indicates surprise over unexpected information about something that happened or was decided upon some time ago.

3. カロリーの高(たか)いものばかり食(た)べていたら

ばかり, "nothing but," expresses the idea of performing a certain action (in this case, eating) repeatedly with just one thing.

4. へえ。ベジタリアンに

へえ is an interjection made upon hearing an unexpected piece of information. The following utterance, ベジタリアンに, goes to the heart of what Mr. Nakano has just said and confirms its significance. Such reiteration conveys to Mr. Nakano what part of his comments Ms. Martin finds important and interesting.

5. いろいろな方法(ほうほう)があるんですか

In this sentence, Ms. Martin takes out いろいろな方法(ほうほう)がある, the crucial part of Mr. Nakano's earlier statement, いろいろな方法(ほうほう)があることがわかりました, to reflect it back to him in the form of a question. By doing this, Ms. Martin signals to Mr. Nakano what part of his comments she finds important while encouraging him to speak more on the topic.

6. ちがう野菜(やさい)をくみあわせてうえるとか

とか is used to list examples of something you are trying to give details about. Below, for instance, it gives tomatoes and lettuce as examples of vegetables. Particles after とか are frequently omitted. とか shows up mostly in speech. In writing and in formal situations, ～や～など is used.

> あの農場(のうじょう)では、トマトとか、レタスとか（の）野菜(やさい)を作(つく)っています。
> At that farm, they grow tomatoes and lettuce and other such vegetables.

GRAMMAR & PATTERN PRACTICE

I Expressing Completion/Incompletion of Past, Present, or Future Actions

１０年前(ねんまえ)までレストランをけいえいしていました。

Be careful when choosing between ～ている and its past form, ～ていた, to convey tense.

～ている indicates that an action either goes on or is repeated over a period of time. The form ～ている is used for actions in the present and future, ～ていた for those in the past.

使(つか)う

今(いま)、パソコンを使(つか)っています。
I am using the computer right now.

仕事(しごと)をするとき、いつもパソコンを使(つか)っています。
I always use a computer when I work.

この仕事(しごと)を始(はじ)めてから、ずっとこのパソコンを使(つか)っています。
I have been using this computer ever since I started working here.

きのうの午後(ごご)、このパソコンを使(つか)っていました。
I was using this computer yesterday afternoon.

先週(せんしゅう)の土曜日(どようび)まで、このパソコンを使(つか)っていました。
I was using this computer until last Saturday.

A second function of ～ている and ～ていた is to express completion, i.e., that an action is/was/will be completed at a specified point in the present, past, or future. The negative forms ～ていない and ～ていなかった indicate that the action is/was/will still be incomplete at that point. This meaning of "completed action" is particularly easy to see with verbs showing not ongoing action but states in effect.

着(つ)く

Present:

にもつはもうくうこうに着(つ)いています。
My luggage has arrived at the airport already.

にもつはまだくうこうに着(つ)いていません。
My luggage has not arrived at the airport yet.

Past:

けさ私(わたし)がくうこうに着(つ)いたとき、にもつはもう着(つ)いていました。
When I got to the airport this morning, my luggage had already arrived.

けさ私(わたし)がくうこうに着(つ)いたとき、にもつはまだ着(つ)いていませんでした。
When I got to the airport this morning, my luggage had not yet arrived.

Future:

あした、私(わたし)がくうこうに着(つ)いたとき、にもつは先(さき)に着(つ)いているでしょう。
When I get to the airport tomorrow, my luggage will probably already have arrived.

あした、私(わたし)がくうこうに着(つ)いたとき、にもつはまだ着(つ)いていないでしょう。
When I get to the airport tomorrow, my luggage will probably have not yet arrived.

Complete the sentences by changing the verbs to the appropriate forms.

1) 教(おし)えます

→ 今(いま)、日本(にほん)の大学(だいがく)でえいごを________

→ 去年(きょねん)まで、中国(ちゅうごく)の大学(だいがく)でえいごを________

2) けっこんします

→ 日本(にほん)に来(き)たとき、もう________

→ 日本(にほん)に来(き)たとき、まだ________

3) ねます

→ 私(わたし)がきのううちに帰(かえ)ったとき、妻(つま)は先(さき)に________

4) 始(はじ)まります

→ けさ、テレビをつけたとき、ニュースはもう________

5) 終(お)わります

→ 私(わたし)が会社(かいしゃ)に着(つ)いたときには、会議(かいぎ)はたぶん________でしょう。

II Describing Change (3): Effected Changes

体を悪くしてしまったんです

The adverbial form of an adjective (e.g., 大きく, きれいに) + する expresses the idea of making something change into a certain state. In Book II (p. 117) the pattern "adverbial form of an adjective + なる" was introduced as meaning to change into a certain state. The difference between the two is that ～く／にする is transitive (e.g., 大きくする, "to make something big"), while ～く／になる is intransitive (e.g., 大きくなる, "to become big"). にする and になる may also be used with potential verbs and verbs that express states, e.g., できるようにする, できるようになる. The example above from the Target Dialogue, 体を悪くします, is virtually synonymous with 体が悪くなります. Although Mr. Nakano did not actually intentionally "make" himself unhealthy, he still uses 悪くする to express his belief that he became unwell as a consequence of his own actions.

客： このテーブルは安くなりますか。
店員： ええ、安くしますよ。
customer: Could this table become cheaper?
salesperson: Yes, we'll make it cheaper.

Complete the sentences as in the example.

例）みじかい
→ 会議の時間をみじかくしてください。

1) あかるい
→ 電気をつけて、部屋を..

2) シンプル
→ ドレスのデザインを..

3) 少ない
→ しゅくだいを..

4) かんたん
→ テストを..

5) きびしい
→ れんしゅうをもっと..

III Expressing Purpose (2)

けんこうをとりもどすために、ベジタリアンになりました。

ため（に）as used here indicates the purpose of an action. In Lesson 3 (p. 49), ため（に）was introduced as an expression for indicating a cause or reason. ため, like よう (p. 72) a noun that cannot stand by itself, means "cause" or "reason." Since fulfilling a purpose constitutes one reason for doing something, the "cause" and "purpose" meanings of ため（に）may be regarded as being intrinsically the same.

家を買うために、ちょきんしています。
I am saving money to buy a house.

中国語をれんしゅうするために、中国の会社でアルバイトを始めました。
I started working part-time at a Chinese company to practice my Chinese.

ために is somewhat similar to ように. The difference is that ように expresses a state you hope will eventually come about, while ために indicates your purpose for doing something.

つうやくになれるように、毎日えいごを勉強しています。
I am studying English every day so I can become an interpreter.

つうやくになるために、毎日えいごを勉強しています。
I am studying English every day to become an interpreter.

Complete the sentences using ために and the proper form of the verbs in parentheses.

1) 新しい食品を________、プロジェクトチームを作りました。
(開発します)

2) 仕事の前にヨガを________、7時に会社に来ました。
(ならいます)

3) くうこうに両親を________、会社をはやく出ました。
(むかえに行きます)

4) つうやくのしかくを________、えいかいわ学校にかよっています。
(とります)

5) 新しいことに________、会社をやめました。
(ちょうせんします)

VOCABULARY

ちょきんする	save money
アルバイト	part-time job
かよう	attend, commute

IV Describing Simultaneous Actions

しぜん農法(のうほう)の農場(のうじょう)を手(て)つだいながら、勉強(べんきょう)しました。

The *-masu* stem of a verb + ながら indicates two actions performed simultaneously by the same subject. In the example above, Mr. Nakano uses ながら to explain how he studied organic agriculture, i.e., while helping out at organic farms. ～て (p. 70) also indicates means, but differs in usage from ながら, as illustrated below.

バスが来(こ)なかったので、あるいて駅(えき)に行(い)きました。
The bus didn't come, so we walked to the station.

時間(じかん)がなかったので、駅(えき)まであるきながら、話(はな)しました。
We were short on time, so we talked while walking toward the station.

Here ～て and ながら each form a subordinate clause that modifies the following main clause. ～て indicates the means/attendant circumstances of the action in the main clause, while ながら highlights the simultaneity of the actions in the main and subordinate clauses. Thus, あるいて describes the speaker's means of going to the station, while あるきながら gives focus to what the speaker did while walking toward the station, i.e., talk.

Complete the sentences using ながら and the proper form of the verbs in parentheses.

1) ....、大学(だいがく)にかようのはたいへんですね。(はたらく)
2) いいおんがくを..............................、おいしいコーヒーを飲(の)むのがすきです。(聞(き)く)
3) このおんせんは、うみを..............................、おふろに入(はい)れます。(ながめる)
4) このきょうざいは、ゲームを..............................、えいごの勉強(べんきょう)ができます。(たのしむ)

VOCABULARY

ながめる (R2)	gaze at, look at
きょうざい	teaching materials

PRACTICE 1 Giving and Listening to News

PHRASE POWER

I. Breaking news to someone:

① じつは
Actually . . .

② もう聞(き)きましたか
Have you heard already?

③ もう知(し)っていると思(おも)いますが
I imagine you may know already, but . . .

④ ごぞんじだと思(おも)いますが
I imagine you are aware of this, but . . . (polite)

⑤ ごぞんじかもしれませんが
You may be aware of this, but . . . (polite)

⑥ ごぞんじのように
As you are aware, . . . (polite)

II. Responding to news:

① ほんとうですか。
Really?

② そうなんですか。
Is that so?

③ そうだったんですか。
Was that so?

④ それはおもしろいですね。
That's interesting, isn't it?

⑤ それは知(し)りませんでした。
I didn't know that.

⑥ へえ、初(はじ)めて聞(き)きました。
Really, that's the first I've heard of that.

⑦ ほんとうにそうなんですか。
Is that really so?

⑧ しんじられません。
I can't believe it.

VOCABULARY

ごぞんじです	know, be aware of (politer way of saying しっている)
しんじる (R2)	believe

SPEAKING PRACTICE

TRACK 18

I. Mr. Suzuki informs Ms. Martin of some news that is going around the office.

鈴木：　マリーさん、聞きましたか。パリ支社のシモンさんが、今度のオリンピックのマラソンだいひょうにきまったそうです。

マルタン：えっ、シモンさんが？　知りませんでした。どこで聞いたんですか。

鈴木：　さっき社内メールが来たんです。マリーさんはシモンさんと親しいんですか。

マルタン：ええ。私がパリ支社にいたころも毎朝仕事の前にはしっていました。

Suzuki: Have you heard, Marie? I hear that Mr. Simon of the Paris branch office has been selected to represent his [home] country in the marathon at the next Olympics.

Martin: What? Mr. Simon? No, I didn't know. Where did you hear this?

Suzuki: I just got a message through the employee mailing list. Do you know Mr. Simon well, Marie?

Martin: Yes. He used to go running every morning before work even while I was at the Paris branch office.

II. Ms. Nakamura informs Mr. Mills of some news that is going around the office.

中村：　あのう、もうごぞんじかもしれませんが、加藤さんのお母様がゆうべなくなったそうです。

ミルズ：ええ。さっき鈴木さんから聞いて、おどろいています。急だったんですか。

中村：　いいえ、1年前からずっと入院していたそうです。加藤さんはお母さんのかんびょうをするために、週末はほとんど病院に行っていたそうです。

ミルズ：そうだったんですか。ずっとたいへんだったんですね。

Nakamura: Um, you may be aware of this already, but Mr. Kato's mother passed away last night, I've been told.

Mills: Yes. I just heard from Mr. Suzuki, and I'm surprised. Was it sudden?

Nakamura: No, from what I understand she had been hospitalized for the entire past year. Mr. Kato was at the hospital nearly every weekend to look after her, from what I hear.

Mills: Is that how it was? He must have had it hard all that time.

VOCABULARY

シモン	Simon (surname)
オリンピック	Olympics
マラソン	marathon
だいひょう	representative
しゃないメール	employee mailing list
したしい	close, on familiar terms (with)
おかあさま	mother (respectful way of referring to someone else's mother)
きゅう(な)	sudden
にゅういんする	be hospitalized
かんびょうをする	look after (someone who is sick), nurse

PRACTICE 2 Giving Career Histories

WORD POWER

しけん	を うける に うかる／おちる

しかく	めんきょ	を とる
しゅうしごう	はくしごう	

べんごし	ぜいりし	こうにんかいけいし
いし	かんごし	きょうし
びようし	ちょうりし	けんちくし
こうむいん	ししょ	がくげいいん
つうやく（しゃ）	ほんやくしゃ	システムエンジニア
しょうけんアナリスト	システムアナリスト	

会社（かいしゃ）を始（はじ）める・作（つく）る・せつりつする・けいえいする
レストランを開（ひら）く

マスコミかんけいの仕事（しごと）をする
どくりつする
しゅうにゅうをえる
のうりょくを生（い）かす

VOCABULARY

うかる	pass (an exam)	ほんやくしゃ	translator
めんきょ	license	システムエンジニア	systems engineer
しゅうしごう	master's degree	しょうけんアナリスト	investment analyst
はくしごう	doctorate	システムアナリスト	systems analyst
ぜいりし	tax accountant	せつりつする	set up, found
こうにんかいけいし	certified public accountant	ひらく	open, establish
いし	doctor	マスコミ	mass media
びようし	beautician, hairstylist	～かんけいのしごとをする	work in (a job field)
ちょうりし	(licensed) cook	どくりつする	become independent
けんちくし	architect	しゅうにゅう	income
ししょ	librarian	える (R2)	gain, earn
がくげいいん	curator	のうりょく	ability, qualification
つうやくしゃ	interpreter	いかす	put to use, take advantage of
～しゃ	-er, -or, -ant (person who performs a certain job)		

SPEAKING PRACTICE

I. An interviewer questions an applicant during a job interview.

面接官：　今の会社では、どんな仕事をしているんですか。
応募者：　ソフトウェアの開発をしています。
面接官：　今の会社に入る前はどんな仕事をしていたんですか。
応募者：　コンビニでアルバイトをしていました。アルバイトをしながら学校にかよって、システムエンジニアのしかくをとりました。
面接官：　なぜうちの会社に入りたいとかんがえたんですか。
応募者：　こちらで開発しているソフトウェアに前からきょうみがあったんです。

interviewer: What kind of work are you doing at your present company?
applicant: I'm working in software development.
interviewer: What kind of work were you doing before you joined your present company?
applicant: I worked part-time at a convenience store. While working part-time, I attended school and got certified as a systems engineer.
interviewer: Why did you think of joining our company?
applicant: I've always been interested in the software being developed here.

II. A magazine reporter interviews the president of a venture company founded while the president was still in college.

雑誌記者：　この会社は学生じだいに始めたと聞きましたが……。
会社社長：ええ、２年生のときゼミの友人とせつりつしました。
雑誌記者：　大学の勉強をつづけながら、会社もけいえいしていたんですか。
会社社長：ええ。とてもたいへんでしたが、４年生になった時、会社はかなり大きくなっていました。スタッフが５０人いじょういました。
雑誌記者：　５０人も。
会社社長：ええ。ですから、大学をやめました。仕事にせんねんすることにしたんです。

reporter: I heard that you started this company in your college years . . .
president: Yes, I founded it during my second year with a friend taking the same seminar.
reporter: So you were running your company while also continuing your studies at university?
president: Yes. It took a lot of hard work, but by the time I was in my fourth year, the company had grown quite large. I had a staff of over fifty.
reporter: Fifty, that many.
president: Yes. So I quit college. I decided to concentrate on my work.

VOCABULARY

めんせつかん	interviewer	ゼミ	seminar
おうぼしゃ	applicant	５０にんも	as many as fifty people
ソフトウェア	software	せんねんする	concentrate, focus on
がくせいじだい	college years		

PRACTICE 3 Asking for Reasons and Histories

SPEAKING PRACTICE

I. While at a bar, Ms. Martin calls out to Mr. Honda, the barkeeper, to remark on his collection of car photographs.

マルタン：この店(みせ)は車(くるま)のしゃしんがたくさんあるんですね。全部(ぜんぶ)レース用(よう)の車(くるま)ですね。

本田(ほんだ)：ええ。全部(ぜんぶ)私(わたし)がうんてんしていた車(くるま)なんです。

マルタン：ええっ？　マスターがうんてんしていた車(くるま)なんですか。

本田(ほんだ)：ええ、そうです。学生(がくせい)じだいからレースに出(で)ていたんです。かいがいのレースに出(で)たこともありますよ。

マルタン：へえ。すごいですね。今(いま)も出(で)ているんですか。

本田(ほんだ)：いえ、３年前(ねんまえ)にやめました。毎日(まいにち)車(くるま)のことばかりかんがえていたら、妻(つま)がうちを出(で)て行(い)ってしまったんです。妻(つま)とのかんけいをとりもどすために、レースに出(で)るのをやめたんです。

マルタン：そうだったんですか。

Martin: This place has a lot of photographs of cars, doesn't it? They're all racing cars, no?
Honda: Yes. They're all cars I've driven myself.
Martin: What? All cars you've driven?
Honda: Yes, that's right. I started entering races in my college days. I've even entered some races abroad.
Martin: Really? That's incredible. Do you still race even now?
Honda: No, I quit three years ago. My wife left me because I kept on thinking about nothing but cars every day. I quit entering races to rebuild my relationship with my wife.
Martin: Was that so?

VOCABULARY

レース	race	でていく	leave
ほんだ	Honda (surname)	〜との	with ——
マスター	barkeeper		
いえ	no (shortened, colloquial form of いいえ)		

II. A visitor to a private photography exhibit calls out to the photographer.

客(きゃく)： すばらしいしゃしんですね。
写真家(しゃしんか)： ありがとうございます。
客(きゃく)： むかしの東京(とうきょう)と今(いま)の東京(とうきょう)をくみあわせたしゃしんはおもしろいですね。いつからこういうしゃしんをとり始(はじ)めたんですか。
写真家(しゃしんか)： ３年前(ねんまえ)からです。それまではサラリーマンをしていたんですが、あるとき、東京(とうきょう)のまちをあるいていたら、こうそうビルのとなりに古(ふる)いおてらがあるのが見(み)えたんです。それで、こういうたてものがなくなる前(まえ)に、しゃしんをとっておこうと思(おも)ったんです。
客(きゃく)： これは昭和(しょうわ)の初(はじ)めの家(いえ)ですね。どこでとったんですか。
写真家(しゃしんか)： 全部(ぜんぶ)東京(とうきょう)です。浅草(あさくさ)とか、新宿(しんじゅく)とか、たくさんこういう家(いえ)がのこっていますよ。

visitor: These are spectacular photographs.
photographer: Thank you.
visitor: It's interesting to see photographs combining [images of] old Tokyo with Tokyo today, isn't it? Since when did you start taking such photographs?
photographer: From three years ago. Up until then I was working as a businessman, but one time while I was walking around Tokyo I came across an old temple standing next to a high-rise building. So I decided to capture photographs of these kinds of structures before they disappeared.
visitor: These are houses from the early Showa era, aren't they? Where did you photograph them?
photographer: All in Tokyo. There are many houses like these left in areas such as Asakusa and Shinjuku.

VOCABULARY

しゃしんか	photographer
こういう	these kinds of
とりはじめる (R2)	start taking (photos)
こうそう	high-rise
しょうわ	the Showa era (1926–1989)
のこる	be left over, remain

KANJI PRACTICE

料
料金 (りょうきん)
無料 (むりょう)

ingredients
fee

理
料理 (りょうり)
物理 (ぶつり)
無理 (むり)

reason
ration

悪
悪い (わるい)
悪口 (わるぐち)
最悪 (さいあく)

bad

晩
毎晩 (まいばん)
今晩 (こんばん)
朝晩 (あさばん)

night

勉
勉強 (べんきょう)

endeavor

強	強い (つよ) 勉強 (べんきょう)
strong	

法	方法 (ほうほう) 農法 (のうほう)
law method	

力	力 (ちから) 入力 (にゅうりょく) 電力 (でんりょく)
power force	

地	土地 (とち) 地下 (ちか)
ground base	

切	切る (き) 切手 (きって) 大切 (たいせつ) 親切 (しんせつ)
cut	

LESSON 6 GLOBAL WARMING

TARGET READING & DIALOGUE

地球おんだん化は、２１せいきの世界にとって、しんこくな問題です。ＩＰＣＣによると、今の地球のへいきん気温は、１００年前より０．７度以上高いそうです。何年か前にへいきん気温が上がったと聞いたときは、じっかんがわきませんでしたが、最近は、地球おんだん化のえいきょうを強くかんじるようになりました。日本でも、12月になっても、あきの花がさきつづけていたり、１月にはるの花がさいたりしています。また、世界かくちで、こうずいやかんばつが起きています。

→p. 103 →p. 105

地球おんだん化をふせぐために、私たちは何ができるのでしょうか。こくさい社会では、いろいろなとりくみが始まっています。私たちも、ごみをリサイクルしたり、電気をせつやくしたり、ひとりひとりができることをしなければなりません。

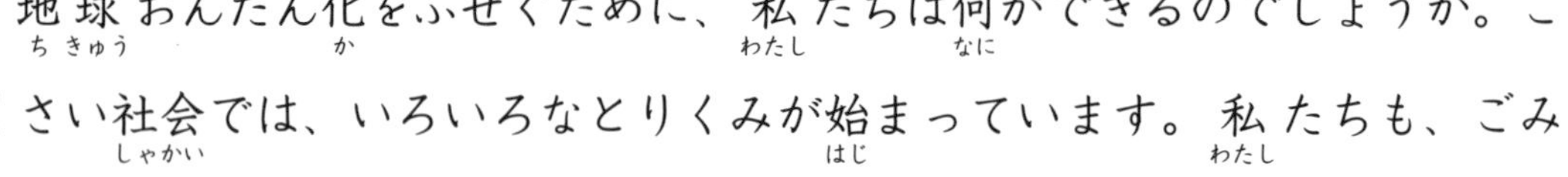

Global warming is a serious problem for the world in the twenty-first century. According to the IPCC, average global temperatures today are over 0.7 degrees higher than they were a hundred years ago. Just a few years ago, when we heard that average temperatures had risen, the reality of it did not strike home; but recently we have begun to strongly feel the effects of global warming. Even in Japan, we see such things happening as autumn flowers continuing to bloom even into December and spring flowers blooming in January. Moreover, floods and droughts are occurring in many parts of the world.

What can we do to prevent global warming? All kinds of endeavors are starting up within the international community. We, too, must recycle waste, conserve electricity, and do whatever else is possible for each and every one of us to do.

While walking around town with Mr. Kato, Ms. Martin notices a solar panel installed on the roof of a house.

マルタン：あの家のやねについているの、ソーラーパネルですよね。

加藤：　ああ、そうですね。最近、つけている家がふえてきました。

マルタン：コストパフォーマンスはどうなんでしょうか。

加藤(かとう)：　かなりいいらしいですよ。ソーラーパネルのメーカーにつとめている友人(ゆうじん)に聞(き)いたんですが、天気(てんき)がいい日(ひ)は十分(じゅうぶん)に発電(はつでん)できるので、電力会社(でんりょくがいしゃ)から電力(でんりょく)を買(か)わなくてもいい →p. 104 そうです。それに、電気(でんき)があまったら、売(う)れるそうです。

マルタン：そうですか。じゃ、電気料金(でんきりょうきん)が安(やす)くなりますね。

加藤(かとう)：　ええ。じつは、今度(こんど)うちもつけることにしたんです →p. 106。きょうみがあるなら →p. 107、その友人(ゆうじん)をしょうかいしましょうか。少(すこ)し安(やす)く買(か)えると思(おも)いますよ。

マルタン：でも、うちはマンションですから。

加藤(かとう)：　そうでしたね。

Martin:	Those are solar panels on the roof of that house over there, aren't they?
Kato:	Oh, you're right. These days, homes with solar panels are on the increase.
Martin:	How is the cost performance?
Kato:	Quite good, I hear. I heard this from a friend employed at a solar panel manufacturer: on days when the weather is nice, the panels apparently produce sufficient power, so you don't need to buy power from the electric company. Moreover, if any power remains, you can sell it, apparently.
Martin:	Is that so? So the electricity bill gets cheaper, does it?
Kato:	That's right. In fact, we want to put solar panels on our own home in the near future. If you're interested, I can introduce you to that friend of mine. You will probably be able to buy panels [from his company] rather cheaply.
Martin:	But I live in an apartment building.
Kato:	That's right, I forgot.

VOCABULARY

地球(ちきゅう)おんだん化(か)	global warming
おんだん化(か)	warming
２１せいき	twenty-first century
～にとって	to ——, for —— (see Note 1 on next page)
しんこく(な)	serious, grave
ＩＰＣＣ	Intergovernmental Panel on Climate Change
へいきん	average
気温(きおん)	temperature
じっかんがわく	seem real
じっかん	feeling of reality
わく	arise
えいきょう	effect, influence
かんじる	feel
～でも／～ても	even if —— (see p. 103)
さきつづける	continue to bloom
～たり	(see p. 105)

また	also, moreover
かくち	many places throughout, all over
こうずい	flood
かんばつ	drought
ふせぐ	prevent
こくさい社会（しゃかい）	international community
社会（しゃかい）	society
とりくみ	measure, endeavor
せつやくする	conserve
ひとりひとり	each one, each and every person
ソーラーパネル	solar panel
コストパフォーマンス	cost performance
メーカー	manufacturer
十分（じゅうぶん）（な）	sufficient, enough
発電（はつでん）する	generate electricity
電力会社（でんりょくがいしゃ）	electric company
電力（でんりょく）	electricity
あまる	be left over

NOTES

1. ２１せいきの世界（せかい）にとって

にとって indicates the standard for a judgment or an evaluation that follows.

> この日本語（にほんご）のテストは、ミルズさんにとってむずかしくないですが、ホワイトさんにとってむずかしいです。
>
> This Japanese-language test is not difficult for Mr. Mills, but it is difficult for Mr. White.

2. 何年（なんねん）か前（まえ）に

Attaching the question marker か to a numerical question word (e.g., 何年（なんねん）か, 何人（なんにん）か, 何日（なんにち）か, いくつか) gives the meaning "a few" (years, people, days, things, etc.).

3. さきつづけて (compound verb)

Attaching the *-masu* stem of a verb to another verb results in a compound verb. Common compound verbs using さく include, in addition to さきつづける given here, さき始（はじ）める, "to begin blooming," and さき終（お）わる, "to stop blooming."

4. できるのでしょうか

As covered in Lesson 1 (p. 8), でしょうか is used to raise an issue with or to consult someone. In writing meant to raise awareness of a problem, such as here, it forms a rhetorical question inviting the reader to think about that problem.

5. ソーラーパネルですよね

よね is an ending used in spoken Japanese to ask someone for confirmation about a statement one has made. Here Ms. Martin uses it merely to strike up a conversation with Mr. Kato, for she knows full well that what she is seeing are indeed solar panels.

6. そうでしたね

Saying そうでしたね in response to someone's statements tells that person you "already knew" or "were just reminded of" that information.

GRAMMAR & PATTERN PRACTICE

I Expressing Ideas that Run Contrary to Expectation (2)

１２月(がつ)になっても、あきの花(はな)がさきつづけています。

〜ても (the *-te* form of a verb/adjective + the particle も) is used to make a statement about something that goes contrary to what would naturally be expected from the set of conditions described before 〜ても. When coming after *-na* adjectives and nouns, 〜ても becomes 〜でも.

とおくても、あるいて行(い)きます。
I'm going to walk there even if it's far.

せつめいを読(よ)んでも、よくわかりません。
I don't get it very well even after reading the explanation.

あした、ひまでも、パーティーには行(い)きません。
I won't go to the party tomorrow even if I have the time.

あした、雨(あめ)でも、ゴルフに行(い)きます。
I'm going to go golfing tomorrow even if it's raining.

Earlier (p. 35), のに was introduced as an expression for joining together two statements that go against each other. The difference between のに and 〜ても is that のに connotes feelings of surprise or regret, while 〜ても conveys either a positive or neutral attitude. Thus のに cannot be used for making requests or invitations, while 〜ても can.

薬(くすり)を飲(の)んでも、かぜがなおりませんでした。
My cold didn't go away even after I took some medicine. (straightforward statement of fact)

薬(くすり)を飲(の)んだのに、かぜがなおりませんでした。
My cold didn't go away even though I took some medicine. (stresses the feeling that something is wrong)

あしたは天気(てんき)が悪(わる)くても、ゴルフに行(い)きましょう。
Let's go golfing tomorrow even if the weather is bad.

Complete the sentences using ～ても with the words in parentheses.

1) ケーキをたくさん……………………、ぜんぜんふとりません。(食べる)
2) その会社は、インターネットで……………………、見つかりません。(しらべる)
3) こうつうが……………………、この家に住みたいと思います。(ふべん)
4) れんしゅうが……………………、やめないでつづけます。(きびしい)
5) むずかしい……………………、できると思います。(仕事だ)

II Expressing Lack of Obligation

電力会社から電力を買わなくてもいいそうです。

～なくてもいい conveys the idea of not having to do something. The opposite expression is ～なければならない, "must." ～なくてもいい and ～なければならない often come up when talking or asking about social or institutional rules and obligations. ～なければならない connotes that you feel what you must do to be a burden, ～なくてもいい that you feel yourself free from such a burden.

毎日はたらかなければなりません。(need)
I have to work every day.

毎日はたらかなくてもいいです。(no need)
I don't have to work every day.

To state whether a certain action *can* be done (i.e., is permitted) or not, meanwhile, the following expressions are used:

ビルの前に車をとめてもいいです。(permitted)
You may park your car in front of the building.

ビルの前に車をとめてはいけません。(not permitted)
You must not park your car in front of the building.

Read the sentences while paying attention to the uses of the expressions introduced above.

1) インターネットで買い物をすれば、店に行かなくてもいいです。
2) 東京はこうつうがべんりなので、車を買わなくてもいいです。
3) 前に住んでいたまちでは、ごみをすてるとき、もえるごみともえないごみに分けなければなりませんでした。今住んでいるまちは分けなくてもいいです。分けるきかいがあるそうです。

III Giving Examples of Events or Actions

１２月になっても、あきの花がさきつづけていたり、１月にはるの花がさいたりします。

～たり is used to list examples of actions or things that all fall into the same general category. In the statement above, for example, it gives two instances of things that happened as a result of global warming.

Q：週末は何をしていたんですか。
A：家にいました。そうじをしたり、せんたくをしたりしていました。
Q: What were you doing over the weekend?
A: I was at home. I cleaned house and did the laundry and other such things.

Q：このスポーツクラブでは何ができるんですか。
A：およいだり、ヨガをしたりすることができます。
Q: What can you do at this sports club?
A: You can swim and do yoga, among other things.

～たり may be used even with just one example.

休みにはパリに行って、びじゅつ館をたずねたりしたいです。
Over the vacation I want to go to Paris to visit museums and do other such things.

Complete the sentences using ～たり .

1) ガーデニングをする、バーベキューをする
→ 庭のある家に住んで、日曜日には、........................、
........................したいです。

2) ミュージカルを見る、買い物をする
→ ロンドンに行ったら、........................、
........................したいです。

3) 毎朝ジョギングをする、にくを食べるのをやめる
→ やせるために、........................、
........................しましたが、あまりこうかがありませんでした。

VOCABULARY ～てはいけない must not —— (from previous page)

IV Stating Decisions

今度(こんど)、うちもつけることにしたんです。

As covered in Book II, Lesson 2 (p. 23), the verb します is used when stating a decision made from among several alternatives.

これにします。(e.g., when selecting something at a store)
I'll take this.

ことにします／する means to decide to do something. It is typically used to inform people about decisions you have already made, and so often appears in the past form, i.e., ことにしました／した. In the first sentence below, for example, ことにしました conveys the speaker's decision to go study abroad.

来年(らいねん)イギリスにりゅうがくすることにしました。
I have decided to study abroad in Great Britain next year.

会社(かいしゃ)をやめることにしましたが、まだ部長(ぶちょう)に話(はな)していません。
I've decided to quit my job, but haven't told the department manager yet.

ことになる／なった, meanwhile, expresses that something is/was decided upon. In short, ことになる is intransitive, while ことにする is transitive. When talking about decisions, Japanese people tend to say ことにする and ことになる more often than they say きめる or きまる.

会社(かいしゃ)をやめることにしました。
I have decided to quit my job.

会社(かいしゃ)をやめることになりました。
It has been decided that I am to quit my job.

The first sentence above makes it clear that the decision to quit was the speaker's own, while the second leaves it ambiguous whether the decision was dictated by the company or other outside circumstances.

来年(らいねん)イギリスにりゅうがくすることになりました。
It has been decided that I am to study abroad in Great Britain next year.

会社(かいしゃ)のほうしんで、プロジェクトをちゅうしすることになりました。
It has been decided that we are to cancel the project in accordance with the wishes of the company.

VOCABULARY

りゅうがくする	study abroad
ほうしん	policy

Making Suggestions Based on Supposition

きょうみがあるなら、その友人をしょうかいしましょうか。

In Book II (p. 222) you were introduced to なら as the conditional form of a *-na* adjective or noun + です. なら also follows the plain forms of verbs. It is used to make a suggestion in reaction to what someone has just said or based on what you suppose they are thinking.

Ａ：今晩はステーキを食べようと思います。
Ｂ：ステーキを食べるなら、ＡＢＣフーズのステーキソースを使ってみてください。おいしくなりますよ。

A: I think I'll eat steak tonight.
B: If you're going to eat steak, try using the steak sauce from ABC Foods. It'll taste better.

Read the dialogues while paying attention to the uses of なら.

1) Ａ：新しいパソコンを買おうと思っているんですが。
Ｂ：新しいパソコンを買うなら、のぞみ電気がいいですよ。店員がとても親切です。

2) Ａ：大阪のホテルを予約したいんですが。
Ｂ：ホテルの予約をするなら、インターネットを使えばかんたんですよ。

3) Ａ：大学をそつぎょうしたら、ＩＴかんけいの仕事をしたいんです。
Ｂ：ＩＴかんけいの仕事をしたいなら、ＩＴの仕事をしている友人をしょうかいしましょう。

VOCABULARY

ステーキソース	steak sauce
のぞみでんき	Nozomi Electronics (fictitious store)
ＩＴ	information technology

PRACTICE 1 Discussing Weather and Its Effects

WORD POWER

① はれ
はれる

② くもり
くもる

③ 雨（あめ）
雨（あめ）がふる

④ 風（かぜ）
風（かぜ）がふく

⑤ 台風（たいふう）
あらし

⑥ 雪（ゆき）
雪（ゆき）がふる

⑦ 雪（ゆき）がつもる

⑧ こおり
こおりがはる

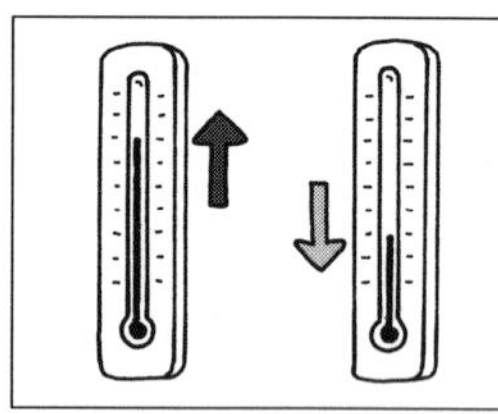

⑨ 気温（きおん）が上（あ）がる
気温（きおん）が下（さ）がる

⑩ 雪（ゆき）がとける
こおりがとける

⑪ こうずい

⑫ かんばつ

VOCABULARY

はれ	sunny	ゆきがつもる	snow piles up
くもり	cloudy	つもる	pile up
くもる	become cloudy, cloud up	こおりがはる	ice freezes over
かぜがふく	wind blows	はる	freeze over
たいふう	typhoon	こおりがとける	ice melts
あらし	storm	とける (R2)	melt

SPEAKING PRACTICE

I. While preparing to go out on a rainy day, Mr. Suzuki is stopped in front of his apartment by the building manager.

管理人(かんりにん)：鈴木(すずき)さん、お出(で)かけですか。
鈴木(すずき)：　これからサッカーを見(み)に行(い)くんです。
管理人(かんりにん)：ええっ？　こんなに雨(あめ)がふっているのに行(い)くんですか。
鈴木(すずき)：　ええ。サッカーは、雨(あめ)がふっても、しあいをするんです。だから、ぼくたち、サポーターも、どんなにさむくても、おうえんに行(い)くんです。
管理人(かんりにん)：かぜをひかないようにしてくださいね。

manager: Are you going out, Mr. Suzuki?
Suzuki: I'm going to go see a soccer match.
manager: What? Are you going even when it's raining this hard?
Suzuki: That's right. In soccer, matches are held even when there is rain. So we supporters also go to cheer our team no matter how cold it is.
manager: Take care you don't catch cold.

II. Mr. Mills and Mr. Kato are about to leave the office to go on a business trip to Kyushu.

ミルズ：急(きゅう)に空(そら)がくもってきましたね。
加藤(かとう)：　ええ、風(かぜ)も出(で)てきましたね。天気(てんき)よほうによると、台風(たいふう)が九州(きゅうしゅう)に近(ちか)づいているらしいです。
ミルズ：ひこうきは予定(よてい)どおりにとぶでしょうか。
加藤(かとう)：　ひこうきがとばなくても、今日中(きょうじゅう)に九州(きゅうしゅう)に行(い)かなければなりませんよ。
ミルズ：じゃ、新幹線(しんかんせん)にしましょうか。のぞみなら、今日中(きょうじゅう)に着(つ)きますから。

Mills: The sky has suddenly started to cloud up, hasn't it?
Kato: Yes, the wind is starting to blow, too. According to the weather forecast, there apparently is a typhoon approaching Kyushu.
Mills: Will the plane fly as scheduled, do you suppose?
Kato: Even if the plane doesn't fly, we still have to get to Kyushu sometime today.
Mills: Shall we go by the Shinkansen, then? We'll get there today if we take the Nozomi.

VOCABULARY

こんなに	to this extent, this much
だから	so, therefore
サポーター	supporter, fan
どんなにさむくても	no matter how cold it is
どんなに〜ても	no matter how . . .
おうえん	cheering
かぜがでる	wind starts to blow
きゅうしゅう	Kyushu (southernmost of Japan's four largest islands)
ちかづく	approach, come near
のぞみ	Nozomi (the fastest of the three types of Shinkansen trains running between Tokyo and Fukuoka)

III. Mr. Suzuki and Mr. Kato are in the office, chatting.

鈴木（すずき）：今年（ことし）はだんとうで、２月（がつ）になっても、スキー場（じょう）にぜんぜん雪（ゆき）がつもっていないそうです。

加藤（かとう）：そういえば、鈴木（すずき）さんは北海道（ほっかいどう）しゅっしんでしたね。けさの新聞（しんぶん）によると札幌（さっぽろ）の雪（ゆき）まつりで雪（ゆき）のぞうがとけ始（はじ）めたらしいですよ。

鈴木（すずき）：札幌（さっぽろ）がそんなにあたたかいのは、ほんとうにめずらしいです。東京（とうきょう）ももうウメがさいていますしね。

加藤（かとう）：ふゆのコートがぜんぜん売（う）れなかったり、ビジネスにもえいきょうが出（で）ているらしいですよ。

Suzuki: I understand that this year we're having a warm winter and the ski resorts don't have any snow at all even though it's February.

Kato: That reminds me, you're from Hokkaido, aren't you, Mr. Suzuki? According to the paper this morning, the snow statues at the Sapporo Snow Festival have apparently started to melt.

Suzuki: It's really unusual for it to be so warm in Sapporo. Not to mention that in Tokyo, too, the plums are blooming already.

Kato: Businesses are supposedly being affected, too, what with winter coats and other things not selling at all.

IV. Mr. Kato is asking about solar generators from a friend who works for an electronics manufacturer.

加藤（かとう）：ソーラー発電機（はつでんき）は、くもっていても、発電（はつでん）できるんですか。

青田（あおた）：いいえ、空（そら）がくもっていると、発電（はつでん）できません。

加藤（かとう）：そうなんですか。うちにつけたら、どのぐらい発電（はつでん）できるんでしょうか。

青田（あおた）：うちの会社（かいしゃ）のサイトで、シミュレーションすることができますよ。住（す）んでいる場所（ばしょ）ややねのかたちを入力（にゅうりょく）すると、１年間（ねんかん）にどのぐらい発電（はつでん）できるかわかります。

加藤（かとう）：そうですか。じゃ、やってみます。

Kato: Can solar generators produce electricity even when it's cloudy?

Aota: No, they can't generate electricity when the sky is clouded over.

Kato: Is that right? How much electricity do you suppose we could generate if we installed one on our house?

Aota: You can run a simulation on our company website. Once you enter the location of your house and the shape of your roof, you can find out how much electricity you'll be able to produce in one year.

Kato: Is that so? I'll try it out, then.

VOCABULARY

だんとう	warm winter	ウメ	plum	シミュレーションする	run a simulation
スキーじょう	ski resort	はつでんき	generator	かたち	shape
～しゅっしん	from ——	あおた	Aota (surname)		
そんなに	to that extent, so . . .	サイト	website		

PRACTICE 2 Discussing Global Warming

WORD POWER

地球（ちきゅう）	the Earth
かんきょう	the environment
しぜん	nature
地球（ちきゅう）おんだん化（か）	global warming
せんしん国（こく）	developed countries
とじょう国（こく）	developing countries

PHRASE POWER

げんいん	causes
温室効果（おんしつこうか）ガス	greenhouse gases
二酸化炭素（にさんかたんそ）のはいしゅつ	carbon dioxide emissions
たいさく	countermeasures
二酸化炭素（にさんかたんそ）のはいしゅつりょうをきせいする	regulate carbon dioxide emissions
しげんをせつやくする	conserve (natural) resources
えいきょう	effects
大気中（たいきちゅう）に二酸化炭素（にさんかたんそ）がふえる	carbon dioxide in the atmosphere increases
きこうがかわる	the climate changes
南極（なんきょく）や北極（ほっきょく）のこおりがとける	the polar ice caps melt
ひょうががなくなる	glaciers disappear

VOCABULARY

せんしんこく	developed country	はいしゅつりょう	amount of emission
とじょうこく	developing country	きせいする	regulate
げんいん	cause	しげん	(natural) resource
おんしつこうかガス	greenhouse gas	たいき	air, atmosphere
おんしつ	greenhouse	きこう	climate
ガス	gas	なんきょく	South Pole
にさんかたんそ	carbon dioxide	ほっきょく	North Pole
はいしゅつ	emission	ひょうが	glacier
たいさく	countermeasure		

SPEAKING PRACTICE

The following dialogues depict a schoolteacher answering questions from students about global warming. Study the dialogues and practice asking and answering similar questions about specialized topics.

TRACK 23

I. Global warming:

生徒（せいと）：先生（せんせい）、地球（ちきゅう）おんだん化（か）というのは、何（なん）のことですか。
教師（きょうし）：地球（ちきゅう）があたたかくなることです。
生徒（せいと）：あたたかくなると、何（なに）かこまることがあるのですか。
教師（きょうし）：ええ。地球（ちきゅう）があたたかくなると、いろいろな問題（もんだい）が起（お）こります。
生徒（せいと）：どんな問題（もんだい）ですか。
教師（きょうし）：世界中（せかいじゅう）のきこうがかわって、こうずいが起（お）きたり、かんばつが起（お）きたりします。そうすると、しょくぶつがそだたなくなったり、病気（びょうき）がふえたりします。

student: Teacher, what is global warming?
teacher: It's when the Earth gets warmer.
student: Is there anything to be concerned about if it gets warmer?
teacher: Yes. All sorts of problems come up when the Earth gets warmer.
student: What kinds of problems?
teacher: Climates change all over the world, so that floods and droughts occur, for example. That leads to other things, such as plants failing to grow and illnesses spreading.

II. Effects of global warming:

生徒（せいと）：地球（ちきゅう）おんだん化（か）がこのまますすむと、地球（ちきゅう）はどうなるのでしょうか。
教師（きょうし）：このまますすむと、１００年後（ねんご）には、へいきん気温（きおん）が今（いま）より６度以上（どいじょう）高（たか）くなるそうです。６度以上（どいじょう）高（たか）くなると、南極（なんきょく）や北極（ほっきょく）のこおりがとけて、かいめんが６０（ろくじゅっ）センチぐらい上（あ）がるそうです。ちょっと、かんがえてみてください。かいめんが上（あ）がると、どんなことが起（お）こると思（おも）いますか。
生徒（せいと）：地球（ちきゅう）のりくちが少（すく）なくなります。
教師（きょうし）：そのとおりです。いくつかのしまには、人間（にんげん）が住（す）めなくなってしまうそうです。

student: What will happen to the Earth if global warming goes on the way it is doing now?
teacher: If global warming goes on this way, then from what I understand, a hundred years from now average temperatures will rise to over six degrees from what they are now. If temperatures rise more than six degrees, then the ice at the South and North Poles will melt and the level of the sea will rise about sixty centimeters. Now try and think a bit. What kinds of things do you think will happen if the sea level rises?

VOCABULARY

おこる	happen, occur	センチ	centimeter
そだつ	grow	りくち	land
このまま	in this way, as is	しま	island
かいめん	sea level		

student: The area of land on the Earth will decrease.

teacher: That's correct. I understand that people will not be able to live anymore on some islands.

III. Causes of global warming:

生徒：地球おんだん化のげんいんは何ですか。

教師：地球おんだん化のげんいんは、温室効果ガスです。大気の中にこのガスがふえると、気温が上がります。

生徒：温室効果ガスというのは、どんなガスですか。

教師：はい。いろいろありますが、一番多いのは、二酸化炭素です。火を使ったり、車をうんてんしたりすると、出るガスです。地球の人口がふえて、さんぎょうがはったつしたために、急に多くなりました。

student: What are the causes of global warming?

teacher: The cause of global warming is greenhouse gases. When the level of these gases in the atmosphere increases, then temperatures rise.

student: What types of gases are greenhouse gases?

teacher: Good question. There are many, but the one that we have the most of is carbon dioxide. This is the gas that is given off when you do things like use fire or drive cars. Its levels suddenly rose because the population of the world increased and industry developed.

IV. Countermeasures to global warming:

生徒：おんだん化をふせぐためには、どうすればいいのですか。

教師：二酸化炭素を出さないようにして、温室効果ガスを少なくすることがひつようです。

生徒：そのために、私たちにできることがありますか。

教師：はい、あります。できるだけ、電気を使わないようにしたり、車にのらないようにしたりしてせいかつしましょう。

student: What should we do to prevent global warming?

teacher: First we need to reduce greenhouse gases by trying not to emit carbon dioxide.

student: Is there anything that we can do to achieve this?

teacher: Yes, there is. Let's try as much as possible to go about our lives without using electricity or riding in cars, among other things.

VOCABULARY

はい	good question
さんぎょう	industry
はったつする	develop

PRACTICE 3 Talking about Environmental Issues

SPEAKING PRACTICE

TRACK 24

I. Mrs. Kato comes up to Taro while he is at the sink washing his face.

加藤（妻）：太郎！　もったいない。かおをあらうとき、おゆを出しっぱなしにしちゃだめよ。それから、部屋を出るときは、かならず電気をけしなさい。エネルギーをむだにしてはいけませんよ。

太郎：　ごめんなさい。わかってるんだけど、ついわすれちゃうんだ。

加藤（妻）：温室効果ガスをへらすには、ひとりひとりができることをしないと。

太郎：　わかった。これからは、エネルギーをむだにしないようにするよ。

Mrs. Kato: Taro! How wasteful! You shouldn't leave the hot water running while you wash your face. And when you leave a room, always turn the lights off. You mustn't waste energy.

Taro: I'm sorry. I keep on forgetting, even though I know I shouldn't.

Mrs. Kato: To reduce greenhouse gases, each and every one of us needs to do what we can.

Taro: I get it. I'll try not to waste energy from now on.

VOCABULARY

もったいない	wasteful, uneconomical	かならず	always, without fail	むだにする	waste
だしっぱなし	left running (of water), left lying out	けしなさい	turn off (imperative; see p. 198)	つい	unintentionally
〜ちゃだめ	shouldn't —— (colloquial for 〜してはいけません)	エネルギー	energy	へらす	decrease
				しないと	must do, need to do

II. While looking through the newspaper, Mr. Suzuki remarks to Mr. Mills about an article he just read.

鈴木(すずき)： また、せきゆがね上(あ)がりしていますね。ガソリンも高(たか)くなるなあ。
ミルズ：ガソリンが高(たか)いと思(おも)うなら、車(くるま)にのらなければいいんですよ。東京(とうきょう)は、車(くるま)がなくても、だいじょうぶですからね。私(わたし)は東京(とうきょう)では車(くるま)を買(か)わないことにしたんです。
鈴木(すずき)： たしかに、ちゅうしゃ料金(りょうきん)も高(たか)いですからね。
ミルズ：外国(がいこく)のとしでは、マイカーのきせいをしているところが多(おお)いですよ。
鈴木(すずき)： そうだそうですね。東京(とうきょう)でもそろそろ始(はじ)まるかもしれません。

Suzuki: The price of oil has gone up again. Gasoline is going to get expensive.
Mills: If you think that gasoline is expensive, then just don't drive cars. In Tokyo you can get around all right even if you don't have a car, you know. I've decided not to buy a car in Tokyo.
Suzuki: You have a point, especially considering how expensive parking fees are, too.
Mills: A lot of cities abroad place restrictions on private cars.
Suzuki: That's what I hear. Maybe restrictions like that will start up in Tokyo sometime soon, too.

VOCABULARY

せきゆ	oil	マイカー	private car, one's own car
ねあがり	price rise		
ガソリン	gasoline		
とし	city, metropolitan area		

KANJI PRACTICE

球

地球 (ちきゅう)
野球 (やきゅう)

ball

化

文化 (ぶんか)
～化 (か)

change
-zation

世

世話 (せわ)
世界 (せかい)

world

界

世界 (せかい)
世界中 (せかいじゅう)

world
bounds

題

問題 (もんだい)

title
theme

温
warm

気温 (きおん)
温度 (おんど)

以
from
than

以上 (いじょう)
以下 (いか)
以外 (いがい)
以来 (いらい)

起
rise

起きる (お)
起こる (お)
起こす (お)

台
stand
base

台風 (たいふう)

風
wind

風 (かぜ)
台風 (たいふう)

Quiz 2 Unit 2 (Lessons 4–6)

I Fill in the blanks with the appropriate particle.

1) おきゃくさんが何時に来る（　　　）知っていますか。
2) しりょうしつのしりょうはだれで（　　　）えつらんできます。
3) しぜん農法にはいろいろな方法（　　　）あります。
4) 来月ひっこすこと（　　　）しました。
5) この農場ではりんごを無農薬（　　　）せいさんしています。

II Choose the most appropriate word from among the alternatives (1–4) given.

1) ニュース（　　　）台風が近づいているそうです。

1. にとって　　2. について　　3. によると　　4. によって

2) 学生（　　　）このけんきゅうはむずかしいと思います。

1. にとって　　2. について　　3. によると　　4. によって

3) A：なぜ、会社をやめたんですか。
B：毎日いそがしくて、ぜんぜん休めなかったんです。（　　　）会社をやめたんです。

1. それで　　2. それに　　3. それは　　4. それが

4) A：ちょっと聞きたい（　　　）があるんですが。
B：何でしょうか。

1. の　　2. こと　　3. もの　　4. ん

5) A：先生が田中さんに会った（　　　）はいつですか。
B：きのうです。

1. の　　2. こと　　3. もの　　4. ん

III Change the form of the word given in parentheses to complete the sentence in a way that makes sense.

1) この仕事にきょうみが（　　　）なら、いっしょにしませんか。（あります）
2) あした天気が（　　　）ても、ゴルフに行きます。（悪いです）
3) よく（　　　）ように、ゆっくり話してください。（わかります）
4) べんごしに（　　　）ために、ほうりつの勉強をしています。（なります）
5) 時間がないので、駅まで（　　　）ながら、話しましょう。（あるきます）

IV Choose the most appropriate word or phrase from among the alternatives (1–4) given.

1) 子(こ)どものかずがへっていることは（　　　）もんだいです。

　1. 安全(あんぜん)な　　2. 大切(たいせつ)な　　3. しんこくな　　4. ひつようくな

2) ソーラーパネルをつけると、天気(てんき)がいい日(ひ)は電気料金(でんきりょうきん)が（　　　）かかりません。

　1. すっかり　　2. ずっと　　3. さっそく　　4. まったく

3) このこうじょうでは毎月(まいつき)たくさんのせいひんを（　　　）しています。

　1. あんない　　2. せいさん　　3. けいえい　　4. せつめい

4) 地球(ちきゅう)おんだん化(か)の（　　　）がしんぱいです。

　1. けんこう　　2. きぎょう　　3. えいきょう　　4. ひょうばん

5) 地球(ちきゅう)おんだん化(か)を（　　　）ために、できることをしましょう。

　1. ふせぐ　　2. おきる　　3. つける　　4. さがす

V Fill in the blanks with the correct reading of each kanji.

1) 広い　　土地を買いました。

（　　　）（　　　）

2) この店では世界中の　野菜を使った料理が食べられます。

（　　　）（　　　）（　　　）

3) 切手のあつめ方を教えてください。

（　　　）　（　　　）

4) へいきん気温が５度　以上　高くなるのは、大きな問題です。

（　　）（　　）　（　　）

UNIT 3

CRIME & EDUCATION

We live in constant interaction with others. It is therefore important for us to be able to appropriately convey our feelings—gratitude, frustration, dissatisfaction, whatever they may be. It is also important that we be able to express our attitudes toward social issues such as crime or child education and safety (covered in this unit) when they rear their heads. Here you will learn authentic expressions for effectively relaying your emotions in Japanese. Study how the expressions are used, then try them out on your own. Your Japanese is sure to sound much more natural after completing this unit.

LESSON
7 ASKING SOMEONE TO TAKE OVER WORK

TARGET DIALOGUE

Ms. Nakamura was suddenly invited to go to a concert with a friend. She approaches Mr. Suzuki to ask him whether he would be willing to take over work in her place.

中村(なかむら)：　鈴木(すずき)さん、ちょっとおねがいがあるんですが。

鈴木(すずき)：　はい、何(なん)でしょうか。

中村(なかむら)：　じつは、今日(きょう)の午後(ごご)6時(じ)から7時(じ)の間(あいだ)に、新商品(しんしょうひん)のカタログがとどくことになっているんですけど、用事(ようじ)ができてしまったんです。すみませんが、代(か)わりにうけとってもらえませんか。→p. 125

鈴木(すずき)：　用事(ようじ)って、デートですか。

中村(なかむら)：　ええ、まあ。行(い)きたかったコンサートのチケットが急(きゅう)に手(て)に入(はい)ったんです。

鈴木(すずき)：　そうなんですか。じゃあ、ぼくがうけとっておきますよ。ほんとうはスポーツクラブに行(い)くつもりだったんですけど……。→p. 128

中村(なかむら)：　ごめんなさい。今度(こんど)お礼(れい)にごちそうしますね。

In the lobby of the concert hall:

中村(なかむら)：　今日(きょう)はさそってくれて、ありがとう。→p. 126

スミス：仕事(しごと)はだいじょうぶだった？

中村(なかむら)：　ええ、鈴木(すずき)さんに代(か)わってもらえたから、だいじょうぶ。

(*curtain bell*)

スミス：あ、始(はじ)まるよ。行(い)こう。

Nakamura: Mr. Suzuki, there's a little something I'd like to ask you to do for me.
Suzuki: Yes, what is it?
Nakamura: Actually, the catalogs for the new products are set to be delivered today between six and seven p.m., but something has come up. I'm sorry, but would you [stay here and] receive them for me in my place?
Suzuki: By "something," do you mean a date?
Nakamura: Well, more or less. I suddenly got tickets to a concert that I wanted to go to. [lit., "The tickets for a concert that I wanted to go to came into my possession suddenly."]
Suzuki: Is that so? In that case, I'll [stay around to] receive them. I was actually planning to go to the sports club, but . . .
Nakamura: I'm sorry. I'll take you out for a meal sometime in return.
. . . . . .
Nakamura: Thank you for inviting me today.
Smith: Was everything all right at work?
Nakamura: Yes, I had Mr. Suzuki fill in for me, so it's all right.
(*curtain bell*)
Smith: Oh, it's starting. Let's go [inside].

VOCABULARY

～の間(あいだ)に	between
できる (R2)	come into existence, come up
代(か)わりに	instead
うけとる	receive
～てもらう	have (someone) do (something) (see p. 125)
まあ	more or less, sort of
手(て)に入(はい)る	be obtained, come into one's possession
ほんとうは	truth be told . . .
つもり	intention, plan
ごめんなさい	I'm sorry
お礼(れい)	gratitude, return for a favor
ごちそうする	treat, take out to eat
～てくれる	do (something) for me (see p. 126)
代(か)わる	take over, fill in, cover for

NOTES

1. 6時(じ)から7時(じ)の間(あいだ)に

間(あいだ), meaning "interval," may be used in either a temporal or spatial sense.

銀行(ぎんこう)と本屋(ほんや)の間(あいだ)にパン屋(や)があります。
Between the bank and the bookstore there is a bakery.

2. ことになっている

ことになっている indicates that something "is to be so," for example because it is dictated by rules or customs based on precedent or because arrangements or preparations have already been made for it. As used in this dialogue, it indicates that everything has already been set for Ms. Nakamura to receive the catalogs at the appointed time.

このたてものの中では、たばこをすえないことになっています。
There is to be no smoking inside this building.

そのことについては、午後の会議で話し合うことになっています。
We are to discuss that matter at the meeting this afternoon.

3. ええ、まあ

まあ is used when you want to be vague about an answer. Here Ms. Nakamura uses it to vaguely intimate that she is going on a date while avoiding saying it outright.

4. 手に入る

手に入る means for something "to come into one's possession," with 入る used in the sense of something metaphorically "entering" one's reach. 手に入る is intransitive, as opposed to 手に入れる, which means "to make one's own" and so is transitive.

めずらしいワインが手に入ったので、いっしょに飲みませんか。
I got hold of some rare wine [lit., "Some rare wine came into my possession"], so won't you have a drink of it with me?

コンサートのチケットを手に入れるために、4時間もならびました。
I stood in line for four whole hours to get the concert tickets.

5. ごめんなさい

ごめんなさい is an apology that tends to be used in more informal situations compared to すみません. Unlike すみません, which may express apology or thanks, ごめんなさい strictly means "I'm sorry." The more casual ごめん is commonly used among speakers on close terms.

おそくなって、ごめんなさい。
I'm sorry I'm late.

おそくなって、ごめん。
Sorry I'm late.

6. お礼に

に here indicates method of use.

おみやげにゆかたを買いました。
I bought a yukata as a souvenir.

けっこんのおいわいにワイングラスをおくりました。
I gave them wine glasses as a wedding present.

GRAMMAR & PATTERN PRACTICE

I Describing the Actions of Giving and Receiving Services

すみませんが、代わりに（カタログを）うけとってもらえませんか。
さそってくれて、ありがとう。

As discussed repeatedly elsewhere (Book I, p. 110; Book III, p. 29), the verbs もらう, くれる, and あげる express the giving or receiving of objects. The *-te* form of a verb + もらう／くれる／あげる (hereafter ～てもらう, ～てくれる, ～てあげる), meanwhile, indicates the giving or receiving of services (i.e., doing something for someone or having someone do something for you). These expressions, in essence, allow you to describe the exchanging of favors or benefits. The constructions introduced here apply to when the benefactor and beneficiary both belong to the same social level. Those for when the two are of different levels will be covered in Unit 4 (pp. 181–82).

1. ～てもらう

友だちは私に店の名前を教えました。
My friend told me the name of the store.

私は友だちに店の名前を教えてもらいました。
I had my friend tell me the name of the store.

Changing the first sentence above by adding ～てもらう while putting yourself in the subject position allows you not only to state the fact that your friend told you the name of the store, but also to convey that you received benefit from and are grateful toward this service. ～てもらう is often, but certainly not always, used to talk about things done for you by others at your own request. The benefactor is marked by the particle に.

～てもらう can describe favors exchanged not only between you and others but also between third parties.

中村さんは鈴木さんに仕事を代わってもらいました。
Ms. Nakamura had Mr. Suzuki take over some work for her.

～てもらう is also frequently used to make requests, in which case it changes to the potential form and becomes ～てもらえますか.

Conversation between two diners at a restaurant:

A：デザートも食べたいですね。メニューをもらいませんか。
B：そうですね。(*to the waiter*) すみません、メニューをもってきてもらえますか。

A: I'd like to have dessert, how about you? Shall we ask to get the menu?
B: Yes, let's. (*to the waiter*) Excuse me, will you bring us the menu?

The form もらいませんか is used by A to suggest to B that they get the menu, ～てもらえますか by B to ask the waiter to perform them a service, i.e., bring them the menu.

～てもらえますか sounds nearly like a command, so that in asking someone to accommodate you it is more often softened to ～てもらえませんか, "would you [please] . . . ?" or ～てもらいたいんですが, "I'd appreciate it if you would . . ."

2. ～てくれる

～てくれる indicates a service done by someone toward you or members of your family. Because the benefactor is the subject, ～てくれる carries the feeling of the service having been performed spontaneously on the person's own initiative. As such, you can use it to thank people for actions conducted on your behalf.

> 友だちが（私に）スキーを教えてくれました。
> My friend taught me how to ski.
>
> 友だちが母を病院につれていってくれました。
> My friend took my mother to the hospital for me.
>
> にもつをもってくれて、ありがとう。
> Thank you for holding my bags for me.

～てくれませんか may be used to form requests. But because it effectively calls on someone to do something for you of their own volition, you should only use it when speaking to those close to or younger than you.

> 妻：　悪いけど、ちょっと手つだってくれない？
> 夫：　いいよ。
> wife: I'm sorry, but give me a hand for a second, will you?
> husband: Sure.

3. ～てあげる

～てあげる indicates a service done by the subject toward someone else. When the beneficiary is someone of lower status or an animal, then ～てやる is sometimes used (see also p. 29).

> 私は田中さんにフランス語を教えてあげました。
> I taught Ms. Tanaka French.
>
> 私はおとうとのしゅくだいを手つだってやりました。
> I helped my younger brother with his homework.

～てあげる implies doing someone a favor and so runs the risk of sounding pushy when said directly to the beneficiary of the action. Thus（私(わたし)は）～てあげる should only be used toward family or those close to you. In the form ～てあげてください, in which the speaker is asking their listener to perform a service for a third person, ～てあげる may be used, but only if both the recipient and the listener are junior staff members or others of lower social status than the speaker.

鈴木(すずき)さんにレポートのないようをせつめいしてあげてください。
Please explain the contents of the report to Mr. Suzuki.

1 Complete each sentence while pretending to be 私(わたし).

1) ミルズ 私(わたし)

私(わたし)はミルズさんににもつをはこんで（　　　　　）。

2) 

マリーさんが私(わたし)にケーキを作(つく)って（　　　　　）。

3) 

私(わたし)は鈴木(すずき)さんに友(とも)だちをしょうかいして（　　　　　）。

2 Read the following while paying attention to their meanings.

1) 子(こ)どものとき、よく両親(りょうしん)に動物(どうぶつ)えんにつれていってもらいました。

2) かんじがわからなくてこまっていたら、親切(しんせつ)な人(ひと)が教(おし)えてくれました。

3) A：すてきなコートですね。
B：父(ちち)に買(か)ってもらったんです。

4) A：パーティーのじゅんび、たいへんだったでしょう？
B：友(とも)だちが手(て)つだってくれたので、すぐ終(お)わりました。

VOCABULARY

ないよう	content
はこぶ	carry
どうぶつえん	zoo

II Expressing Intention (1)

つもり is used to indicate intention, or in other words something that you have already settled on doing in your mind without being certain whether it will actually be carried out. つもり behaves like a noun, and so verbs preceding it take plain forms.

毎日中国語を勉強して、しょうらい中国語のつうやくになるつもりです。
I intend to study Chinese every day and someday become an interpreter in the language.

もうたばこをすわないつもりです。
I intend not to smoke anymore.

Ａ：来週の新年会にしゅっせきしますか。
Ｂ：ええ、そのつもりです。
A: Will you attend the New Year party next week?
B: Yes, I'm planning on it.

For things you are definitely going to do in the near future, use the *-masu* form or dictionary form, not つもり.

今電車にのっているので、おりたらこちらから電話します。
I'm on the train now, so I'll call you when I get off.

In Book II (p. 166), we introduced ～う／ようと思っています as an expression for indicating plans for the future. つもり carries a stronger sense of determination than ～う／ようと思っています, which is often used to talk about plans you still are not definite about or that you just came up with right then and there.

今度両親と旅行をしようと思っているんです。(Book II, p. 164)
I'm thinking of traveling with my parents.

おなかがすいたから、昼ごはんを食べに行こうと思うんだけど、いっしょに行かない？
I'm hungry, so I'm thinking about going out to eat lunch. Won't you come with me?

When used in the past tense, as in the example from the Target Dialogue, つもり indicates that something you meant to do did not come to pass for some reason. As such, it is often used to make excuses.

スポーツクラブに行くつもりだったのに、ざんぎょうで行けなくなりました。
I meant to go to the sports club, but couldn't because I had to work late.

ほんとうはやるつもりだったんですが、なかなか時間がなくて……。
I honestly meant to do it, but just never had the time . . .

VOCABULARY しゅっせきする attend

Read the following while paying attention to the uses of the expressions introduced on the previous page.

1) A：今年(ことし)のもくひょうは何(なん)ですか。
B：日本語(にほんご)のしけんにごうかくすることです。毎日(まいにち)かんじを5もじおぼえるつもりです。

2) 私(わたし)はずっといなかに住(す)みたいと思(おも)っていました。たいしょくしたら、いなかにひっこして、農業(のうぎょう)を始(はじ)めるつもりです。

3) マルタン：日曜日(にちようび)のバーベキューに何(なに)をもっていきますか。
鈴木(すずき)：にくと野菜(やさい)はミルズさんが用意(ようい)すると言(い)っていましたから、ぼくは飲(の)み物(もの)をもっていくつもりです。
マルタン：じゃあ、私(わたし)はくだものをもっていこうかな。

4) あまいものは食(た)べないつもりだったのに、おいしそうだったので、つい食(た)べてしまいました。

VOCABULARY

もじ	letter, character
のうぎょう	farming, agriculture
もっていく	take, bring

PRACTICE 1 Requesting Services

PHRASE POWER

① パソコンをしゅうりしてもらえますか。
Will you repair my computer for me?

② Sサイズを M サイズにとりかえてもらえますか。
Will you exchange this size S for a size M for me?

③ おさらがよごれているので、とりかえてもらえますか。
Will you change these dishes for me, since they're dirty?

④ 今日中(きょうじゅう)ににもつをとりに来(き)てもらえませんか。
Would you please come pick up the package for me sometime today?

⑤ にもつを今日(きょう)の5時(じ)にとどけてもらえませんか。
Would you please deliver the package for me at five o'clock today?

⑥ しんさつの予約(よやく)の時間(じかん)をかえてもらいたいんですが……。
I'd appreciate it if you'd change the time of my doctor's appointment.

SPEAKING PRACTICE

TRACK 26

I. Ms. Martin asks for an item she is buying at a department store to be delivered.

マルタン：これ、おねがいします。プレゼントなので、つつんでもらえますか。
店員(てんいん)：しょうちしました。
マルタン：この住所(じゅうしょ)にとどけてもらいたいんですが……。
店員(てんいん)：では、こちらにお書(か)きください。

Martin: I'd like this. It's a gift, so will you wrap it up for me?
salesperson: Of course.
Martin: I'd like you to deliver it to this address for me.
salesperson: Then please write [the address] here.

VOCABULARY

しゅうりする	repair
よごれる (R2)	become dirty
しんさつ	medical examination

II. Mr. Suzuki requests repairs at a computer shop.

鈴木(すずき)：　このパソコン、こちらで買(か)ったんですが、こわれてしまったんです。しゅうりしてもらえますか。
店員(てんいん)：　しょうちしました。
鈴木(すずき)：　何日(なんにち)ぐらいかかりますか。
店員(てんいん)：　そうですね。こしょうのげんいんをしらべてみないとわかりませんが……。
鈴木(すずき)：　３日(みっか)ぐらいでしゅうりしてもらえませんか。急(いそ)いでいるんです。
店員(てんいん)：　今(いま)、サービスセンターに聞(き)いてみますので、少々(しょうしょう)＊お待(ま)ちください。

Suzuki: I bought this computer here, but it broke down. Will you repair it for me?
salesperson: Of course.
Suzuki: About how many days will it take?
salesperson: Well, we won't know until we look into the cause of the malfunction.
Suzuki: Would you please repair it for me in three days or so? I'm in a hurry, you see.
salesperson: I'll try asking the service center right now, so please give me a moment.

＊々 is a character indicating repetition of the kanji coming before it, e.g., 人々(ひとびと), "people," 国々(くにぐに), "countries."

III. Mr. Mills has called a dentist to have his appointment changed.

受付の人(うけつけのひと)：田中歯科(たなかしか)でございます。
ミルズ：　あのう、あしたの１０時(じ)に予約(よやく)した、ミルズです。すみませんが、予約(よやく)の時間(じかん)をかえてもらいたいんですが……。
受付の人(うけつけのひと)：何時(なんじ)がよろしいですか。
ミルズ：　１１時(じ)は空(あ)いていますか。
受付の人(うけつけのひと)：はい、だいじょうぶです。それでは、あしたの１１時(じ)にお待(ま)ちしております。
ミルズ：　よろしくおねがいします。

receptionist: Tanaka Dental Office.
Mills: Uhh, I'm Mills, who made a reservation for ten o'clock tomorrow. If possible, I'd appreciate it if you'd change the time of the reservation.
receptionist: What time would be agreeable?
Mills: Is eleven o'clock available?
receptionist: Yes, that would be fine. We'll see you tomorrow at eleven, then.
Mills: Thank you.

VOCABULARY

サービスセンター	service center
たなかしか	Tanaka Dental Office (fictitious dentist's office)
しか	dentist's office

PRACTICE 2 Thanking Others for Their Service

PHRASE POWER

① 部屋のかたづけを手つだってくれて、ありがとう。
Thank you for helping out with the cleaning of the room.

② わざわざ駅までむかえに来てくれて、ありがとう。
Thank you for going out of your way to come and greet me at the station.

③ 私のすきな料理を作ってくれて、ありがとう。
Thank you for making my favorite dish.

④ 私のためにパーティーを開いてくれて、ほんとうにありがとう。
Thank you very much for throwing a party for me.

⑤ しけんのけっかを知らせてくれて、ありがとう。
Thank you for letting me know your exam results.

⑥ 今日はランチにさそってくれて、ありがとう。
Thank you for inviting me out for lunch today.

⑦ ホテルの予約をしておいてくれて、たすかったよ。
It was a great help, you know, your making hotel reservations for us.

⑧ きのうは仕事を代わってもらって、たすかりました。
It was a great help, you know, your taking over work for me yesterday.

⑨ 無理を言って予約をかえてもらって、すみません。
I'm sorry for asking so much of you [lit., "asking the impossible"] and having you change our reservations.

⑩ 手に入りにくいチケットをとってもらって、すみませんでした。
Thank you [lit., "I apologize"] for having you get those hard-to-get-hold-of tickets for me.

VOCABULARY

かたづけ	cleaning, tidying up	ランチ	lunch
わざわざ〜する	go out of one's way to do, take the trouble to do	むりをいう	ask too much
ひらく	have, hold (a party, etc.)		

READING PRACTICE

Hiro, Ms. Nakamura's friend, thanks Ms. Nakamura by e-mail for visiting her at the hospital.

今日はわざわざお見まいに来てくれて、ありがとう。ひさしぶりに会えて、うれしかった。もってきてくれた本、おもしろいね。おいしゃさんの話では、あと１か月ぐらいしたら、たいいんできるって。たいいんしたら、また会おうね。
ヒロ

Thank you for taking time out just to come visit me at the hospital today. I was happy to have been able to see you after such a long time. The book you brought me is really fun reading. According to the doctor, I'll be able to leave the hospital in about another month. Let's meet again once I'm out of the hospital.
Hiro

SPEAKING PRACTICE

Emi Morita strikes up a conversation with Ms. Martin.

森田エミ：マリーさんのブログ、見ましたよ。チェロをひいている写真、すてきでした。
マルタン：見てくれて、うれしいわ。なかなかひょうばんがいいのよ。
森田エミ：フランス料理のレシピも書いてあって、おもしろいですね。料理がすきな友だちに教えてあげました。

Emi Morita: I saw your blog, Marie. That photograph of you playing your cello was lovely.
Martin: I'm glad you took a look at my blog. It's gotten quite a bit of positive feedback.
Emi Morita: It's interesting to look at, isn't it, especially with all those French recipes written down in it. I told a friend who likes to cook about it.

VOCABULARY

(お) みまい	visit to someone who is sick or injured
たいいんする	leave (a hospital after a stay)
なかなか	quite, fairly

PRACTICE 3 Making Excuses

PHRASE POWER

① はやく起(お)きるつもりだったんですが……。

I meant to get up early, but . . .

② ～さんに知(し)らせるつもりだったんですが……。

I meant to tell Mr./Ms.——, but . . .

③ 自分(じぶん)でやるつもりだったんですが……。

I meant to do it myself, but . . .

④ 今日中(きょうじゅう)にこの仕事(しごと)をすませるつもりだったんですが……。

I planned on finishing this work today, but . . .

⑤ もっとはやくじゅんびをするつもりだったんですが、なかなか時間(じかん)がなくて……。

I meant to prepare earlier, but I just didn't have the time . . .

⑥ 話(はな)すつもりだったんですが、なかなか言(い)いにくくて……。

I meant to talk [to you about it], but it was just so hard to bring it up . . .

⑦ はやく来(く)るつもりだったんだけど、電車(でんしゃ)にのりおくれちゃって ……。

I meant to come earlier, but I missed my train . . .

⑧ うちに帰(かえ)ったらすぐやるつもりだったんだけど、ついわすれちゃって ……。

I meant to do it as soon as I got home, but I just carelessly forgot . . .

VOCABULARY のりおくれる (R2) miss (a train, etc.)

SPEAKING PRACTICE

I. During lunch Mr. Suzuki talks with a junior colleague who is about to switch jobs.

鈴木(すずき)：　てんしょくするって聞(き)いたけど……。
品川(しながわ)：　すみません。鈴木(すずき)さんにはもっとはやく知(し)らせるつもりだったんですが……。来月(らいげつ)いっぱいでやめることにしました。
鈴木(すずき)：　そうか。やめてしまうのはざんねんだなあ。近(ちか)いうちに一度(いちど)飲(の)みに行(い)こう。
品川(しながわ)：　ありがとうございます。

Suzuki: I heard you're going to switch jobs.
Shinagawa: I'm sorry. I meant to tell you earlier, but . . . I've decided to quit at the end of next month.
Suzuki: Well, it's too bad you're going to quit. Let's go out for a drink once sometime in the near future.
Shinagawa: Thank you.

II. Aiko's boyfriend makes excuses to Aiko for being late for a date.

愛子(あいこ)：　おそい。
ボーイフレンド：おくれて、ごめん。今日(きょう)ははやく来(く)るつもりだったんだけど、さいふをうちにわすれちゃって、とりに帰(かえ)ったんだ。
愛子(あいこ)：　おくれるときは、けいたいに電話(でんわ)してくれない？
ボーイフレンド：それが、けいたいのでんちが切(き)れちゃって……。

Aiko: You're late.
boyfriend: Sorry I'm late. I meant to get here early today, but I forgot my wallet at home and went back to get it.
Aiko: Won't you call me on my cell phone when you're going to be late?
boyfriend: The thing is, the batteries were out on my cell phone.

VOCABULARY

しながわ	Shinagawa (surname)
いっぱいで	at the end of
ちかいうちに	in the near future
ボーイフレンド	boyfriend
きれる (R2)	run out

KANJI PRACTICE

商
商品 (しょうひん)
commerce
merchandise

代
代わる (か)
代わりに (か)
年代 (ねんだい)
時代 (じだい)
substitute
generation

貸
貸す (か)
貸し出し (か だ)
lend
rent

借
借りる (か)
borrow
rent

送
送る (おく)
送別会 (そうべつかい)
send

映

映画 えいが

reflect

画

映画 えいが

picture

写

写真 しゃしん

copy

真

写真 しゃしん

true
genuine

歌

歌 うた
歌う うた

song
sing

LESSON 8
MY PASSPORT WAS STOLEN

TARGET DIALOGUE

A phone call comes into the office from Mr. Suzuki, who was scheduled to come back today from an overseas business trip.

中村(なかむら)：　部長(ぶちょう)、鈴木(すずき)さんから電話(でんわ)です。パスポートをすられて、今日(きょう)は帰(かえ)れないそうです。 →p. 141

佐々木(ささき)：えっ、それはたいへん。

………………

佐々木(ささき)：鈴木(すずき)さん？　パスポートをすられたんですって？

鈴木(すずき)：　ええ、さいふもこうくう券(けん)もとられてしまいました。できるだけ早(はや)く帰(かえ)れるようにどりょくしますが、明日(あす)の会議(かいぎ)には出席(しゅっせき)できないだろうと思(おも)います。

佐々木(ささき)：わかりました。予定(よてい)がわかったら、知(し)らせてください。

鈴木(すずき)：　はい。もうしわけありません。

After Mr. Suzuki comes back, Mr. Mills questions him more closely about the time he was pickpocketed.

ミルズ：たいへんでしたね。いったいどこですられたんですか。

鈴木(すずき)：　たぶん、ショッピングセンターだろうと思(おも)います。エレベーターに乗(の)ろうとしたとき、後(うし)ろから走(はし)ってきた男(おとこ)におされたんです。そのとき、すられたんだと思(おも)います。 →p. 144

ミルズ：そのときは気(き)がつかなかったんですか。

鈴木(すずき)：ええ。その後(あと)、店(みせ)でさいふを出(だ)そうとして、ポケットに手(て)を入(い)れたら、何(なに)もなかったんです。

ミルズ：それで、どうしたんですか。

鈴木(すずき)：すぐホテルにもどって、フロントの人(ひと)にそうだんしました。チェックアウトした後(あと)だったのに、とても親切(しんせつ)にしてくれました。けいさつでじじょうを説明(せつめい)している間(あいだ)→p. 145、いっしょにいて通訳(つうやく)してくれたんです。ほんとうにたすかりました。

ミルズ：よかったですね。

Nakamura: Manager Sasaki, we have a phone call from Mr. Suzuki. He said he had his passport stolen and can't come back today.
Sasaki: What? That's awful!
. . . . . .
Sasaki: Mr. Suzuki? I hear you got your passport stolen.
Suzuki: Yes, my wallet and plane tickets were taken, too. I'll make an effort so I can get back as soon as possible, but I think I'm probably not going to be able to attend tomorrow's meeting.
Sasaki: I understand. Please let us know once you know your schedule.
Suzuki: Yes. I'm sorry for the trouble.
. . . . . .
Mills: That was some experience you had, wasn't it? Wherever were you pickpocketed?
Suzuki: I think probably at the shopping center. Just as I was about to get onto the elevator, I was pushed by a man who came running from behind me. I think that was when I was pickpocketed.
Mills: Didn't you notice at the time?
Suzuki: No. But later at a store, when I put my hand in my pocket to try to get my wallet out, there was nothing there.
Mills: And then what did you do?
Suzuki: I went back to the hotel right away and consulted the person at the front desk. He was very helpful, although it was already after I had checked out. He stayed and interpreted for me all while I was explaining my situation to the police. It really was a big help.
Mills: That was fortunate.

VOCABULARY

すられる (R2)	get pickpocketed	とられる (R2)	get stolen, get taken
する	pickpocket	とる	steal, take
こうくう券(けん)	plane ticket	どりょくする	strive, make an effort

明日(あす)	tomorrow
いったい	what- (how-, when-, etc.) ever (used with a question word to add emphasis)
ショッピングセンター	shopping center
気(き)がつく	notice
チェックアウトする	check out (of a hotel)
じじょう	situation, circumstance
間(あいだ)	while
通訳(つうやく)する	interpret

NOTES

1. すられたんですって?

   ～んですって? is a colloquial expression used often by women. It is spoken with a rising intonation and says, in effect, "I heard . . . , but is it true? Tell me more." The plain-style equivalent, ～んだって?, is used by both men and women.

2. 後(うし)ろから走(はし)ってきた男(おとこ)

   走(はし)ってきた indicates that the man "came running" in the direction of Mr. Suzuki, the speaker. The opposite expression, 走(はし)っていった (went running), would indicate that the man ran away from Mr. Suzuki. Other compound verbs using きた and いった include 入(はい)ってきた (came in), 近(ちか)づいてきた (came near), 出(で)ていった (went out), and にげていった (ran away).

   男(おとこ) and 女(おんな) are sometimes used in place of 男(おとこ)の人(ひと) and 女(おんな)の人(ひと), as 男(おとこ) is done here. Care needs to be taken with these words, however; while 男(おとこ) and 女(おんな) are strictly neutral in connotation when describing gender, they can sound rude when used to point to specific individuals. In the dialogue, Mr. Suzuki intentionally adopts the less polite 男(おとこ) to describe the man who came running from behind because he believes he was a pickpocket.

3. それで、どうしたんですか

   どうしたんですか by itself means "What's the matter?" and is often used to initiate a conversation. それで、どうしたんですか, "And then what did you do?" is used to encourage someone to go on with what they are already talking about.

4. チェックアウトした後(あと)

   A verb preceding 後(あと) (after) takes the *-ta* form regardless of the tense in the main clause.

GRAMMAR & PATTERN PRACTICE

I Using Passive Structures

パスポートをすられて、今日(きょう)は帰(かえ)れないそうです。

すられる is a verb in the passive form. The passive form is constructed as follows.

Regular I verbs: *-nai* stem + れる

言(い)う	→ 言(い)われる	たのむ	→ たのまれる
おす	→ おされる	とる	→ とられる

Regular II verbs: *-nai* stem + られる (same as the potential form)

あつめる	→ あつめられる	すてる	→ すてられる
わすれる	→ わすれられる	見(み)る	→ 見(み)られる

Irregular verbs:

する	→ される	来(く)る	→ 来(こ)られる

Passive verbs conjugate like Regular II verbs, except that they have no potential form.

おされない　おされます　おされれば　おされて　おされた

1. Passive structures whose subject is a person

In Japanese, as in English, passive sentences are formed by placing the receiver of the action described by the verb in subject position. Compare the following two sentences, both of which describe the same occurrence but from differing points of view:

男(おとこ)の人(ひと)が鈴木(すずき)さんをおしました。
A man pushed Mr. Suzuki. (focus on the man)

鈴木(すずき)さんは男(おとこ)の人(ひと)におされました。
Mr. Suzuki was pushed by a man. (focus on Mr. Suzuki)

Passive sentences function to place emphasis on the effect exerted by an action on the receiver of that action. The person who performs the action is identified by the particle に.

むすこは私(わたし)のパソコンをこわしました。
My son broke my computer.

私(わたし)はむすこにパソコンをこわされました。
I got my computer broken by my son.

As the second example here shows, when that which is adversely affected by the action is a person's belonging, that person becomes the topic of the sentence.

Sentences that use passive verbs tend to show that the action is or was unwelcome.

雨(あめ)がふりました。
It rained.

（私(わたし)は）雨(あめ)にふられました。
I got rained on.

Choosing between a passive verb versus ～てもらう or ～てくれる allows you to give differing renditions of how you feel about the action described, even if the action itself is the same. Passive sentences are often used to convey a sense of damage. ～てもらう and ～てくれる, by contrast, show that the speaker is thankful for the action.

知(し)らない人(ひと)に写真(しゃしん)をとられました。
I got my picture taken by someone I didn't know.

知(し)らない人(ひと)に写真(しゃしん)をとってもらいました。
I had someone I didn't know take my picture for me.

2. Passive structures whose subject is a thing

Passive sentences that take as their subject an inanimate object are often used to depict objective reality. Such sentences carry none of the connotations of adverse effect discussed above. When the agents are unspecified, unknown, or irrelevant, they are simply omitted.

このおてらは１０００年前(ねんまえ)に建(た)てられました。
This temple was built a thousand years ago.

京都(きょうと)でこくさい会議(かいぎ)が開(ひら)かれました。
An international conference was held in Kyoto.

When mentioned, the agent usually takes によって.

『ハムレット』はシェイクスピアによって書(か)かれました。
Hamlet was written by Shakespeare.

VOCABULARY

たてる (R2)	build	～によって	by ——
こくさいかいぎ	international conference		
『ハムレット』	*Hamlet*		
シェイクスピア	Shakespeare		

1 Change each verb to its passive form.

1) 使(つか)う → ……………………

2) すすめる → ……………………

3) 作(つく)る → ……………………

4) えらぶ → ……………………

5) まちがえる → ……………………

6) しょうたいする → ……………………

2 Change each sentence to a passive one.

1) 父(ちち)は私(わたし)をなぐりました。

→ 私(わたし)は ……………………

2) 先生(せんせい)は私(わたし)をほめました。

→ 私(わたし)は ……………………

3) スミスさんは中村(なかむら)さんを映画(えいが)にさそいました。

→ 中村(なかむら)さんは ……………………

4) 女(おんな)の人(ひと)が私(わたし)の足(あし)をふみました。

→ 私(わたし)は ……………………

3 Complete the sentences by changing the verbs in parentheses to a form of their passive counterparts that makes sense.

1) ベニスは水(みず)の都(みやこ)と……………………いる。(よぶ)

2) 最近(さいきん)めずらしいペットが……………………いる。(ゆにゅうする)

3) 日本(にほん)のアニメが初(はじ)めて……………………のは１９６０年代(ねんだい)だ。(ゆしゅつする)

4) きのう……………………特別(とくべつ)ばんぐみはおもしろかった。(ほうそうする)

5) かれは先月(せんげつ)……………………せんきょでとうせんした。(行(おこな)う)

VOCABULARY

しょうたいする	invite	ベニス	Venice	ばんぐみ	program (TV or radio)	とうせんする	be elected
なぐる	hit, strike	みやこ	capital	ほうそうする	broadcast	おこなう	hold, carry out
ほめる (R2)	praise	ゆにゅうする	import	せんきょ	election		
ふむ	step on	ゆしゅつする	export				

II Expressing Intention (2)

エレベーターに乗(の)ろうとしたとき、男(おとこ)におされました。
さいふを出(だ)そうとして、ポケットに手(て)を入(い)れました。

The volitional form of a verb + とする indicates either that you are just about to carry out a pre-planned action or that you are trying to do something without so far being successful.

晩(ばん)ごはんを食(た)べようとしたとき、電話(でんわ)がかかってきました。
Just as I was about to eat dinner, I got a phone call.

ねむろうとしましたが、ねむれませんでした。
I tried to sleep, but couldn't.

1 Complete the sentences using ～う／ようとしたとき.

1) タクシーに乗(の)る
→ ……………………、けいたいがなりました。

2) 家(いえ)を出(で)る
→ ……………………、雨(あめ)がふってきました。

3) 電車(でんしゃ)に乗(の)る
→ ……………………、ドアが閉(し)まってしまいました。

2 Complete the sentences using ～う／ようとしましたが.

1) にもつをはこぶ
→ ……………………、おもくてはこべませんでした。

2) 勉強(べんきょう)する
→ ……………………、おとうとにじゃまされて、できませんでした。

VOCABULARY

でんわがかかる	get a phone call
なる	ring, sound
じゃまする	hinder, get in the way (of)

III Indicating a Span of Time During Which an Action or Event Occurs

The noun 間(あいだ) follows any number of modifiers to form a subordinate clause setting out a span of time throughout which an action or event, expressed in the main clause, continues or continued. Verbs preceding 間(あいだ) almost always appear in the 〜ている form regardless of the tense of the main clause. Nouns, meanwhile, are joined to 間(あいだ) by adding の in between.

Unlike with ながら (p. 91), which indicates two actions performed simultaneously by the same subject, the subjects in the 〜間(あいだ) clause and main clause do not necessarily have to match.

(私(わたし)が) けいさつでじじょうを説明(せつめい)している間(あいだ)、(ホテルの人(ひと)は) ずっといっしょにいてくれました。

[The person from the hotel] stayed with me all while [I] was explaining matters to the police.

間(あいだ) + に indicates that the action in the main clause takes place in one portion of the time span delineated by 間(あいだ).

子(こ)どもがねている間(あいだ)に、買(か)い物(もの)に行(い)ってきました。

I went shopping while my child was asleep.

Complete the sentences using the words given.

1) 入院(にゅういん)しています

→ ....間(あいだ)、とてもたいくつでした。

2) 買(か)い物(もの)をしています

→ 妻(つま)が..間(あいだ)、私(わたし)はきっさ店(てん)でコーヒーを飲(の)んでいました。

3) 出(で)かけています

→ ....間(あいだ)に、にもつがとどきました。

4) 旅行(りょこう)しています

→ ....間(あいだ)に、花(はな)がかれてしまいました。

5) なつ休(やす)み

→ ....間(あいだ)、毎日(まいにち)アルバイトをしていました。

VOCABULARY

たいくつ (な)	boring, tedious
きっさてん	coffee shop
かれる (R2)	die (of plant), wither

PRACTICE 1 Talking about Unpleasant Experiences

PHRASE POWER

① 犬(いぬ)にかまれた。
I got bitten by a dog.

② みんなにわらわれた。
I got laughed at by everyone.

③ 友(とも)だちにいじめられた。
I got bullied by my friends.

④ 友(とも)だちにだまされた。
I got cheated by a friend.

⑤ 悪口(わるぐち)を言(い)われた。
I had bad things said about me.

⑥ 日本語(にほんご)が下手(へた)だと言(い)われた。
I was told my Japanese was bad.

⑦ 子(こ)どもにカメラをこわされた。
I got my camera broken by my child.

⑧ 母(はは)に大事(だいじ)なものをすてられた。
I had a precious item thrown away by my mother.

⑨ じょうしにしかられた。
I got scolded by my boss.

⑩ どうりょうに仕事(しごと)のじゃまをされた。
I was interrupted at work by a colleague.

⑪ ハッカーにデータをぬすまれた。
I got my data stolen by a hacker.

⑫ 部長(ぶちょう)に名前(なまえ)をまちがえられた。
I got my name bungled by the department manager.

VOCABULARY

かむ	bite, chew	へた (な)	bad at, unskilled
いじめる (R2)	bully, pick on	しかる	scold
だます	fool, cheat, deceive	ハッカー	hacker
わるぐち	slander, insult	ぬすむ	steal

⑬ こうつうじこにあった。

I got into a traffic accident.

⑭ だれかに車(くるま)をぶつけられた。

I got bumped into by someone's car.

⑮ ちゅうしゃいはんでつかまった。

I got caught on a parking violation.

⑯ スピードいはんでつかまった。

I got caught on a speeding violation.

⑰ どろぼうに入(はい)られた。

My house got broken into by thieves.

⑱ さぎにあった。

I was deceived in a scam.

⑲ ゆうかいされた。

I got kidnapped.

⑳ 知(し)らない男(おとこ)になぐられた。

I got hit by a man I didn't know.

㉑ すりにさいふをすられた。

I got my wallet pickpocketed.

㉒ どろぼうだと思(おも)われた。

I was mistaken for a thief.

㉓ 雨(あめ)にふられて、びしょぬれになった。

I was rained on and got soaking wet.

㉔ あかんぼうになかれて、ぜんぜんねられなかった。

The baby kept on crying [lit., "The baby cried on me"], so I couldn't sleep at all.

㉕ 妻(つま)に死(し)なれて、こまっている。

My wife died [lit., "My wife died on me"] and I'm at a loss.

VOCABULARY

ぶつける (R2)	hit, bump into	さぎにあう	be deceived in a scam	びしょぬれ	soaking wet
ちゅうしゃいはん	parking violation	さぎ	scam, swindle		
つかまる	get caught	ゆうかいする	kidnap		
スピードいはん	speeding violation	すり	pickpocket		

SPEAKING PRACTICE

TRACK 30

I. Ms. Nakamura lived overseas between the ages of two and ten.

鈴木(すずき)：　中村(なかむら)さんは帰国子女(きこくしじょ)だから、外国語(がいこくご)ができていいですね。
中村(なかむら)：　でも、いいことばかりじゃないんですよ。小学校(しょうがっこう)では、かんじが読(よ)めなくてわらわれたり、日本語(にほんご)の発音(はつおん)がへんだって言(い)われたり。
鈴木(すずき)：　そうだったんですか。たいへんだったんですね。
中村(なかむら)：　ええ。最初(さいしょ)の半年(はんとし)ぐらいはつらくて、学校(がっこう)に行(い)くのがいやでした。

Suzuki: Ms. Nakamura, it must be good to be an overseas returnee and be able to speak a foreign language.
Nakamura: But not everything about it is good, you know. In elementary school I got laughed at for not being able to read kanji and was told my pronunciation of Japanese was strange, among other things.
Suzuki: Was that so? It must have been hard for you.
Nakamura: Yes. I found it so difficult for about the first six months that I hated going to school.

II. Mr. Inuyama calls the police after discovering that his house was broken into.

警官(けいかん)：　はい、１１０番(ひゃくとおばん)です。じけんですか、じこですか。
犬山(いぬやま)：　じけんです！　どろぼうに入(はい)られました！
警官(けいかん)：　どろぼうは今(いま)そこにいますか。*
犬山(いぬやま)：　いいえ。うちに帰(かえ)ったら、まどガラスがわれていて、部屋(へや)の中(なか)がめちゃくちゃになっていたんです。
警官(けいかん)：　けが人(にん)はいますか。
犬山(いぬやま)：　いいえ、いません。とにかくはやく来(き)てください！

officer: This is 110. Are you reporting a crime, or an accident?
Inuyama: A crime! My house was broken into by thieves!
officer: Are the thieves there now?
Inuyama: No. When I came home, the windowpanes were broken and the room was a mess.
officer: Has anyone been injured?
Inuyama: No, nobody. In any case, come right away!

> * Although this question might seem strange, the officer asks it in order to assess whether the person reporting the crime is in immediate danger, given that if the thieves *were* still nearby, any hasty action by the police, such as even approaching the scene in a patrol car, might put the person at risk of harm.

VOCABULARY

きこくしじょ	overseas returnee (someone who came back to Japan after spending their childhood abroad)	まどガラス	windowpane
		われる (R2)	break, smash
はつおん	pronunciation	めちゃくちゃ（な）	messed up, disordered
つらい	hard, difficult, trying	けがにん	injured person
１１０ばん	110 (emergency phone number)	とにかく	anyway, in any case
じけん	incident, crime		

PRACTICE 2 Describing What Happened

SPEAKING PRACTICE

I. Mr. Suzuki has just been rear-ended by a car while driving and is now at the scene of the accident, together with the woman who was in the other car, describing to a police officer what happened.

警官：　じこのじょうきょうをくわしく説明してください。
鈴木：　このかどを左にまがろうとしたとき、急に子どもがとび出してきたんです。それで、あわててブレーキをふんだら、後ろの車についとつされたんです。
女の人：すみません。急にとまるとは思わなかったんです。

officer: Please describe to me in detail the situation at the time of the accident.
Suzuki: A child suddenly came running out just as I was about to turn left on this corner. So when I hastily braked, I was rear-ended by the car behind me.
woman: I'm sorry. I didn't think you were going to stop so suddenly.

II. Ms. Martin is talking to Mr. Mills about the time she forgot her wallet.

マルタン：タクシーでお金をはらおうとしたとき、さいふがないのに気がついたんです。
ミルズ：　え、それで、どうしたんですか。
マルタン：タクシーのうんてん手さんにめいしをわたして、お金を借りたんです。うんてん手さんが親切な人で、たすかりました。
ミルズ：　そうですか。さいふはあったんですか。
マルタン：ええ。会社におきわすれていたんです。

Martin: Right when I was about to pay my fare for the taxi, I noticed my wallet wasn't there.
Mills: Oh, and then what did you do?
Martin: I handed the taxi driver my business card and borrowed some money. I was lucky the driver was a nice person.
Mills: Is that so? Did you find your wallet?
Martin: Yes. I'd left it behind at the office.

VOCABULARY

じょうきょう	situation, circumstance
くわしい	detailed
とびだす	jump out, run out
あわてる (R2)	move hastily, become flustered
ブレーキ	brake
ついとつする	bump into from behind, rear-end
おきわすれる (R2)	leave behind, forget

PRACTICE 3 Relating Troubles

SPEAKING PRACTICE

I. Mr. Mills greets Mr. Suzuki, who has just come into the office.

ミルズ：(*cheerfully*) 鈴木さん、おはようございます。
鈴木：　あ、ミルズさん、大きな声を出さないでください。ふつかよいであたまがいたいんです。
ミルズ：え？　ゆうべそんなに飲んだんですか。
鈴木：　ええ。バーでかのじょを待っている間、ずっと。
ミルズ：どのぐらい待っていたんですか。
鈴木：　２時間ぐらいだったかな。けっきょく、仕事が終わらないからって、来なかったんですけど。

Mills: (*cheerfully*) Good morning, Mr. Suzuki!
Suzuki: Oh, Mr. Mills, please don't talk in a loud voice. I have a headache from a hangover.
Mills: Really? Did you drink so much last night?
Suzuki: Yes, the entire time while I was waiting at the bar for my girlfriend.
Mills: How long were you waiting?
Suzuki: About two hours, it must have been. In the end she didn't come because she wasn't able to finish work.

II. Ms. Martin asks Ms. Nakamura about the seminar she came back from yesterday.

マルタン：中村さん、きのうのセミナーはどうでしたか。
中村：　とてもおもしろかったんですが……。
マルタン：どうかしたんですか。
中村：　こうしの先生が話している間、くしゃみがとまらなくて、たいへんだったんです。
マルタン：かふんしょうですか。
中村：　ええ、そうなんです。きのうは薬をわすれてしまって、大しっぱいでした。

Martin: How was the seminar yesterday, Ms. Nakamura?
Nakamura: It was very interesting, except . . .
Martin: Did something go wrong?
Nakamura: I had an awful time because I couldn't stop sneezing while the lecturer was talking.
Martin: Was it hay fever?
Nakamura: Yes, it was. I forgot my medicine yesterday, so I really messed up!

VOCABULARY

けっきょく	in the end, after all
セミナー	seminar
こうし	lecturer
だいしっぱい	big mistake, fiasco

III. Mr. Mills consults Mr. Suzuki about a piece of mail he has no idea about.

ミルズ：鈴木(すずき)さん、今(いま)ちょっといいですか。きのう、うちにこんなしょるいが送(おく)られてきたんですけど……。

鈴木(すずき)：え？　どんなしょるいですか。(*takes the papers from Mr. Mills*) これ、せいきゅう書(しょ)ですよ。１００万円(まんえん)ふりこんでくださいって。

ミルズ：えーっ！　１００万円(まんえん)？　どうしてですか。

鈴木(すずき)：「入会金(にゅうかいきん)として」って書(か)いてありますよ。ミルズさん、このグループに入会(にゅうかい)したんですか。

ミルズ：いいえ、入会(にゅうかい)していませんよ。そんなグループ、知(し)らないです。*

鈴木(すずき)：じゃあ、このせいきゅう書(しょ)は、むしすればいいですよ。

ミルズ：だいじょうぶでしょうか。むししている間(あいだ)に、何(なに)かまずいことが起(お)きませんか。

鈴木(すずき)：だいじょうぶです。あやしい手紙(てがみ)やメールは、むしするのがいちばんいいそうですよ。

Mills: Mr. Suzuki, could I bother you for a moment right now? These papers were sent to me yesterday . . .

Suzuki: Oh? What kind of papers? (*takes the papers from Mr. Mills*) This is a bill. It says to deposit one million yen [into their bank account].

Mills: What? One million yen? Why?

Suzuki: It says "for registration fees." Did you join this group, Mr. Mills?

Mills: No, I didn't. I don't know [anything about] such a group.

Suzuki: Then you should just ignore this bill.

Mills: Will that be all right, do you suppose? Won't something bad happen while I'm ignoring it?

Suzuki: There'll be no problem. I hear it's best to ignore suspicious letters and e-mails.

* 知(し)らないです means the same as 知(し)りません. The pattern "*-nai* form + です" is often used in place of the negative form in everyday speech (see also p. 215).

VOCABULARY

せいきゅうしょ	bill, invoice
にゅうかいきん	registration fee
にゅうかいする	join (an organization)
むしする	ignore
まずい	bad, untoward

KANJI PRACTICE

券 ticket
券（けん）

席 seat
席（せき）
出席（しゅっせき）

乗 ride
乗る（の）

走 run
走る（はし）

説 explain
説明する（せつめい）

明	明るい (あか) 明日 (あす) 説明 (せつめい)
bright	

通	通る (とお) 通う (かよ) 青山通り (あおやまどお) 左側通行 (ひだりがわつうこう)
pass commute	

訳	通訳する (つうやく) 通訳 (つうやく)
translate	

死	死ぬ (し)
die	

建	建てる (た) 建物 (たてもの)
build construct	

LESSON 9

PROTECTING ONE'S CHILDREN

TARGET READING

最近学校の行き帰りに、小学生がまきこまれる事件が多い。子どもをはんざいからまもるため、けいたい電話やぼうはんブザーを持たせる親がふえている。→p. 156 だが、子どもにぼうはん商品を持たせ、その使い方を教えておけば、子どもは安全なのだろうか。

けいさつや学校は、ぼうはん教育に力を入れ始めた。小学校にポスターをはって、「いかのおすし」というあいことばを小学生におぼえさせている。これは、「知らない人について行かない」「知らない人の車に乗らない」「たすけて！と大声を出す」「あぶないと思ったら、すぐにげる」「何かあったら、すぐ大人に知らせる」という意味だ。

家庭でも、「知らない人に声をかけられたら、どうする？」「道を聞かれたら、どうする？」など、親子で話し合っておくことがひつようだ。大切なのは、子どもに自分をまもる方法を自分で考えさせることだ。

いか…………いかない
の……………のらない
お……………おおごえをだす
す……………すぐにげる
し……………しらせる

Recently there are many cases of elementary schoolchildren getting involved in criminal incidents on their way to and from school. To protect children against crimes, more and more parents are making them carry cellular phones or security buzzers. But if you make your children carry crime-prevention goods and teach them how to use them, then does that really make them safe?

Police and schools have started to put effort into educating children about crime prevention. They are putting up posters in elementary schools to get students to learn the slogan いかのおすし (squid sushi). This word means [i.e., is an acronym made up of the initial sounds of the important words in]

"Don't go with strangers," "Don't get into cars driven by strangers," "Cry 'Help!' in a loud voice when you get into trouble," "Run away immediately when you feel you're in danger," and "Let adults know immediately when something happens to you."

At home, too, it is necessary for parents and children to discuss with each other such questions as "What should you do when strangers approach you?" or "What should you do when someone asks you for directions?" The important thing is to make children think on their own about ways of protecting themselves.

VOCABULARY

行(い)き帰(かえ)り	going to and returning from
まきこむ	involve, mix (someone) up (in)
はんざい	crime
まもる	protect
けいたい電話(でんわ)	cellular phone
ブザー	buzzer
持(も)たせる (R2)	have (someone) carry
親(おや)	parent
だが	but (used mainly in writing)
教育(きょういく)	education
力(ちから)を入(い)れる (R2)	put effort (into)
ポスター	poster
いか	squid
あいことば	slogan, catchphrase
ついて行(い)く	follow, go with
たすけて！	help!
たすける (R2)	help
大声(おおごえ)	loud voice
意味(いみ)	meaning
声(こえ)をかける (R2)	call out to, approach
道(みち)を聞(き)く	ask for directions
話(はな)し合(あ)う	talk over, discuss

NOTES

1. 安全(あんぜん)なのだろうか

   だろうか, the plain-style equivalent of でしょうか, is used to raise an issue with or consult someone. Here it functions as a rhetorical question calling on the reader to think about measures for protecting children against crime.

2. いかのおすし

   To make a set of rules or statements easier to remember, often the initial sounds of each item will be taken out and devised into a meaningful acronym. いかのおすし here is such a mnemonic that puts together the initial sounds of the important words in five crime-prevention rules to make up a phrase easily understood even by children.

3. 「　　　」

   Called かぎかっこ, these symbols are used to set off dialogue and quotations and to indicate emphasis. To add parenthetical information or to give readings for kanji, meanwhile, use（　　）, which are called かっこ.

GRAMMAR & PATTERN PRACTICE

I Using Causative and Causative-passive Structures

親は子どもにぼうはんブザーを持たせる。

The causative form of a verb indicates that the subject of the sentence either "makes" or "lets" someone else perform the action described by that verb. The causative form is constructed as follows.

Regular I verbs: -*nai* stem + せる

行く → 行かせる

待つ → 待たせる

-*nai* stem + す (short form)

行かす

待たす

Regular II verbs: -*nai* stem + させる

食べる → 食べさせる

Irregular verbs:

する → させる

来る → 来させる

Causative verbs conjugate in the same way as Regular II verbs (行かせない、行かせます、行かせれば、行かせよう、行かせて、行かせた).

Clauses that use causative verbs fall into three main patterns, each of which requires different particles to mark the person who actually performs the action (i.e., the person "made to do" something).

1. Person に

If the verb in the clause has an object, then the person performing the action is always marked by the particle に. Whether the sentence indicates coercion or permission is determined by the context.

母はおとうとに部屋をそうじさせました。
My mother made my younger brother clean his room.

2. Person を or person に

If the verb in the clause does not have an object, then the person performing the action takes either を or に. を tends to indicate coercion.

私は子どもを外国に行かせました。
I made my child go abroad.

私は子どもに外国に行かせました。
I let my child go abroad.

3. Person を

Causative structures may be used to express situations in which the actions of the person in subject position (however inadvertently or unknowingly) end up inducing certain feelings in another. This use typically involves verbs having to do with emotions, such as がっかりする (to be let down), こまる (to be at a loss), or しんぱいする (to worry). The person experiencing the emotions takes を.

> 子(こ)どものとき、よく病気(びょうき)になって両親(りょうしん)をしんぱいさせました。
> When I was little, I used to get sick and make my parents worry a lot.

> せいとがさわいで、先生(せんせい)をこまらせました。
> The students created a commotion and made trouble for the teacher.

4. Other constructions that use the causative form

1) The *-te* form of a causative verb + ください

The pattern "*-te* form of a causative verb + ください" is used to make offers or to ask for permission. In the latter case, the politer forms ～せ／させていただけませんか and ～せ／させていただきたいんですが are often used.

> 私(わたし)にこの仕事(しごと)をやらせてください。
> Please let me do this job.

> すみませんが、ぐあいが悪(わる)いので、先(さき)に帰(かえ)らせていただけませんか。
> I'm not feeling well, so I'm sorry, but will you allow me to go home early?

2) The causative-passive form

The causative-passive form, so called because it combines the causative form with the passive form, indicates an action performed by the subject unwillingly under coercion. It is formed by dropping the る from the causative form and adding the auxiliary られる.

Regular I verbs:	行(い)かせる→行(い)かせられる（行(い)かす→行(い)かされる）
	待(ま)たせる→待(ま)たせられる（待(ま)たす→待(ま)たされる）
Regular II verbs:	食(た)べさせる→食(た)べさせられる
Irregular verbs:	させる→させられる
	来(こ)させる→来(こ)させられる

> 子(こ)どものとき、私(わたし)は母(はは)にピアノを習(なら)わせられました。
> When I was little, I was made by my mother to learn piano (i.e., although I didn't want to).

VOCABULARY

しんぱいする	worry
さわぐ	make noise, cause a commotion
ぐあい	(physical) condition

Complete the sentences by changing the verbs in parentheses to a form of their causative counterparts that makes sense.

1) しょうらい子どもに中国語を…………………たいです。(習う)

2) 部長はひしょにコーヒーを…………………ました。(持ってくる)

3) 今すぐ部下にデータのまちがいを…………………ます。(しらべる)

4) 先生はせいとにえいごで…………………ました。 (こたえる)

5) 私はむすこにバイクのめんきょを…………………つもりです。(とる)

6) 子どもをあぶないところで…………………ないでください。(あそぶ)

7) 私はむすめに外国の大学で…………………つもりです。(勉強する)

8) スミスさんはよくじょうだんを言って、みんなを…………………ます。(わらう)

9) 私にも意見を…………………ください。(言う)

10) 小学生のとき、毎日かんじを…………………られました。(おぼえる)

11) 子どもがじゅくに行きたくないと言ったのに、親は子どもをじゅくに…………………ました。(行く)

12) 子どもがもっと勉強したいと言ったので、親は子どもにじゅくに…………………ました。(行く)

VOCABULARY

まちがい	mistake, error
こたえる (R2)	answer
バイク	motorcycle
じょうだん	joke

GRAMMAR NOTE

Stating Other People's Desires and Thoughts

To speak of your own desires, you can use either the *-tai* form of a verb or ほしい.

(私は) 車を／が買いたいです
I want to buy a car

(私は) 車がほしいです
I want a car.

ほしい is an *-i* adjective used to express desire for an object; the thing being desired takes the particle が. Given that other people's desires may be truly known only by them and not you, however, in Japanese they are distinguished from your own through use of the different expressions たがっています and ほしがっています. Here the thing being desired takes the particle を. Since wishes are often private, it is considered rude to refer openly to the desires of others, especially of those above you; thus たがっています and ほしがっています should only be used in relation to individuals who are close to or younger than you.

Similarly, in Japanese a distinction is made between your own thoughts and those of others by using と思います for the former and と思っています for the latter. と思っています, however, can also be used to state thoughts of your own that you have been holding over for some time.

むすこはサッカーせんしゅになりたがっています。
My son wants to be a soccer player.

子どもがゲームのソフトをほしがっていたので、たんじょう日に買ってやりました。
My child wanted game software, so I bought some for him for his birthday.

中野さんは無農薬でりんごが作れると思っています。
Mr. Nakano thinks that it is possible to grow apples without using pesticides.

(私は) 子どもに安全な野菜を食べさせたいと思っています。
I am always thinking that I would like to have my child eat safely grown vegetables.

PRACTICE 1 Discussing Education and Childrearing

WORD POWER

Things you want to get your children to do:

じゅく	ピアノのレッスン	たいそうきょうしつ	に通(かよ)う
語学(ごがく)	がっき	スポーツ	を習(なら)う
ペット	しょくぶつ	きょうだい	の世話(せわ)をする

家事(かじ)を手(て)つだう
部屋(へや)をかたづける
食事(しょくじ)のあとかたづけをする
るすばんをする

がまんする
やくそくをまもる
ただしいことばを使(つか)う

SPEAKING PRACTICE

I. Mrs. Kato and Mrs. Inuyama talk about children and chores.

加藤(かとう)（妻(つま)）：おたくではお子(こ)さんに家事(かじ)を手(て)つだわせていますか。
犬山(いぬやま)（妻(つま)）：いいえ。ほんとうはさせたいんですが……。へいじつはじゅく、週末(しゅうまつ)はたいそうきょうしつに通(かよ)わせているので、時間(じかん)がないんです。
加藤(かとう)（妻(つま)）：うちもそうでした。でも、勉強(べんきょう)より手(て)つだいが大事(だいじ)だと夫(おっと)に言(い)われて、食事(しょくじ)のあとかたづけをさせることにしました。
犬山(いぬやま)（妻(つま)）：うちも何(なに)かさせようかな。

Mrs. Kato: Do you have your child help out with housework?
Mrs. Inuyama: No, although I actually would like to . . . I'm having him attend cram school on weekdays and gym classes on the weekend, so there's no time.
Mrs. Kato: That was how it was at our house, too. But I decided to get my son to clear up after

VOCABULARY

たいそう	exercise, gymnastics	かじ	housework	がまんする	endure, exercise self-control
きょうしつ	class	あとかたづけ	putting things away, clearing up after	まもる	keep (a promise, rules, etc.)
ごがく	language study	るすばん	staying home alone		
がっき	musical instrument				

meals after being told by my husband that it's more important for children to help out at home than to study.

Mrs. Inuyama: We, too, should get our son to do some housework.

II. Ms. Martin and Ms. Sasaki talk about child safety.

マルタン：日本は最近安全じゃなくなったと言われていますけど、ほかの国とくらべるとずっと安全だと思います。

佐々木：　そうですか。

マルタン：私の国では11さいぐらいまで子どもをひとりで学校に通わせません。しんぱいですから。

佐々木：　親がむかえに行けない場合は、どうするんですか。

マルタン：かならずベビーシッターにたのみます。

佐々木：　へえ、そうなんですか。

Martin: It's said that Japan has become unsafe recently, but I think it's still much safer compared to other countries.

Sasaki: Is that so?

Martin: In my country, you wouldn't let children go to and from school by themselves until they get to be about eleven years old. It would be too much of a worry.

Sasaki: What do parents do if they can't go pick their children up?

Martin: They always arrange for a babysitter.

Sasaki: Wow, really?

III. Ms. Sasaki and Mr. Kato complain about the way children are raised nowadays.

佐々木：このごろのわかい親は、子どもにあまいと思いませんか。

加藤：　そうですね。子どもがほしがるものは何でも買ってあげるし、おそくまでテレビを見せるし。

佐々木：この間、電車の中で子どもがさわいでいたので注意したら、その子どものお母さんに、おこられてしまいました。

加藤：　どうして最近の親は子どもをしからないんでしょうか。

佐々木：ほんとうですね。子どもにがまんさせることも大切なのに。

Sasaki: Don't you think that young parents nowadays are too easy on their children?

Kato: That's true. They buy their children whatever they want and let them watch television until late, too.

Sasaki: The other day when I cautioned a child for being noisy on the train, I was told off by the child's mother.

Kato: Why don't parents these days scold their children, I wonder.

Sasaki: I agree. It's important to make children exercise self-control.

VOCABULARY

ほか	other	このごろ	nowadays
ずっと	much more	あまい	easy, lax
かよう	commute (to)	ちゅういする	warn, caution
ベビーシッター	babysitter		

PRACTICE 2 Asking for Permission to Do Something

SPEAKING PRACTICE

TRACK 34

I. Ms. Chan asks Ms. Sasaki to hold off on a reply.

佐々木(ささき)：チャンさん、ちょっといいですか。
チャン：はい、何(なん)でしょうか。
佐々木(ささき)：じつはシンガポール支社(ししゃ)で、えいごと中国語(ちゅうごくご)のできる人(ひと)をさがしているんですけど、チャンさんはこの話(はなし)にかんしんがありますか。
チャン：はあ。今(いま)すぐおへんじしなければなりませんか。急(きゅう)なことなので、すみませんが、少(すこ)し考(かんが)えさせてください。
佐々木(ささき)：もちろん、へんじはよく考(かんが)えてからで、いいですよ。

Sasaki: May I speak to you a moment, Ms. Chan?
Chan: Yes, what is it, may I ask?
Sasaki: Actually, they're looking for someone who can speak English and Chinese at the Singapore branch office. Would you be interested in this offer?
Chan: Ah, would I need to answer you right away? I'm sorry, but it's sudden, so please let me think about it a little.
Sasaki: Of course it'll be all right to give me your answer after you've given it plenty of thought.

II. Mr. Suzuki offers to help Mr. Kato move to a new house.

鈴木(すずき)：加藤(かとう)さん、土曜日(どようび)のひっこし、ぼくに手(て)つだわせてください。
加藤(かとう)：ありがとう。でも、いいよ。休(やす)みの日(ひ)に悪(わる)いから。
鈴木(すずき)：学生(がくせい)のころ、ひっこしのアルバイトをしたことがあるんです。ぜひ、やらせてください。
加藤(かとう)：そう、じゃ、たのむよ。ありがとう。

Suzuki: Please let me help you move on Saturday, Mr. Kato.
Kato: Thanks, but you don't have to. I feel bad [to impose on you] on your day off.
Suzuki: I once worked part-time for a moving company while I was a college student. Please let me do it, by all means.
Kato: Well, in that case, I'll ask the favor of you. Thanks.

VOCABULARY

はあ — well . . . , um . . . (a response to a question less definite than はい; spoken with a falling intonation)

III. Mrs. Kato and Mrs. Inuyama are getting ready to pay the bill at a restaurant.

加藤(かとう)（妻(つま)）：ああ、おいしかったですね。そろそろ行(い)きましょうか。
犬山(いぬやま)（妻(つま)）：そうですね。今日(きょう)は私(わたし)にはらわせてください。
加藤(かとう)（妻(つま)）：いえいえ、いつもごちそうになっていますから、私(わたし)がはらいます。
犬山(いぬやま)（妻(つま)）：それはこまります。私(わたし)にはらわせてください。

Mrs. Kato: Well, that was delicious, wasn't it? Shall we get going soon?
Mrs. Inuyama: Yes, let's. Please, let me pay today.
Mrs. Kato: Oh no, I get treated by you all the time, so I'll pay.
Mrs. Inuyama: I can't have that. Let me pay.

VOCABULARY ごちそうになる get treated (to a meal)

PRACTICE 3 Talking about Things You Wish Your Spouse/Partner Would Do

PHRASE POWER

① 家(いえ)をきれいにそうじしてほしい
I want my spouse to keep the house clean.

② おさけをあまり飲(の)まないでほしい
I want my spouse not to drink very much.

③ なやみを何(なん)でも話(はな)してほしい
I want my spouse to talk to me about anything that is troubling him/her.

④ 話(はなし)を聞(き)いてほしい
I want my spouse to listen to what I have to say.

⑤ けっこんきねん日(び)をわすれないでほしい
I want my spouse not to forget our wedding anniversary.

⑥ 子(こ)どもとあそんでほしい
I want my spouse to play with the children.

⑦ お金(かね)をたくさん使(つか)わないでほしい
I want my spouse not to spend a lot of money.

⑧ もっとお金(かね)をかせいでほしい
I want my spouse to earn more money.

⑨ 自分(じぶん)が悪(わる)いと思(おも)ったら、すぐあやまってほしい
I want my spouse to apologize right away when he/she feels himself/herself to be wrong.

⑩「ありがとう」と言(い)ってほしい
I want my spouse to say "thank you" to me.

VOCABULARY

なやみ	trouble, concern
かせぐ	earn

SPEAKING PRACTICE

Mrs. Kato and Mrs. Inuyama complain about their husbands.

加藤（妻）：犬山さん、聞いてくださいよ。うちの夫、ぜんぜん私の話を聞いてくれないんです。私が話しかけても、ちゃんと聞いていないみたい。

犬山（妻）：うちもそうですよ。子どものことを話しても、そうだんにのってくれないんです。

加藤（妻）：なやみやぐちも聞いてほしいのに……。

犬山（妻）：ほんとうにそうですね。

Mrs. Kato: Listen to this, Mrs. Inuyama. My husband never listens at all to what I have to say. Even when I talk to him, he doesn't seem to be paying proper attention.

Mrs. Inuyama: That's how it is at our house, too. My husband won't talk things over with me even when I'm telling him about our child.

Mrs. Kato: I want him to listen to my concerns and complaints . . .

Mrs. Inuyama: I hear you.

USAGE NOTE

～てほしい

As discussed on p. 159, ～がほしい means "to want something." The pattern "*-te* form of a verb + ほしい," meanwhile, expresses the idea of wanting someone to act in a certain way. The person whom you want to get to perform the action is marked with the particle に.

私は子どもにもっと勉強してほしいです。
I want my child to study more.

～ないでほしい

To express the idea of wanting someone to refrain from doing something, you can use the *-nai* form of a verb + で + ほしい.

うちの前に車をとめないでほしいんですが……。
I'd appreciate it if you'd not park your car in front of our house.

VOCABULARY

はなしかける (R2)	talk (to)
ぐち	complaint

KANJI PRACTICE

件
affair
matter

件（けん）
事件（じけん）
件名（けんめい）

持
hold

持つ（もつ）
持ち物（もちもの）
気持ち（きもち）

育
raise

育つ（そだつ）
教育（きょういく）

道
way
street

道（みち）
茶道（さどう）

考
think

考える（かんがえる）

歩

歩く (ある)
歩道 (ほどう)

walk

習

習う (なら)

learn

運

運ぶ (はこ)
運転 (うんてん)
運動 (うんどう)

carry

転

自転車 (じてんしゃ)
回転ずし (かいてん)

roll
turn

注

注意する (ちゅうい)

pour
focus

Quiz 3 Unit 3 (Lessons 7–9)

I Fill in the blanks with the appropriate particle.

1) むすめは先生（　　）ほめられました。
2) 私は友だち（　　）にもつをはこんでもらいました。
3) 会社（　　）さいふをおきわすれてしまいました。
4) かど（　　）まがろうとしたら、犬がとびだしてきました。
5) 私（　　）その仕事をやらせてください。

II Choose the most appropriate word from among the alternatives (1–4) given. The same word cannot be used twice in the same dialogue/sentence.

1) A：田中さん、おそいですね。（　　）どうしたんでしょう。
   B：（　　）ねぼうしたんでしょう。
   1. ぜひ　2. たぶん　3. いったい　4. できれば

2) 休みの日に（　　）手つだいに来てくれて、ありがとう。
   1. わざわざ　2. なかなか　3. すっかり　4. だんだん

3) もうおそいですね、（　　）帰りましょうか。
   1. それから　2. それより　3. いろいろ　4. そろそろ

4) （　　）あした休むつもりでしたが、仕事がいそがしいので、行くことにしました。
   1. ほんとうは　2. ちゃんと　3. ちょうど　4. すぐ

III Change the form of the word given in parentheses to complete the sentence in a way that makes sense.

1) マリーさんが仕事を（　　　）くれました。(代わります)
2) くうこうにおきゃくさんをむかえに（　　　）ことになっています。(行きます)
3) 家を（　　　）としたとき、友だちが来ました。(出ます)
4) 子どもにけいたい電話を（　　　）ています。(持ちます)
5) おとうとにカメラを（　　　）て、かなしかったです。(こわします)

IV Choose the most appropriate word or phrase from among the alternatives (1–4) given.

1) 田中(たなか)さんが入院(にゅういん)したので、花(はな)を持(も)って（　　　）行(い)った。

　1. お礼(れい)に　　2. お見(み)まいに　　3. 代(か)わりに　　4. むかえに

2) 電車(でんしゃ)に（　　　）、夫(おっと)はずっとねていた。

　1. 乗(の)るとき　2. 乗(の)っている間(あいだ)　3. 乗(の)っている間(あいだ)に　4. 乗(の)ろうとしたとき

3) けさ駅前(えきまえ)においたバイクがないんです。（　　　）らしいんです。

　1. えらばれた　　2. だまされた　　3. すられた　　4. ぬすまれた

4) おとうとは大学(だいがく)のしけんにごうかくして、両親(りょうしん)を（　　　）。

　1. しんぱいさせました　　2. がっかりさせました

　3. こまらせました　　4. よろこばせました

5) パーティーのじゅんびを（　　　）ほしいんですが、いいですか。

　1. まもって　　2. 習(なら)って　　3. そうだんして　　4. 手(て)つだって

V Fill in the blanks with the correct reading of each kanji.

1) 説明を聞いてから、意見を言ってください。

（　　　）　　（　　　）

2) １９５０年代に　建てられたビルの写真をとりました。

（　　　）（　　　）　（　　　）

3) 道を　歩きながら、仕事のことを考えました。

（　　　）（　　　）　　（　　　）

4) エミさんは自転車で学校に通っています。

（　　　）（　　　）

UNIT 4

BUSINESS

Have you ever had the experience of coming across a lot of unfamiliar expressions when being spoken to while out shopping or at a restaurant? What about when someone you didn't know asked you for directions? Such situations require formal language. Unit 4 introduces you to examples and usage of honorific language and explains how to adjust your register depending on audience, topic, or occasion, or on whether you are speaking or writing. Through the skills gained in this unit, you will be able to enrich your expressive powers as well as interact more smoothly with others and develop better interpersonal relationships.

LESSON **10**

BUSINESS GREETINGS

TARGET DIALOGUE

Mr. Kato, the section chief of the sales department of the ABC Foods Tokyo branch, is visiting Nozomi Department Store with Mr. Green, the branch president. Mr. Kato introduces Mr. Green to Mr. Kuroda, the managing director of Nozomi Department Store.

加藤：　黒田常務、支社長のグリーンでございます（→p. 177）。支社長、こちら、黒田常務でいらっしゃいます（→p. 177）。

グリーン：グリーンともうします（→p. 178）。よろしくおねがいいたします（→p. 178）。

黒田：　黒田です。こちらこそ、よろしくおねがいします。

グリーン：バレンタイン・フェアに出店させていただける（→p. 181）ことになって、米国本社も、たいへんよろこんでおります（→p. 178）。ありがとうございました。

黒田：　いえいえ。おんしゃの新商品は、ひょうばんがいいようですね。

グリーン：はい、おかげさまで、最近売り上げがのびてきています。

加藤：　バレンタイン・フェアむけに、新しいパッケージのデザインをけんとうしております。

黒田：　そうですか。はいけんする（→p. 179）のが楽しみですね。

加藤：　来月の初めに、お持ちして（→p. 180）見ていただこうと思っております。

The conversation concludes, and Mr. Kato takes his leave.

加藤(かとう)：　本日(ほんじつ)はおいそがしいところ、お時間(じかん)をいただき、ありがとうございました。

黒田(くろだ)：　こちらこそ、わざわざおいでいただき、ありがとうございました。

グリーン：では、今後(こんご)ともよろしくおねがいいたします。

加藤(かとう)：　失礼(しつれい)いたします。

Kato: Director Kuroda, this is [Frank] Green, our branch president. President, this is Director Kuroda.
Green: I'm Green. Please extend us your kind consideration.
Kuroda: I'm Kuroda. Please, we're the ones who should be asking for yours.
Green: Our parent company in the United States, too, is extremely pleased that we are going to be allowed to put out a booth for your Valentine's Day Fair. Thank you very much.
Kuroda: Not at all. Your new product seems to be popular, doesn't it?
Green: Yes, thanks to you, sales are recently on the rise.
Kato: We're considering introducing a new package design for the Valentine's Day Fair.
Kuroda: Is that so? I look forward to having a look.
Kato: We're planning to bring you a sample for your inspection at the beginning of next month.
. . . . . .
Kato: Thank you for giving us time out of your busy schedule today.
Kuroda: Please, thank you for taking the time just to come here.
Green: Well then, please do continue to extend us your kind consideration now as always.
Kato: We'll be taking our leave now.

VOCABULARY

黒田(くろだ)	Kuroda (surname)
常務(じょうむ)	managing director
でいらっしゃいます	this is . . . (honorific way of introducing someone)
～ともうします	I am ——, my name is —— (humble way of introducing oneself)
バレンタイン・フェア	Valentine's Day Fair
出店(しゅってん)する	put out a store/booth, exhibit
～させていただく	be allowed to do (humble way of saying ～させてもらう)
米国(べいこく)	United States
おんしゃ	your company (formal way of referring to someone else's company)
けんとうする	consider, discuss
はいけんする	see, look at (humble way of saying 見(み)る)

お持(も)ちする	bring (humble for 持(も)つ)
お〜する	(basic pattern for turning a verb into a humble expression)
本日(ほんじつ)	today (formal way of saying 今日(きょう))
ところ	time, moment (おいそがしいところ = at a busy time)
おいでいただく	come (to where one is) (honorific expression)
今後(こんご)とも	into the future, now as always

NOTES

1. HONORIFIC LANGUAGE

Honorific language, or honorifics, conveys speakers' perceptions of the circumstances and interpersonal relationships prevailing within a conversation. One basic principle is that speakers employ *honorific expressions* to elevate their listeners, and thereby show respect for them, while using *humble expressions* to talk humbly about themselves. Within the office, workers employ honorific expressions toward their bosses while speaking of themselves using humble expressions.

When a conversation also includes clients or other people from an out-group (see the Culture Note on p. 176), as in this dialogue, the speakers employ honorific expressions toward the out-group while using humble expressions for members of their in-group just as they would for themselves. This is done regardless of the member's status within the in-group itself, even if, for example, the person is the 80-year-old president of the company. (Thus, 〜さん and other such terms need to be left out in speaking of people from one's own in-group with those outside of it.)

Honorifics reflect differences in not only status but also degree of familiarity. When people speak to strangers, they use honorific language, perhaps progressing to the *desu/masu* style and then to the plain style as they grow closer. The use of honorifics also depends on setting and topic, so that colleagues who are on familiar terms may still use honorific language when addressing each other at formal business meetings, for example.

2. 〜させていただく

The pattern "*-te* form of a causative verb + いただく (humble way of saying もらう)" often occurs in expressions of gratitude, as is the case here. It is sometimes adopted for the sake of demonstrating respect toward another even when talking about something they did not particularly do.

きのうは楽(たの)しい時間(じかん)をすごさせていただき、ありがとうございました。
Thank you for allowing me to spend an enjoyable time yesterday.

3. 米国(べいこく)

Some foreign country and geographical names have kanji designations, e.g., 米国(べいこく) (the United States), 英国(えいこく) (the United Kingdom), 欧州(おうしゅう) (Europe), and 欧米(おうべい) (Europe and North America). Although newspapers and the like also often use single-kanji designations—独(どく) for Germany, 仏(ふつ) for France, 露(ろ) for Russia, or 豪(ごう) for Australia, to give a few—as shorthand for those countries or in speaking of relations between two or more of them (e.g., 日米(にちべい), "Japanese-U.S."), these are generally not used in colloquial speech, at least when referring to a single country by itself.

4. おんしゃ（御社(おんしゃ)）

A business term meaning "your company." The corresponding term for "my company" is 弊社(へいしゃ).

5. おかげさまで

おかげ, introduced on p. 49 in the form おかげで, is often used for the sake of polite conversation even for things that may not actually be "owed" to the listener.

おげんきですか。
おかげさまで（げんきです）。
Have you been well?
[Yes,] thanks to you.

6. けんとうしております

While けんとうしております is used in this dialogue in a literal sense, in some business or political contexts, being told けんとうしておきます, "We'll consider it," in reply to a question such as いかがでしょうか, "What do you think [of the possibilities of this proposal]?" is tantamount to being brushed off without a clear answer in prelude to being refused later.

7. おいそがしいところ

おいそがしいところ is an idiom expressing feelings of gratitude or apology toward having someone spend time on your account. Another common idiom that uses ところ in a time-related sense is 今(いま)のところ, "for the moment," as in 今(いま)のところ、お話(はなし)できることは何(なに)もありません, "For the moment I have nothing I can say to you."

CULTURE NOTE

In-groups and Out-groups

In Japanese, speakers do not employ honorific expressions toward family when talking about them with people outside of it. Japanese regard family as in-group and therefore to be treated similarly to their own selves, meanwhile setting off all others as part of the out-group. Through extension, not only one's own family but also the larger society, company, and organizations to which one belongs are considered to be in-group and those falling outside these affiliations to be out-group, giving rise to distinctions that are in turn reflected in language. These notions of in-group/out-group influence honorific language as well as expressions of giving and receiving. The Japanese word for in-group, ウチ, is fundamentally the same as the word うち meaning "home" or "inside." Similarly, うちの indicating possession or affiliation in such expressions as うちの子(こ)ども (our child) or うちの部長(ぶちょう) (our department manager) may also be traced back to Japanese distinctions between in-groups and out-groups.

GRAMMAR & PATTERN PRACTICE

I Honorifics (1): Key Expressions

Note 1 and the Culture Note at left outlined some of the basic traits of Japanese honorific language. This section will present some common honorific verbs while demonstrating how to use them in expressions for giving introductions or greeting someone you are meeting for the first time.

1. Neutral expression: です

Honorific and humble expressions for です are as follows.

Humble (hereafter given as "HUM"): でございます。
Honorific (hereafter given as "HON"): でいらっしゃいます。

Both are frequently used in making introductions, conducting business, or otherwise interacting in formal situations.

While exchanging business cards:

加藤(かとう)：　ＡＢＣフーズの加藤(かとう)でございます。
高橋(たかはし)：　のぞみデパートの高橋(たかはし)でございます。
Kato: I'm Kato from ABC Foods.
Takahashi: I'm Takahashi from Nozomi Department Store.

Introduction scene from the Target Dialogue, in which Mr. Kato introduces President Green, his boss (in-group), to their client, Managing Director Kuroda (out-group):

加藤(かとう)：黒田(くろだ)常務(じょうむ)、支社長(ししゃちょう)のグリーンでございます。
支社長(ししゃちょう)、こちら、黒田(くろだ)常務(じょうむ)でいらっしゃいます。
Kato: Director Kuroda, this is Green, our branch president. President, this is Director Kuroda.

でございます and でいらっしゃいます are also commonly used when speaking to guests or customers, calling out to someone you are meeting for the first time, or talking over the phone to people with whom you are not on familiar terms.

Calling out to someone you do not yet know:

Ａ：　失礼(しつれい)ですが、ミルズさんでいらっしゃいますか。
ミルズ：はい、ミルズです。
A: Excuse me, but are you Mr. Mills?
Mills: Yes, I'm Mills.

VOCABULARY しつれいですが　excuse me, but . . .

Over the phone:

ミルズ：　もしもし、加藤(かとう)さんのおたくでいらっしゃいますか。
加藤(かとう)（妻(つま)）：はい、加藤(かとう)でございます。
Mills: Hello, is this Mr. Kato's residence?
Mrs. Kato: Yes, this is Kato.

2. Neutral expression: name といいます

The first expression below is used to give your own name or those of your in-group members in formal situations, the second to politely introduce someone else's name.

HUM: ～ともうします。
HON: ～さん／～様(さま)／～ (position or title) とおっしゃいます。

高橋(たかはし)：　こちらは、ＡＢＣフーズの方(かた)で、ジョン・ミルズさんとおっしゃいます。
ミルズ：ミルズともうします。よろしくおねがいいたします。
Takahashi: This is Mr. John Mills from ABC Foods.
Mills: I'm Mills. Please extend me your kind consideration.

3. Special verbs

Listed below are several other special verbs, for example もうします and おっしゃいます, that are commonly used to show respect or humility. Study the expressions to make sure you are able to understand and use them.

HONORIFIC VERBS	NEUTRAL VERBS	HUMBLE VERBS
なさいます *	します	いたします
いらっしゃいます * おいでになります	来(き)ます	まいります うかがいます
いらっしゃいます *	行(い)きます	まいります うかがいます
いらっしゃいます *	います	おります
めしあがります	食(た)べます 飲(の)みます	いただきます
おっしゃいます *	言(い)います	もうします もうしあげます (R2)
くださいます *	くれます	

	もらいます	いただきます
	あげます	さしあげます (R2)
ごらんになります	見ます	はいけんします
	聞きます	うかがいます
ごぞんじです	知っています	ぞんじております
	会います	お目にかかります

NOTE 1: The honorific verbs marked with ⋆ (なさいます, いらっしゃいます, おっしゃいます and くださいます) conjugate like Regular I verbs (e.g., なさる, いらっしゃる, おっしゃる, くださる), except that the r-sound is dropped from the *-masu* forms.

NOTE 2: The humble verbs いたします, まいります, おりますand もうします can also be used simply for added politeness, in which case they do not express humility.

Complete the dialogues by changing the words in parentheses to their honorific or humble equivalents.

1) A：もしもし、加藤さんのおたく……………………か。(です)
   B：はい、加藤……………………(です)

2) A：いつ日本に……………………か。(来ました)
   B：3年前に……………………(来ました)

3) A：おくさまのお名前は何と……………………か。(いいます)
   B：夏子と……………………(いいます)

4) A：お飲み物は何を……………………か。(飲みます)
   B：赤ワインを……………………(飲みます)

VOCABULARY

なつこ	Natsuko (female name)
あかワイン	red wine

II Honorifics (2): Basic Patterns

This section introduces basic patterns for forming honorific and humble expressions out of verbs other than the special cases covered earlier.

1. Honorific expressions

The pattern "お + *-masu* stem + になります" is used to turn ordinary verbs into honorific ones.

A, a person from outside Mr. Mills's company, is asking B, someone from inside the company, when Mr. Mills is expected to return to the office.

Ａ：ミルズさんは何時ごろおもどりになりますか。
Ｂ：５時にもどる予定です。
A: About what time will Mr. Mills be returning?
B: He's scheduled to come back at five.

2. Humble expressions

The pattern "お + *-masu* stem + します" is used to turn ordinary verbs into humble expressions. (For verbs of the "noun + する" type, use "お／ご + noun + します.") This pattern is frequently used in making offers to others, e.g.,

おもそうなおにもつですね。お持ちしましょうか。
Those bags look heavy. Shall I carry them for you?

While most verbs will take the prefix お, verbs of the form "noun + する" such as あんないする (guide), 電話する (phone), and 説明する (explain) may appear with either お or ご depending on the noun, e.g., ごあんないする, お電話する, ご説明する.

The pattern may be made even more formal by replacing します with its humble equivalent, いたします, in situations requiring especially polite language, such as when speaking to guests or customers.

A waiter at a restaurant is speaking to customers.

お待たせいたしました。ごあんないいたします。
Thank you for waiting. I'll show you to your table now.

VOCABULARY お～になる (basic pattern for turning an ordinary verb into an honorific one)

1 Complete the dialogues by filling in the blanks with the appropriate honorific expressions.

1) A：何時に……………………か。
　 B：9時に出かけます。

2) A：どの新聞を……………………か。
　 B：ＪＢＰ新聞を読みます。

3) A：どなたに……………………か。
　 B：ミルズさんに会います。

2 Complete the sentences by changing the verbs in parentheses to their humble equivalents.

1) 雨がふってきました。かさを……………………か。（貸す）
2) 車で……………………か。（送る）
3) みなさんに……………………か。（しょうかいする）

III Honorifics (3): Honorific Verbs for Giving and Receiving

In honorific language, もらう, くれる, and あげる become いただく, くださる, and さしあげる, respectively. As covered earlier (pp. 125–27), these verbs may be used to express the giving and receiving both of objects and services. Similarly to ～てあげる (pp. 126–27), さしあげる carries the danger of sounding patronizing when said directly to the recipient. ～てさしあげる, indicating a service done by you, sounds particularly pushy and rude, so that it is usually not said to someone face to face.

VOCABULARY

ＪＢＰしんぶん	JBP Newspaper (fictitious newspaper name)
おくる	escort, see/drive (someone somewhere)

1 Read the following sentences describing the giving and receiving of objects while paying attention to the differences between the neutral and polite expressions.

1) Neutral: (私(わたし)は) おとうとに本(ほん)をもらいました。

Polite: (私(わたし)は) 先生(せんせい)に本(ほん)をいただきました。

2) Neutral: (私(わたし)は) 友(とも)だちに本(ほん)をあげます。

Polite: (advertisement) カタログを無料(むりょう)でさしあげます。

3) Neutral: 父(ちち)と母(はは)は (私(わたし)に) 本(ほん)をくれました。

Polite: 先生(せんせい)は (私(わたし)に) 本(ほん)をくださいました。

2 Read the following sentences describing the giving and receiving of services while paying attention to the differences between the neutral and polite expressions. Then fill in the parentheses before each statement with either **A** or **B**, depending on what kind of relationship you think the speaker has with the person being thanked.

1) **A** a close friend
B someone not very close; someone of higher status than the speaker

1. (　　　) この前(まえ)は (ぼくに) スキーを教(おし)えてくれて、ありがとう。

2. (　　　) 先日(せんじつ)はうちの子(こ)にスキーを教(おし)えてくださって、ありがとうございました。

2) **A** a close friend
B someone not very close; someone of higher status than the speaker

1. (　　　) 今日(きょう)は食事(しょくじ)にさそってくれて、ありがとう。

2. (　　　) 今日(きょう)は食事(しょくじ)にさそってくださって、どうもありがとうございました。

PRACTICE 1 Giving Greetings and Introductions

PHRASE POWER

I. Introducing yourself:

HUM: 加藤(かとう)でございます。
I am Kato.

HUM: ＡＢＣフーズのミルズともうします。
I am Mills, from ABC foods.

HUM: 加藤(かとう)の家内(かない)でございます。
I am Kato's wife.

II. Introducing members of your in-group:

HUM: 部長(ぶちょう)の佐々木(ささき)でございます。
This is Sasaki, our department manager.

HUM: 家内(かない)でございます。
This is my wife.

HUM: むすめの愛子(あいこ)ともうします。
This is my daughter, Aiko.

III. Introducing people from an out-group:

HON: こちらは高橋(たかはし)さんでいらっしゃいます。
This is Mr. Takahashi.

HON: こちらはのぞみデパートの高橋(たかはし)さんとおっしゃいます。
This is Mr. Takahashi, from Nozomi Department Store.

SPEAKING PRACTICE

I. Ms. Martin calls Mr. Nakano at his home.

マルタン： 中野(なかの)さんのおたくでいらっしゃいますか。
中野(なかの)（妻(つま)）：はい、中野(なかの)でございます。
マルタン： マルタンともうしますが、中野(なかの)さんはいらっしゃいますか。
中野(なかの)（妻(つま)）：今(いま)、ちょっと出(で)かけておりますが、あと１時間(じかん)ほどで帰(かえ)ると思(おも)います。
マルタン： では、また後(のち)ほどお電話(でんわ)させていただきます。

Martin: Is this the Nakano residence?
Mrs. Nakano: Yes, this is Nakano.
Martin: My name is Martin. Would Mr. Nakano be in?

Mrs. Nakano: He's out at the moment, but I think he'll come back in about an hour.
Martin: Then I'll call again later.

II. Mr. Mills's contact from Nozomi Department Store comes to visit him at ABC Foods.

青木(あおき)： のぞみデパートの青木(あおき)ともうしますが、２時(じ)にミルズさんとお会(あ)いすることになっております。
受付(うけつけ)： 青木様(あおきさま)、お待(ま)ちしておりました。あちらにおかけになってお待(ま)ちください。

The receptionist calls Mr. Mills.

受付(うけつけ)： ミルズさん、のぞみデパートの青木様(あおきさま)が受付(うけつけ)でお待(ま)ちですが。
ミルズ： わかりました。すぐ行(い)きます。

The receptionist approaches Mr. Aoki.

受付(うけつけ)： 青木様(あおきさま)、ミルズはすぐにまいりますので、もう少々(しょうしょう)お待(ま)ちください。

Aoki: I'm Aoki from Nozomi Department Store, and I've arranged to see Mr. Mills at two.
receptionist: Mr. Aoki, we've been expecting you. Please take a seat over there to wait.
. . . . . .
receptionist: Mr. Mills, Mr. Aoki from Nozomi Department Store is waiting for you at the reception desk.
Mills: I understand. I'll come right away.
. . . . . .
receptionist: Mr. Aoki, Mills will come right away, so please be patient a while longer.

III. On the weekend, Mr. Kato goes to pick up his wife at a tennis club.

加藤(かとう)（妻(つま)）：あ、主人(しゅじん)がまいりました。あなた、こちら、いつもいっしょにテニスをしている赤坂(あかさか)さんよ。
加藤(かとう)（夫(おっと)）：あ、どうも。いつも家内(かない)がお世話(せわ)になっております。
赤坂(あかさか)： こちらこそ、いつもおくさまにお世話(せわ)になっております。

Mrs. Kato: Oh, here comes my husband. Dear, this is Mrs. Akasaka, who always plays tennis with me.
Mr. Kato: Oh, hello. My wife is always receiving your assistance.
Akasaka: Please, I'm the one who's always receiving hers.

VOCABULARY

あおき	Aoki (surname)	あなた	Dear (said by a wife to her husband)
かける	sit (on a chair)	あかさか	Akasaka (surname)
おまちです	wait (respectful expression; =おまちになっています)	どうも	hello (when used as a greeting by itself)

PRACTICE 2 Thanking People

PHRASE POWER

① おいしいワインをありがとうございました。
Thank you for the delicious wine.

② 家内(かない)にきれいな花(はな)をありがとうございました。
Thank you for the beautiful flowers you gave to my wife.

③ きちょうなお時間(じかん)をいただき（まして）、ありがとうございました。
Thank you for giving me your valuable time.

④ 私(わたし)のために、パーティーを開(ひら)いてくださって、ありがとうございます。
Thank you for throwing a party for me.

⑤ 今日(きょう)はおまねきいただき（まして）、ありがとうございました。
Thank you for inviting me today.

⑥ 本日(ほんじつ)はわざわざおいでいただき（まして）、ありがとうございました。
Thank you for taking the time just to come here today.

⑦ 先日(せんじつ)はいいお話(はなし)を聞(き)かせていただき（まして）、ありがとうございました。
Thank you for allowing me to hear such a good lecture the other day.

SPEAKING PRACTICE

I. Mr. Kato concludes a meeting with Mr. Takahashi.

加藤(かとう)：　本日(ほんじつ)はおいそがしいところ、お時間(じかん)をいただき、ありがとうございました。
高橋(たかはし)：　こちらこそ、わざわざおいでいただき、ありがとうございました。

Kato: Thank you for giving us time out of your busy schedule today.
Takahashi: Please, thank you for taking the time just to come here.

II. Mr. Mills thanks Mr. Takahashi for his prior assistance.

ミルズ：　先日(せんじつ)はお世話(せわ)になりまして、ありがとうございました。
高橋(たかはし)：　こちらこそ。ミルズさんが通訳(つうやく)をしてくださって、たすかりました。

Mills: Thank you for your assistance the other day.
Takahashi: Please, I should thank you. It was a big help that you interpreted for us.

VOCABULARY

きちょう（な）	valuable
まねく	invite

III. Mr. Kato thanks Ms. Akasaka for a past invitation.

加藤(かとう)： 先日(せんじつ)はごしょうたいいただき、ありがとうございました。とても楽(たの)しくすごさせていただきました。

赤坂(あかさか)： こちらこそ、子(こ)どもにおみやげをいただいて、ありがとうございました。とてもよろこんでおりました。

Kato: Thank you for inviting me the other day. I had a very enjoyable time.
Akasaka: Please, thank you for the souvenirs you gave to my child. He was very happy.

IV. Aiko notices Ms. Martin is at her ballet recital and goes up to her.

愛子(あいこ)： マリーさん、来(き)てくださってありがとうございます。
マルタン：愛子(あいこ)さん、すばらしかったわ。どんどん上手(じょうず)になるわね。
愛子(あいこ)： そうですか。ありがとうございます。
マルタン：これ、どうぞ。(*hands Aiko a bouquet*)
愛子(あいこ)： うわあ、きれいなお花(はな)、ありがとうございます。とてもいいかおり。
マルタン：愛子(あいこ)さんのイメージで、花屋(はなや)さんに作(つく)ってもらったのよ。
愛子(あいこ)： こんなにきれいな花(はな)たばをいただいたの、初(はじ)めてです。うれしい！

Aiko: Thank you for doing me the favor of coming, Marie.
Martin: Aiko, you were fantastic. You're getting better and better.
Aiko: Do you think so? Thank you!
Martin: Here, please take these. (*hands Aiko a bouquet*)
Aiko: Wow, what beautiful flowers, thank you! They smell very good.
Martin: I had the florist make it for me to fit your image.
Aiko: This is the first time I've received such a beautiful bouquet. I'm so happy!

VOCABULARY

イメージ	image
はなや	florist

PRACTICE 3 Making Apologies

PHRASE POWER

① おそくなって、もうしわけありません。
I apologize for being late.

② お待(ま)たせして、もうしわけありません。
I apologize for making you wait.

③ ごめいわくをおかけして、もうしわけありません。
I apologize for giving you such trouble.

④ さそっていただいたのに、うかがえなくて、もうしわけありません。
I apologize for not being able to come even though you were kind enough to invite me.

⑤ せっかく用意(ようい)してくださったのに、もうしわけございません。
I apologize [that I was not able to accept your kindness] when you went through all that trouble to prepare.

SPEAKING PRACTICE

TRACK 39

I. Ms. Martin arrives late to an appointment with Mr. Yamakawa, a fellow member of the community orchestra.

マルタン：お待(ま)たせして、もうしわけありません。
山川(やまかわ)：　マリーさんがやくそくの時間(じかん)におくれるなんてめずらしいね。
マルタン：チェロのれんしゅうをしていたら、時間(じかん)をわすれてしまったんです。すみません。

Martin: I apologize for making you wait.
Yamakawa: It's unusual for you to be late to an appointment, isn't it? [lit., "That you should be late for an appointment is rare, wouldn't you say?"]
Martin: I was practicing my cello, and I lost track of the time. I'm sorry.

II. An unexpected guest arrives while Mr. Kato is not home.

加藤(かとう)（妻(つま)）：　せっかくいらっしゃってくださったのに、あいにく加藤(かとう)が外出(がいしゅつ)しておりまして、もうしわけありません。
加藤(かとう)の知人(ちじん)：いいえ、近(ちか)くまで来(き)ましたので、ちょっとごあいさつしようと思(おも)っただけですから。

VOCABULARY

めいわくをかける	cause/give (someone) trouble	あいにく	unfortunately, contrary to what one would like
せっかく	with trouble, with pains (used to express regret when an effort is ruined or does not pay off)	がいしゅつする	go out
なんて	that	ちじん	acquaintance

Mrs. Kato: I apologize that my husband is unfortunately out, when you kindly took the trouble to visit.
acquaintance: Oh no, I only thought I would stop by to say hello, since I was nearby.

III. A mother apologizes for her son climbing a neighbor's tree.

母：この間はむすこがいろいろごめいわくをおかけして、もうしわけありませんでした。
近所の人：いいえ。げんきなお子さんですね。
母：おたくの大切な木のえだをおってしまって、ほんとうにもうしわけありません。
近所の人：気になさらないでください。それより、けがかなくてよかったですよ。

mother: I apologize for my son putting you through a lot of trouble the other day.
neighbor: Not at all. He's certainly active, isn't he?
mother: I'm really very sorry he broke that branch off your precious tree.
neighbor: Please, don't worry about it. More importantly, it was good that he wasn't hurt.

VOCABULARY おる break, snap

PRACTICE 4 Requesting Services

SPEAKING PRACTICE

TRACK 40

I. Ms. Nakamura arrives at the restaurant where she is to have dinner with Mr. Smith.

中村(なかむら)：　７時(じ)に予約(よやく)した中村(なかむら)です。少(すこ)しはやいんですけど……。
ウェイター：中村様(なかむらさま)ですね。すぐごあんないいたしますので、おかけになってお待(ま)ちいただけますか。

………………

ウェイター：お待(ま)たせいたしました。ごあんないいたします。
中村(なかむら)：　すみません、にもつ、あずかっていただけますか。
ウェイター：はい、おあずかりいたします。(*gives her a tag*) では、お帰(かえ)りのさいに、こちらをおわたしください。

Nakamura: I'm Nakamura, the one with a reservation for seven o'clock. I'm a little early, but . . .
waiter: Ms. Nakamura. I'll show you to your table very soon, so could I please ask you to take a seat and wait?

. . . . . .

waiter: Thank you for waiting. I'll show you to your table.
Nakamura: Excuse me, could you check my bags for me, please?
waiter: Yes, I'll check them. (*gives her a tag*) When you leave, please hand this [to a staff member].

II. Mr. Smith finds a dish he can't eat included in the meal he would like to order.

スミス：　すみません、このコースのかきを、ほかのものにかえてもらえませんか。かきがにがてなので……。
ウェイター：ちょっと聞(き)いてまいりますので、少々(しょうしょう)お待(ま)ちいただけますか。
スミス：　ありがとうございます。

………………

ウェイター：できるそうです。えびでいかがでしょうか。
スミス：　はい。けっこうです。じゃ、このコースをおねがいします。

Smith: Excuse me, could you please change the oysters in this course for me to something else? I'm not fond of oysters, you see.
waiter: I'll go off a moment to ask, so could I please have you wait a little?
Smith: Thank you.

. . . . . .

waiter: I've been told it's possible. Would shrimp do?
Smith: Yes, that's fine. Then I'll take this course, please.

VOCABULARY

ウェイター	waiter
さい	time, occasion (おかえりのさい = at the time you leave)
コース	lit., "course," a menu item that includes several dishes at a set price
かき	oyster
えび	shrimp

PRACTICE 5 Conducting Business

SPEAKING PRACTICE

Mr. Kato makes a phone call to Mr. Takahashi, the manager of the sales department of Nozomi Department Store, to set up an appointment.

高橋(たかはし)：　はい、高橋(たかはし)です。
加藤(かとう)：　ＡＢＣフーズの加藤(かとう)です。いつもお世話(せわ)になっております。
高橋(たかはし)：　こちらこそ。
加藤(かとう)：　バレンタイン・フェアのことでは、いろいろごじょげんいただき、ありがとうございました。さっそくですが、支社長(ししゃちょう)のグリーンが、ぜひごあいさつにうかがいたいと言(い)っているのですが、黒田常務(くろだじょうむ)のご都合(つごう)はいかがでしょうか。
高橋(たかはし)：　そうですか。わざわざありがとうございます。では、予定(よてい)をかくにんして、後(のち)ほどごれんらくします。そちらのご都合(つごう)はいかがですか。
加藤(かとう)：　来週(らいしゅう)でしたら、いつでもけっこうです。
高橋(たかはし)：　わかりました。
加藤(かとう)：　よろしくおねがいします。では、失礼(しつれい)します。

Takahashi: Takahashi here.
Kato: This is Kato from ABC Foods. We're always receiving your assistance.
Takahashi: Oh no, it is we who are always receiving yours.
Kato: Thank you for all the advice you gave us regarding the Valentine's Day Fair. To get right to the point, Green, our branch president, is saying that he would very much like to pay you a visit. May I inquire what Director Kuroda's schedule looks like?
Takahashi: I see. Thank you for taking the trouble [to want to come visit us]. In that case, I'll confirm his schedule and contact you at a later time. When might be convenient for you [to visit]?
Kato: Anytime next week would be fine.
Takahashi: I understand.
Kato: Thank you. Well then, goodbye.

VOCABULARY

じょげん	advice
かくにんする	confirm

KANJI PRACTICE

黒
黒い くろ(い)
黒田 くろだ
black

米
米国 べいこく
rice
America

英
英語 えいご
distinguished
England

楽
楽しい たの(しい)
音楽 おんがく
pleasant
music

色
色 いろ
color

赤

赤い
あか
赤んぼう
あか

red

青

青い
あお

blue

銀

銀行
ぎんこう

silver

茶

お茶
ちゃ
茶色
ちゃいろ

tea

工

工場
こうじょう
工事中
こうじちゅう

craft
construction

LESSON 11 LEAVING AND RELAYING MESSAGES

TARGET DIALOGUE

Mr. Suzuki is looking around the office for Mr. Kato.

鈴木(すずき)：　あれ、加藤(かとう)さんは？

加藤(かとう)の秘書(ひしょ)：先(さき)ほど出(で)かけられましたが、何(なに)か？ →p. 200

鈴木(すずき)：　そうですか。(*furrows his brow*)

加藤(かとう)の秘書(ひしょ)：何(なに)かあったら、連絡(れんらく)するように言(い)われていますが。 →p. 196

鈴木(すずき)：　じゃあ、すみませんが、バレンタイン・フェアの件(けん)で急(いそ)いでごそうだんしたいことがあるので、電話(でんわ)をいただきたいと伝(つた)えてください。 →p. 196

加藤(かとう)の秘書(ひしょ)：わかりました。お伝(つた)えします。

A phone call comes through to Mr. Suzuki from Mr. Kato.

加藤(かとう)：　あ、加藤(かとう)です。

鈴木(すずき)：　おいそがしいところ、すみません。うちの売(う)り場(ば)の件(けん)で、さっきたんとう者(しゃ)から電話(でんわ)がありました。場所(ばしょ)をいどうしてほしいと言(い)っているんです。

加藤(かとう)：　どこにいどうしろって？ →p. 198

鈴木(すずき)：　それが、入口(いりぐち)からかなり遠(とお)くなるらしいんです。

加藤(かとう)：　それはまずいね。今(いま)ごろいどうしろと言(い)われてもこまるよ。

鈴木(すずき)：　加藤(かとう)さんから高橋(たかはし)さんにご連絡(れんらく)いただけませんか。

加藤(かとう)：　わかった。じゃ、すぐ連絡(れんらく)してみるよ。

鈴木(すずき)：　すみません。よろしくおねがいします。

Suzuki: Say, where's Mr. Kato?

Kato's secretary: He went out a little while ago, but did you need anything?

Suzuki: I see. (*furrows his brow*)

Kato's secretary: I've been told to contact him if there is anything [he should know].

Suzuki: In that case, I'm sorry, but please tell him that I'd like for him to call me since I have something I'd like to consult him in a hurry about on the matter of the Valentine's Day Fair.

Kato's secretary: I understand. I'll convey your message.

Kato: This is Kato.

Suzuki: I'm sorry [to bother you] when you're busy. There was a phone call just now on the matter of our booth space from the person in charge. He says he wants us to move to another place.

Kato: Where does he say for us to move to?

Suzuki: The thing is, it's apparently going to be quite a bit farther from the entrance.

Kato: That's not good. It's upsetting to be told to move at this late date.

Suzuki: Could I perhaps have you contact Mr. Takahashi yourself?

Kato: All right. In that case, I'll contact him right away.

Suzuki: Thank you. I appreciate it.

VOCABULARY

先(さき)ほど	a little while ago
～られる	(auxiliary honorific verb; see p. 200) (出(で)かけられる = go out)
～の件(けん)	the matter of ——, the issue of ——
売(う)り場(ば)	selling space, store/booth space
たんとう者(しゃ)	person in charge
いどうする	move, transfer
しろ	do (plain imperative form of する) (いどうしろ = move)
今(いま)ごろ	now, at this point

NOTES

1. 〜が、何(なに)か？

〜が、何(なに)か？ is the expression to use when asking someone whether they need anything after first giving them an idea of how things stand at present.

A：あした、おひまですか。
B：ええ、ひまですが、何(なに)か？

A: Are you free tomorrow?
B: Yes, I'm free, but did you need me for anything?

2. 〜の件(けん)

件(けん) means "matter" or "issue." 〜の件(けん), roughly equivalent to 〜のこと, "about," is often used in formal or serious discussions after a topic or issue to mean "on the matter of" as in バレンタイン・フェアの件(けん), "the matter of the Valentine's Day Fair." It also frequently occurs together with demonstratives (e.g., この件(けん), あの件(けん), その件(けん)) to mean "this matter" or "that matter" in reference to information shared between the speaker and listener.

3. Question word + って？

As covered in Lesson 1 (p. 12), って is a colloquial form of the quotation particle と. When spoken with a rising intonation, as here, って becomes a question.

かれはどこにいるって？
Where did he say he is?

かれは何時(なんじ)に来(く)るって？
When did he say he'd come?

When used interrogatively in a sentence without a question word, って means "Is what I heard true/the same as what you heard?"

ミルズさんはカナダ人(じん)だって？
Is it true that Mr. Mills is Canadian?

中村(なかむら)さんがけっこんするんだって？
Is it true that Ms. Nakamura is going to get married?

4. 加藤(かとう)さんから高橋(たかはし)さんにご連絡(れんらく)いただけませんか

Here, Mr. Suzuki is asking for Mr. Kato to be the one to contact Mr. Takahashi of Nozomi Department Store regarding their booth space. The pattern 〜から〜に is often used when wishing to emphasize that your listener, not you, should talk to the person in question.

加藤(かとう)：(to Mr. Suzuki) 鈴木(すずき)さんからミルズさんに話(はな)してください。
Kato: (to Mr. Suzuki) Please be the one to tell Mr. Mills.

妻(つま)：(to her husband) あなたから太郎(たろう)(子(こ)ども)に言(い)ってよ。
wife: (to her husband) You have a word with Taro [their child].

GRAMMAR & PATTERN PRACTICE

I Leaving and Relaying Messages

電話をいただきたいと伝えてください。

When you leave a message, the level of politeness and honorific expressions to be chosen will change depending on the relationships existing between you, the person spoken to, and the person who is to receive the message.

伝えて or 言って is used to ask someone to convey a statement or instruction to someone else. For leaving questions as messages, an appropriate verb is 聞いて, as in 聞いてください, "please ask."

1. Messages that are statements

1. Leaving a message:

部長：鈴木さん、ミルズさんに会議は3時からだと伝えてください。
department manager: Mr. Suzuki, please tell Mr. Mills the meeting will be from three o'clock.

2. Relaying a message:

鈴木：ミルズさん、部長が会議は3時からだとおっしゃっていました（よ）。
Suzuki: Mr. Mills, the department manager said that the meeting was going to be from three o'clock.

2. Messages that are instructions

1. Leaving a message:

部長：中村さん、ミルズさんにレポートを出すように伝えてください。
department manager: Ms. Nakamura, please tell Mr. Mills to submit his report.

部長：中村さん、鈴木くんにしょるいをわすれないように言ってください。
department manager: Ms. Nakamura, please tell Suzuki-kun not to forget the documents.

2. Relaying a message:

中村：ミルズさん、部長がレポートを出すように（と）おっしゃっていました（よ）。
Nakamura: Mr. Mills, the department manager said for you to submit your report.

VOCABULARY

だす hand in, submit

中村：　鈴木さん、部長がしょるいをわすれないように（と）おっしゃっていました（よ）。

Nakamura: Mr. Suzuki, the department manager said for you not to forget the documents.

Messages that are instructions are put in the form ように. This form is generally used only when leaving behind instructions for those below you or in your in-group, i.e., friends or family. Care needs to be taken in leaving behind instructions for people of the out-group, since such instructions might easily sound like a command and therefore sound rude unless you are intentionally trying to speak down from above. To leave a request as a message, use the pattern 〜てください（と伝えてください）. Consider the difference between the two examples below.

電話するように伝えてください。
Please tell [him/her] to call me.

電話してくださいと伝えてください。
Please ask [him/her] to call me.

1 Complete the request by filling in the blank with each message below, in its proper form.

ミルズ：高橋さんに……………………………………
……………と伝えてください。

1) また後で電話します
2) 送っていただいたにもつがとどきました
3) なるべくはやくおへんじをいただきたいです

2 Complete the request by filling in the blank with the most appropriate Japanese expression for conveying each of Mr. Kato's wishes, below.

加藤：ミルズさんに……………………………………
……………ように言ってください。

1) "Come back to the office immediately."
2) "Get in touch with Mr. Suzuki."
3) "Do not be late for the meeting."

VOCABULARY

なるべく　as . . . as possible

II Using Plain Imperatives: Do and Don't

In Japanese, the plain imperatives discussed here occur by themselves only under limited circumstances, for example during emergencies, while cheering at sports events, or when issuing commands toward someone over whom you have strong authority, such as a parent might over a child.

火事(かじ)だ！　にげろ！　あわてるな！
It's a fire! Run! Don't panic!

行(い)け！　シュートしろ！
Go! Shoot the ball!

もっと 勉強(べんきょう)しろ！
Study harder!

Plain imperatives tend to be used more by men than women. Women typically use the *-te* form of the verb instead, even for emergencies, e.g., 火事(かじ)よ！　にげて！　あわてないで！

To produce the plain imperative form of a Regular II verb, simply drop る from the dictionary form and add ろ. For Regular I verbs, use the *-ba* stem (the conditional form without ば).

Reg. I:	行(い)く	→ 行(い)け		帰(かえ)る	→ 帰(かえ)れ
Reg. II:	食(た)べる	→ 食(た)べろ		にげる	→ にげろ
Irreg.:	来(く)る	→ 来(こ)い		する	→ しろ

For the negative imperative form, just add な to the dictionary form of the verb.

Reg. I:	行(い)く	→ 行(い)くな		帰(かえ)る	→ 帰(かえ)るな
Reg. II:	食(た)べる	→ 食(た)べるな		にげる	→ にげるな
Irreg.:	来(く)る	→ 来(く)るな		する	→ するな

Plain imperatives are also used to indirectly quote orders given by others.

部長(ぶちょう)に明日(あす)までにレポートを書(か)けと言(い)われました。
I was told by the department manager to write the report by tomorrow.

The pattern "plain imperative (+ よ)" is used mostly by men to offer advice, consolation, or encouragement toward others they are on familiar terms with. While such sentences do employ the imperative form, they are not, strictly speaking, meant to be taken as commands.

For more on these and other functions of plain imperatives, see Practice 2, Phrase Power III, p. 204.

VOCABULARY

かじ	fire
シュートする	shoot (a ball)

In addition to plain imperatives, Japanese has another imperative form, the ～なさい form (*-masu* stem of a verb + なさい).

(a mother to her child) 7時(じ)よ。起(お)きなさい。
It's seven o'clock. Get up.

(instruction on a test) つぎのぶんを日本語(にほんご)に訳(やく)しなさい。
Translate the following sentences into Japanese.

Change the verbs into plain imperatives, as in the examples.

例(れい) 1) Reg. I 書(か)く → 書(か)け、書(か)くな

1) 言(い)う → ....
2) 話(はな)す → ....
3) 買(か)う → ....
4) まがる → ....

例(れい) 2) Reg. II 食(た)べる → 食(た)べろ、食(た)べるな

5) 開(あ)ける → ....
6) 見(み)せる → ....
7) かたづける → ....
8) やめる → ....

例(れい) 3) Irreg. 来(く)る → 来(こ)い、来(く)るな
する → しろ、するな

9) 持(も)ってくる → ....
10) 勉強(べんきょう)する → ....

VOCABULARY

ぶん	sentence
やくす	translate

III Honorifics (4): Auxiliary Honorific Verbs

先ほど出かけられましたが、

The honorific expressions covered in Lesson 10 are reserved mostly for receptionists and members of the service industry or for when speaking politely in formal situations. Here you will learn the honorific form of verbs, employed more normally in the office and other business settings.

The honorific form is constructed in the same way as the passive form (p. 141), i.e., by adding the auxiliary ～れる (for Regular I verbs) or ～られる (for Regular II verbs) to the verb's *-nai* stem. For Regular II verbs, then, the honorific form is identical to the potential form; which meaning the form is meant to convey is determined by the context.

部長は明日アメリカに行かれます。
Our department manager will go to the United States tomorrow.

部長、今日は何時に帰られますか。
Manager, what time will you be leaving the office today?

Read the following dialogue, in which a news reporter is interviewing a traveler at Narita International Airport, while paying attention to the uses of れる and られる.

リポーター：すみません、ちょっとうかがってもよろしいですか。今日はどちらに行かれるんですか。
旅行者：イタリアです。
リポーター：何日ぐらいたいざいされる予定ですか。
旅行者：２週間です。
リポーター：そうですか。お気をつけて。

VOCABULARY

リポーター	reporter
りょこうしゃ	traveler
たいざいする	stay (in a country as part of a trip or for an extended period)

PRACTICE 1 Messages

PHRASE POWER

I. Leaving statements as messages:

① 伝言をおねがいしてもよろしいでしょうか。
May I ask you to leave a message?

② ミルズさんに後から行くと伝えてください。
Please tell Mr. Mills I'll follow him later.

③ 鈴木くんにちょっとおくれると伝えてもらえますか。
Will you tell Suzuki for me that I'll be a little late?

④ 部長にお電話をいただきたいとお伝えください。
Please tell the department manager that I would like for her to call me.

⑤ 先生にろんぶんの件でごそうだんしたいことがあるとお伝えいただけますか。
Could you please tell the professor for me that I have something I would like to consult her about regarding my thesis?

⑥ ６時に帰るって、お母さんに伝えて。
Tell Mom I'll get home at six.

⑦ 悪いけど今日は行けなくなったってヒロに言っといて。
Tell Hiro I'm sorry, but it's become impossible for me to go today.

II. Leaving instructions as messages:

① ミルズさんに私に電話するように伝えてください。
Please tell Mr. Mills to call me.

② 鈴木さん、ミルズさんにレポートを書くように言ってください。
Mr. Suzuki, please tell Mr. Mills to write that report.

VOCABULARY

でんごん	message
ろんぶん	paper, thesis

III. Relaying messages:

① 先に行っていると言っていました。
He said he was going to go without you.

② ごそうだんしたいことがあるとおっしゃっていました。
He said he had something he wanted to consult you about.

③ 明日の予定はキャンセルになったそうです。
From what I hear, tomorrow's plans have been canceled.

④ ちょっとおくれるとのことでした。
He said he was going to be a little late.

IV. Telling someone what one has been told to do:

① 連絡するように言われています。
I've been told to contact him.

② 会議室にごあんないするように言われています。
I've been told to take you to the meeting room.

SPEAKING PRACTICE

I. Mr. Kato phones Mr. Takahashi.

加藤：	ＡＢＣフーズの加藤ですが、高橋さんはいらっしゃいますか。
のぞみデパートの社員：	お世話になっております。もうしわけありません。高橋は、ただいま、ほかの電話に出ております。後ほど、こちらからお電話させましょうか。
加藤：	いえ。では、後でまたこちらからお電話するとお伝えください。

Kato:	I'm Kato from ABC Foods. May I inquire if Mr. Takahashi is present?
Nozomi Department Store employee:	I'm sorry, but Takahashi is answering another call right now. Shall we have him call you back at a later time?
Kato:	No. In that case, please tell him I'll call again later.

VOCABULARY

～とのことです (someone) said that —— (formal way of saying ～といっていました; often used in business situations)

II. Ms. Martin gives Mr. Suzuki a message from Mr. Mills.

マルタン：鈴木さん、さっきミルズさんがさがしてましたよ。先に行ってるって言ってましたけど。

鈴木：　あ、しまった！　今日、ミルズさんたちといっしょにジャズ・バーに行くやくそくしてたの、わすれてた！　そうだ、マリーさんもいっしょに行きませんか。ピアノとベースがいいらしいですよ。

マルタン：ほんとう？　じゃ、すぐに用意してきますね。

Martin: Mr. Suzuki, Mr. Mills was looking for you just now. He said he'll be going without you.

Suzuki: Oh no! I'd forgotten I'd promised to go to a jazz bar with him and the others! Say, won't you go too, Marie? The piano and bass players are supposed to be excellent.

Martin: Really? I'll get ready right away, then.

III. Ms. Martin announces to an employee at the Nakano Farm that she has come to see Mr. Nakano.

マルタン：　マルタンともうします。中野さんに2時にお会いすることになっているんですが。

農場の人：　あ、マルタンさんですね。中野から聞いております。はたけの方にごあんないするように言われておりますので、どうぞ。こちらです。

マルタン：　ありがとうございます。

Martin: My name is Martin. I've arranged to meet Mr. Nakano at two.

farm employee: Oh, Ms. Martin. I've heard [that you were coming] from Nakano. I've been told to show you to the fields, so please, come this way.

Martin: Thank you.

VOCABULARY

しまった（あ、しまった！）	oh no, oops! how stupid of me!
ジャズ・バー	jazz bar
ベース	bass

PRACTICE 2 Using Plain Imperatives

PHRASE POWER

I. Having been told to do something:

① 部長にすぐあやまりに行けと言われた。
I was told by the department manager to go apologize right away.

② 夫に長電話をするなと言われた。
I was told by my husband not to talk on the phone so long.

③ 妻に飲みすぎるなと言われた。
I was told by my wife not to drink too much.

④ 父親にもっとしっかり勉強しろと言われた。
I was told by my father to study more diligently.

⑤ 母親にもっと家事を手伝えと言われた。
I was told by my mother to help out more with the housework.

II. Giving the gist of signs:

① 何て書いてあるんですか。
What does this sign say?

② ここに車をとめるなって書いてあります。
It says not to park your car here.

駐車禁止

③ きけんなので、この中に入るなって書いてあります。
It says not to go in here because it's dangerous.

危険！立入禁止

III. Offering encouragement or advice (casual, used mostly by men):

① しけん、がんばれよ。
Be sure to do your best on your exam.

② 車に気をつけろよ。
Watch out for cars.

③ かさ、持っていけよ。
Take your umbrella.

VOCABULARY

ながでんわ	long phone call	なんて	(colloquial form of なんと [なん + particle と])
のみすぎる	drink too much		
すぎる	do too much		
しっかり	diligently		

IV. Exchanging angry words (casual, used mostly by men):

① あやまれ。
Say you're sorry.

② ばかにするな。
Don't make a fool of me.

SPEAKING PRACTICE

I. It is time for a meeting, but Mr. Kato has not shown up.

佐々木：　加藤さんはまだですか。
マルタン：さっき電話があって、じゅうたいでおくれるので、先に始めていてほしいとのことです。
佐々木：　先に始めろと言われても、この件は加藤さんがいないと話ができませんね。じゃあ、会議は加藤さんがもどってからにしましょう。

Sasaki: Isn't Mr. Kato here yet?
Martin: There was a call from him just now, and he said that he wanted us to start without him since there was a traffic jam and he was going to be late.
Sasaki: We may have been told to start without him, but we can't very well discuss this matter unless he's here, can we? Let's have this meeting after Mr. Kato gets back, then.

II. Mr. Mills notices a sign posted in front of a building under construction.

歩行者、頭上注意

ミルズ：鈴木さん、これ、何て書いてあるんですか。
鈴木：　「ほこうしゃ、ずじょう、ちゅうい」歩いている人は、あたまをぶつけたり、上から物がおちてきたりしないか気をつけろって書いてあるんですよ。
ミルズ：じゃ、はやく行きましょう。(*breaks into a half run*)

Mills: Mr. Suzuki, what does this say?
Suzuki: "ほこうしゃ、ずじょう、ちゅうい." It says for people walking to watch out that they don't hit their head or that things don't come falling from above.
Mills: In that case, let's hurry. (*breaks into a half run*)

VOCABULARY

ばかにする	look down on, make a fool of
ほこうしゃ	pedestrian
ずじょう	overhead

III. Mr. Suzuki notices that his friend is not acting her usual self.

鈴木：　むずかしいかおして、どうしたの。
鈴木の友人（女）：仕事でね、部長に今月中に新しいきかくを考えろって言われているんだけど、むずかしくて。もしいいきかくが出せたら、えいぎょうの仕事をさせてもらえるかもしれないの。
鈴木：　へえ、ほんとう。前からやってみたいって言ってたじゃない。チャンスだから、がんばれよ。
鈴木の友人（女）：うん、ありがとう。がんばってみる。

Suzuki: What's with that scowl [lit., "difficult look"] on your face?
friend: Work. I've been told by my department manager to think of a new proposal within the month, but it's so hard. If I can put forward a good proposal, then I may be allowed to do sales work.
Suzuki: I see. You always said you wanted to try doing that. This is your chance, so go for it!
friend: Thanks. I'll try.

IV. Mrs. Kato is worrying about her son.

加藤（妻）：ねえ、今日私が太郎の部屋をそうじしようとしたら、太郎が部屋に入るなって言ったのよ。
加藤（夫）：へえ。
加藤（妻）：最近、学校から帰るとすぐ自分の部屋に入って出てこないし、パソコンばかりやってるし。あなたからあの子に言ってよ、親をしんぱいさせるなって。
加藤（夫）：太郎も大人になってきたんだよ。

Mrs. Kato: You know, today when I tried to clean Taro's room, he told me not to come in.
Mr. Kato: Really?
Mrs. Kato: These days he always shuts himself in his room right after he comes home from school and doesn't come out, on top of which he does nothing but fiddle with his computer. You tell him not to make his parents so anxious.
Mr. Kato: Taro is growing up, that's all.

VOCABULARY

きかく　plan, proposal
チャンス　chance, opportunity

KANJI PRACTICE

連
連れていく (つ)
連絡する (れんらく)
link

絡
連絡する (れんらく)
interlink

伝
伝える (つた)
手伝う (て つだ)
伝言 (でんごん)
transmit

医
医者 (い しゃ)
医学 (い がく)
medical doctor

者
者 (もの)
医者 (い しゃ)
歩行者 (ほ こう しゃ)
person

遠

遠い
とお

far

研

研究する
けんきゅう

研究者
けんきゅうしゃ

grind
sharpen

究

研究する
けんきゅう

carry to extremity

室

教室
きょうしつ

温室
おんしつ

会議室
かいぎしつ

room

図

地図
ちず

図書館
としょかん

diagram
drawing

LESSON 12

THE STORY OF VALENTINE'S DAY

TARGET READING

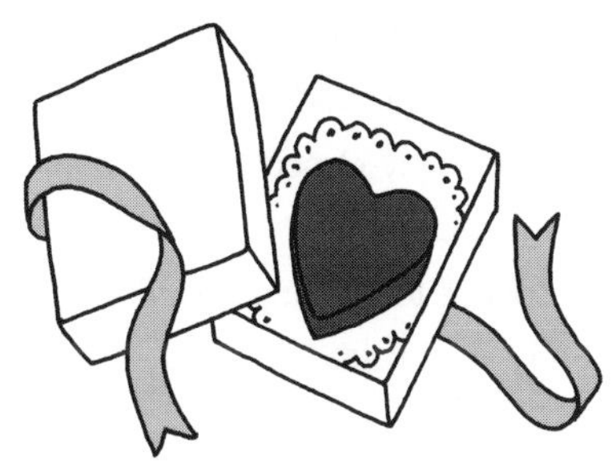

日本では毎年２月になると、デパートのかし売り場やチョコレート専門店の前に長いれつができる。そのれつにならんでいるのは、ほとんどが女性だ。日本には、バレンタインデーに女性から男性へチョコレートをおくる習慣があるからだ。→p. 212

１９３６年に、神戸の洋がしの会社がバレンタインデーむけのチョコレートのこうこくを出した。これがバレンタインデーにチョコレートをおくる習慣の始まりだと言われている。１９５８年には、東京のあるデパートが「バレンタインに女性から男性へチョコレートをおくりましょう」というキャンペーンを行った。しかし、このときは３日間で３つしか売れなかったそうだ。

その後、多くのチョコレート会社やデパートがせんでんに力を入れ、この習慣は１９７０年ごろから広まり始めた。すきな男性にチョコレートをおくるだけでなく、女性社員が男性のじょうしやどうりょうにチョコレートをくばる「ギリチョコ」や、女友だちにおくる「友チョコ」など、新しい習慣も生まれた。

今では、チョコレートの年間しょうひりょうの約１、２割がバレンタインデーのじきに売れているそうだ。このじきには、世界中のチョコレートがデパートにならぶので、ふだんは手に入りにくいチョコレートも買うことができる。最近は、このきかいに、うつくしいパッケージのこうきゅうチョコレートを自分へのプレゼントとして買う女性も増えている。今後も日本のバレンタインデーは、新しい習慣を生み出していくかもしれない。

In Japan, every year in February long lines emerge in front of confectionery sections of department stores and in front of specialty chocolate shops. Most of the people standing in these lines are women. This is because in Japan there is a practice of women giving men chocolates on Valentine's Day.

In 1936, a maker of Western sweets in Kobe put out an advertisement for Valentine's Day chocolates. This is said to be the beginnings of the practice of giving chocolates on Valentine's Day. In 1958, a certain department store in Tokyo carried out a campaign encouraging women to give men chocolates on Valentine's Day. It is said, however, that on this occasion only three were sold in three days.

Later on, many chocolate companies and department stores poured effort into advertising the practice, so that it began to grow widespread from about the 1970s onwards. Not only did women give chocolates to men they liked, but new practices also came into being, for example ギリチョコ, "obligatory chocolates," in which female workers pass out chocolates to male bosses or colleagues, and 友(とも)チョコ, "friend chocolates," given to female friends.

Today it is said that almost a fifth of the chocolate consumed annually is sold around the time of Valentine's Day. Because chocolates from all over the world line department shelves at this time, people can even buy chocolates that are ordinarily hard to obtain. Recently, an increasing number of women are taking advantage of such opportunities to buy beautifully packaged premium chocolates as "gifts" to themselves. It may be that Valentine's Day in Japan will continue giving rise to ever more new practices.

VOCABULARY

かし	sweets
男性(だんせい)	man
習慣(しゅうかん)	custom, practice
あるからだ	be because there is . . .
〜からだ	be because ——
洋(よう)がし	Western sweets
こうこく	advertisement
始(はじ)まり	beginnings, roots
キャンペーン	campaign
その後(ご)	after that, later
多(おお)くの	many (before a noun)
せんでん	advertising
広(ひろ)まる	spread
くばる	pass out, hand out
ギリチョコ	*giri* (obligatory) chocolate; a Valentine's Day chocolate given to a male boss or colleague out of a sense of obligation and not from any romantic feelings (Although ギリ is Japanese in origin, here it is written in katakana since it has been combined with the katakana word チョコ to form a new word.)
ぎり	(sense of) obligation
チョコ	chocolate (short for チョコレート)
女友(おんなとも)だち	female friend
友(とも)チョコ	friend chocolate (a Valentine's Day chocolate given to a female friend)
友(とも)	friend
年間(ねんかん)	annual
しょうひりょう	amount of consumption
じき	time, period
ふだん	usually, ordinarily
こうきゅう	high-class, premium
今後(こんご)	now on, into the future
生(う)み出(だ)す	give rise to, engender

NOTES

1. バレンタインデー

February 14, Valentine's Day, is called in Japanese バレンタインデー or simply バレンタイン.

2. 始(はじ)まりだと言(い)われている

〜と言(い)われている means "it is said that . . ." or "they say that . . ." It is also used when citing folk knowledge or superstition.

> おんせんはけんこうにいいと言(い)われている。
> Hot springs are said to be good for your health.

3. あるデパート

Using ある, "a certain . . . ," before a noun, provides one means of referring to a specific instance of that noun without identifying it outright. Here it is used to avoid revealing the name of the department store in question, although the author actually knows what it is.

4. すきな男性(だんせい)にチョコレートをおくるだけでなく、……「友(とも)チョコ」など、新(あたら)しい習慣(しゅうかん)も生(う)まれた

だけではない means "not only . . ." In the pattern Aだけで（は）なく、Bも, it means "not only A, but also B."

> この店(みせ)は、料理(りょうり)がおいしいだけでなく、サービスもいい。
> This restaurant has not only good food but also excellent service.

5. 自分(じぶん)へのプレゼント

> すきな男性(だんせい)に／へプレゼントをあげます。

The particle に cannot occur with の. Thus when a phrase that may take either に or へ (as in すきな男性(だんせい)に／へ above) is added with の to modify a noun, only への, not にの, may be used. The particles は, が, and を also never come before の.

Examples of phrases with particles that *can* occur with の include the following.

姉(あね)からのメール	e-mail from my older sister
大阪(おおさか)までのきっぷ	ticket to Osaka
ハワイでのけっこんしき	wedding ceremony in Hawaii
とりひき先(さき)との会議(かいぎ)	meeting with a client

GRAMMAR & PATTERN PRACTICE

I Explaining Reasons

日本には、バレンタインデーに女性から男性へチョコレートをおくる習慣があるからだ。

から indicates a reason.

近くて便利ですから、私はよく銀座に行きます。
I go to Ginza a lot because it is close by and convenient.

私はよく銀座に行きます。近くて便利ですから。
I go to Ginza a lot. Because it's close by and convenient.

In the first example above, から forms a dependent clause providing the reason for what is stated in the main clause, 銀座に行きます. In the second example, it fulfills the same role, only the clause is tacked onto the main sentence as a kind of afterthought.

Similar to this pattern is "plain form + からです" used to clearly state a reason when the reason itself is the topic under discussion or a point of contention.

私はよく銀座に行きます。それは、近くて便利だからです。
I go to Ginza a lot. That is because it is close by and convenient.

The "plain form + からです" pattern allows the reason-giving clause to stand by itself as a complete sentence. Here 近くて便利だからです forms the main clause of an independent sentence explaining the reason why the speaker goes to Ginza a lot. それは means the same thing as そのりゆうは, "the reason for that is." The two sentences may also be combined into one as follows.

私がよく銀座に行くのは、近くて便利だからです。
The reason why I go to Ginza a lot is that it is close by and convenient.

からです／からだ sentences treat the why of a matter as its main point and so are often used in answering questions about reasons or in setting out reasons in writing. This pattern sometimes appears as part of the expression なぜなら～からです／からだ, "As to why, it is because . . ."

At a meeting:

加藤： なぜミルズさんをプロジェクトのチーフにえらんだんですか。
佐々木：せきにんかんが強くて、リーダーシップがあるからです。
Kato: Why did you choose Mr. Mills to be the project chief?
Sasaki: That's because he has a strong sense of responsibility and provides good leadership.

VOCABULARY

りゆう	reason
せきにんかん	sense of responsibility
リーダーシップ	leadership

ＣＤの売り上げはだんだんおちてきている。インターネットで音楽をダウンロードする人が増えたからだ。
CD sales are gradually declining. This is because more and more people are downloading music from the Internet.

富士山を世界いさんにするねがいはまだじつげんしていない。なぜなら、富士山はとてもごみの多い山だからだ。
The hope of making Mt. Fuji a World Heritage Site has not yet been realized. As to why, this is because Mt. Fuji is littered with trash.

Choose the appropriate expression from the options given in parentheses.

1) A：たばこをやめたほうがいいですよ。体に（悪いですから／悪いからです）。
B：でも、やめられないんです。

2) シカさんがよく（知っていますから／知っているからです）、聞いてみたらどうですか。

3) ミルズさんがしけんにごうかくしたのは、（どりょくしましたから／どりょくしたからです）。

4) A：ざんぎょうですか。手伝いましょうか。
B：だいじょうぶです。もうすぐ（終わりますから／終わるからです）。

II Understanding Written Styles

This section will outline the different styles used in Japanese writing. As mentioned in Book II (p. 193), most Japanese writing is done in the plain style, except in some genres (e.g., letters) that employ the *desu/masu* style to familiarly address the reader.

The table below lists some common sentence endings for written *desu/masu* and plain style.

		desu/masu style (written)	plain style (written)
Verbs	present aff.	行きます	行く
	present neg.	行きません	行かない
	past aff.	行きました	行った
	past neg.	行きませんでした	行かなかった

-*I* adjectives	present aff.	高(たか)いです	高(たか)い
	present neg.	高(たか)くありません／高(たか)くないです	高(たか)くない
	past aff.	高(たか)かったです	高(たか)かった
	past neg.	高(たか)くありませんでした／高(たか)くなかったです	高(たか)くなかった
-*Na* adjectives/ Nouns + です	present aff.	便利(べんり)です	便利(べんり)だ／便利(べんり)である*
	present neg.	便利(べんり)ではありません	便利(べんり)ではない
	past aff.	便利(べんり)でした	便利(べんり)だった／便利(べんり)であった*
	past neg.	便利(べんり)ではありませんでした	便利(べんり)ではなかった

NOTE: In writing employing the plain style, -*na* adjectives and nouns + です may appear either as だ (e.g., 便利(べんり)だ) or である (e. g., 便利(べんり)である) in the present-affirmative tense (see * above). である sounds more explanatory than だ and often occurs in academic writing. The past form of である is であった (also marked with *).

Below are a few other examples of *desu/masu* style versus plain style. Note the differences between the underlined parts.

desu/masu style		plain style
社会(しゃかい)はかわった<u>のです</u>。	→	社会(しゃかい)はかわった<u>のだ</u>。／かわった<u>のである</u>。
外国人(がいこくじん)が増(ふ)える<u>でしょう</u>。	→	外国人(がいこくじん)が増(ふ)える<u>だろう</u>。

Read the sentences while paying attention to their meanings. Then change the underlined parts to written *desu/masu* style.

1) 友(とも)だちは大切(たいせつ)<u>だ</u>。 → 友(とも)だちは大切(たいせつ) ....
2) はんざいをふせげる<u>だろうか</u>。 → はんざいをふせげる ....
3) かれはちょうせんした<u>のだ</u>。 → かれはちょうせんした ....
4) 母(はは)はわかいころ、かんごし<u>だった</u>。
→ 母(はは)はわかいころ、かんごし ....

VOCABULARY

である	be (plain-style equivalent of です)
わかい	young

III Understanding Spoken Styles

The dialogues in the Speaking Practice presented later in this lesson primarily make use of the plain style. As discussed in Book II (pp. 206–07), the *desu/masu* and plain styles occur not only in prose but also in speech. The table below gives several common sentence endings used in spoken *desu/masu* and plain style. Compare the endings to each other as well as to the corresponding written expressions on pp. 213–14.

		desu/masu style (spoken)	plain style (spoken)
Verbs	present aff.	行きます	行く
	present neg.	行きません／行かないです*	行かない
	past aff.	行きました	行った
	past neg.	行きませんでした／行かなかったです*	行かなかった
-*I* adjectives	present aff.	高いです	高い
	present neg.	高くないです／高くありません	高くない
	past aff.	高かったです	高かった
	past neg.	高くなかったです／高くありませんでした	高くなかった
-*Na* adjectives/ Nouns + です	present aff.	便利です	便利（だ）
	present neg.	便利ではありません／便利じゃありません／便利じゃないです*	便利じゃない
	past aff.	便利でした	便利だった
	past neg.	便利ではありませんでした／便利じゃありませんでした／便利じゃなかったです*	便利じゃなかった

NOTE: The patterns marked with * (e.g., 行かないです , 便利じゃないです) are also used in the spoken language.

Note what becomes of the present-affirmative です after -*na* adjectives and nouns in plain-style speech.

desu/masu style		plain style
げんきですか。	→	げんき？
はい、げんきです。	→	うん、げんき。
かんたんですね。	→	かんたんだね。(used by both men and women)
		かんたんね。(used by women)
雨ですよ。	→	雨だよ。(used by both men and women)
		雨よ。(used by women)

Also take note of the following plain-style equivalents for 〜んです and 〜でしょう.

desu/masu style		plain style
ひつようなのです／ひつようなんです。	→	ひつようなんだ（よ）。(used by both men and women)
	→	ひつようなの。(used primarily by women)
ひつようなのですか／ひつようなんですか。	→	ひつようなの？(used by both men and women)
高(たか)いでしょう？	→	高(たか)いでしょう？(used by both men and women)
		高(たか)いだろう？(used by men)

Spoken plain style frequently makes use of contractions, shown below to the right of the slash. These contractions may sometimes occur in the *desu/masu* style as well.

desu/masu style		plain style
終(お)わってしまいました。	→	終(お)わってしまった。／終(お)わっちゃった。
飲(の)んでしまいました。	→	飲(の)んでしまった。／飲(の)んじゃった。
予約(よやく)しておきます。	→	予約(よやく)しておく。／予約(よやく)しとく。
話(はな)してはいけません。	→	話(はな)してはいけない。／話(はな)しちゃいけない。
行(い)かなければなりません。	→	行(い)かなければならない。／行(い)かなきゃ（ならない）。
行(い)かなくてはいけません。*	→	行(い)かなくてはいけない。／行(い)かなくちゃ（いけない）。

* 〜なくてはいけません, like 〜なければなりません covered earlier (Book II, p. 238), indicates duty, obligation, or necessity. 〜なければなりません is typically used in relation to broad rules or responsibilities that apply to many, whereas 〜なくてはいけません tends to talk about more personal obligations. Both follow the *-nai* stems of verbs.

The following sound changes commonly occur in spoken Japanese:

書(か)いています。／書(か)いている。	→	書(か)いてます。／書(か)いてる。
すみません。	→	すいません。
何(なん)という店(みせ)ですか。	→	何(なん)ていう店(みせ)ですか。
行(い)かなきゃならない。	→	行(い)かなきゃなんない。
いろいろな	→	いろんな
友(とも)だちのうち	→	友(とも)だちんち
ほんとう	→	ほんと

Finally, certain particles are often omitted in plain-style speech. Such omissions, however, usually do not affect the meaning of the sentence, which can be understood from the context, and are unlikely to cause misunderstanding. に (as used after a person), で, and と generally cannot be omitted without compromising meaning.

desu/masu style		plain style
六本木(ろっぽんぎ)で中村(なかむら)さんと映画(えいが)を見(み)ました。	→	六本木(ろっぽんぎ)で中村(なかむら)さんと映画(えいが)見(み)た。
京都(きょうと)に行(い)きませんか?	→	京都(きょうと)行(い)かない?

Read the sentences while paying attention to their meanings. Then change the underlined parts to spoken *desu/masu* style. (Put contractions into their standard forms.)

1) レポート(を)書(か)かなきゃならない。
→ レポートを ....

2) この部屋(へや)に入(はい)っちゃいけない。
→ この部屋(へや)に ....

3) さいふ(を)わすれちゃった。 → さいふを ....

4) いす(を)ならべといて。 → いすを ....

STYLE NOTE

This lesson has so far discussed written and spoken Japanese in terms of two styles, the *desu/masu* style and the plain style. Although the two are treated separately here for the sake of exposition, in reality people mix and match styles and levels of vocabulary according to occasion and purpose, so that no clear boundaries actually exist between them.

While papers, theses, and other formal writing will generally be done in plain style throughout, in more casual writing, such as essays, one style will sometimes be mixed into the other. Some essays, in fact, are written in an entirely conversational tone.

In speech, speakers choose between the *desu/masu* and plain style depending on audience and occasion. Even within the same conversation, however, people will sometimes switch from one style to another in order to fulfill some special intent or purpose. They may, for example, switch to the plain style during a *desu/masu*-style conversation to make an aside, or use the *desu/masu* style to make a polite request in the midst of one otherwise conducted in the plain style.

Manners of speaking will also vary depending on a person's gender, age, and personality. Generally, women tend to speak more politely than men, and gender differences tend to be less evident among younger compared to older segments of the population.

To get used to written and spoken Japanese in different styles, try first to read or to listen, and to understand. The more examples you are exposed to, the better you will be able to choose between styles to accommodate the audience and occasion at hand.

PRACTICE 1 Reading about Customs and Special Occasions

WORD POWER

新年(しんねん)をいわう	celebrate the New Year
しあわせをねがう	wish for happiness
けんこうをねがう	wish for health
ちょうじゅをねがう	wish for long life
ほうさくをいのる	pray for a good harvest

READING PRACTICE

① おせち料理(りょうり)

日本(にほん)には、しょうがつにおせち料理(りょうり)という特別(とくべつ)な料理(りょうり)を食(た)べる習慣(しゅうかん)があります。おせち料理(りょうり)は、年末(ねんまつ)に作(つく)って、じゅうばこに入(い)れておきます。最近(さいきん)は、家庭(かてい)で作(つく)らずに、デパートやスーパーで買(か)う人(ひと)が多(おお)くなりました。

おせち料理(りょうり)は、ひとつひとつの料理(りょうり)に意味(いみ)があります。たとえば、えびは、こしがまがっていておとしよりのようなので、ちょうじゅをねがって使(つか)われます。こんぶは、音(おと)が「よろこぶ」ということばとにているので、しあわせをねがう意味(いみ)があります。ほかに、まめやくりなどの料理(りょうり)があります。

しょうがつには、はなれて住(す)んでいる家族(かぞく)もあつまって、いっしょにおせち料理(りょうり)を食(た)べてゆっくりすごします。

Osechi Cuisine

In Japan, there is a custom of eating a special cuisine called *osechi* during the New Year. *Osechi* is prepared at the end of the year and kept arranged inside stacked boxes. Nowadays, more and more people buy *osechi* from department stores or supermarkets instead of making it at home.

Each and every dish in *osechi* cuisine carries a special significance. For example, shrimp is used to wish for a long life, since its back is bent so that it looks like an old person. Kombu kelp carries the meaning of wishing for happiness because its name sounds like the word よろこぶ ("to have joy"). Other dishes include those made with beans and chestnuts.

VOCABULARY

しんねん	New Year	おせちりょうり	*osechi* cuisine	(お)としより	elderly person, senior citizen
いわう	celebrate	ねんまつ	end of the year	こんぶ	kombu kelp
ねがう	wish for	じゅうばこ	stacked boxes	ほかに	besides, other (than that)
ちょうじゅ	long life, longevity	ひとつひとつの	each and every	まめ	bean
ほうさく	good harvest	たとえば	for example	くり	chestnut
いのる	pray	まがっている	be bent	はなれる (R2)	be apart, be removed

During the New Year's holidays, family members, including those who usually live apart, all gather to eat *osechi* together and relax.

② ねんがじょう

日本には、新年のあいさつとして、ねんがじょうを送る習慣がある。

ねんがじょうは、年末までに出し、がんたんにうけとる。１１月になると、ゆうびんきょくでねんがじょう用のはがきが発売される。店にも「えと」のえがかかれたはがきがならぶ。

ねんがじょうには、まず「明けましておめでとうございます」などの新年をいわうことばを書く。つぎにきんきょうほうこくなどを書き、最後は「今年もよろしくおねがいします」としめくくることが多い。むかしは手書きのものも多かったが、今はパソコンで作ったねんがじょうがしゅりゅうである。

最近は、ねんがじょうを出さずにメールで新年のあいさつをする人が増えている。しかし、ねんがじょうをもらうとうれしいとかんじる人も多いので、ねんがじょうの習慣はかんたんにはなくならないだろう。

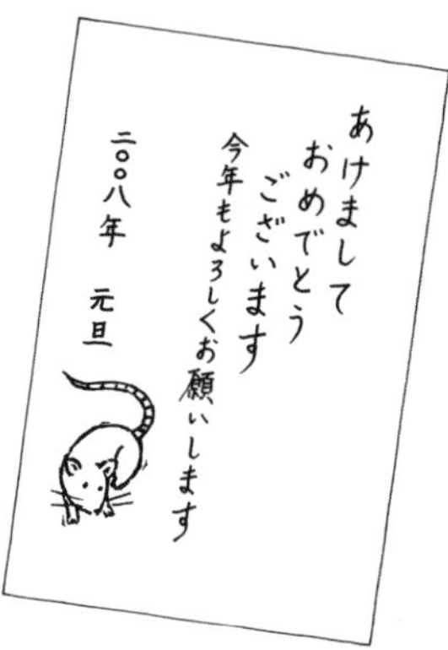

New Year's Cards

In Japan, there is a custom of sending New Year's cards as greetings for the New Year.

People send out New Year's cards before the end of the year and receive [those addressed to them] on New Year's Day. In November, cards for sending out New Year's greetings go on sale at post offices. Cards picturing the animal for the coming year on the twelve-year Oriental zodiac also line store shelves.

On New Year's cards, people first write 明けましておめでとうございます ("Happy New Year") or other greetings used to celebrate the New Year. Next they write messages about their lives recently and other topics, typically wrapping up at the end with 今年もよろしくおねがいします ("Please extend me your kind consideration throughout this year as before"). Although in the past handwritten cards were also common, nowadays those printed using computers are the mainstream.

Recently, an increasing number of people send New Year's greetings by e-mail instead of sending out cards. But given that there are many people who feel a special sense of happiness about receiving New Year's cards, the custom of sending them will most likely not easily go away.

VOCABULARY

ねんがじょう	New Year's card
がんたん	New Year's Day
はつばいする	put on sale
えと	Oriental zodiac (twelve-year cycle in which each year is named after a different animal)
あけましておめでとうございます	happy New Year
きんきょう	recent situation
ほうこく	report
しめくくる	wrap up, end
てがきの	handwritten
しゅりゅう	mainstream

PRACTICE 2 Talking about Customs and Special Occasions

WORD POWER

I. Annual events:

（お）しょうがつ

せいじんの日(ひ)

せつぶん

ひなまつり（３月３日(がつみっか)）

子(こ)どもの日(ひ)（５月５日(がついつか)）

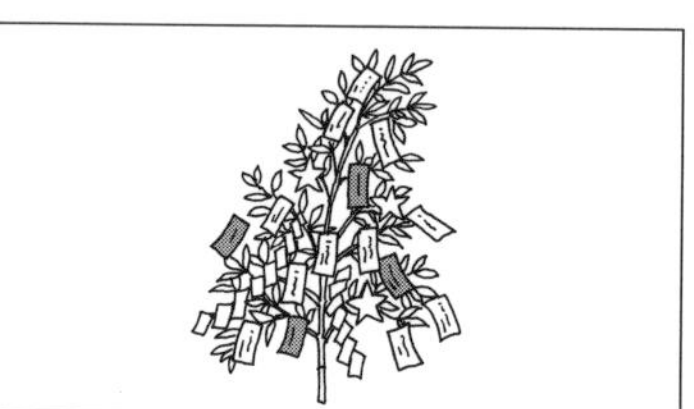

たなばた（７月７日(がつなのか)）

大(おお)みそか（１２月(がつ)３１日(にち)）

II. Ceremonial occasions:

けっこんしき

（お）そうしき

SPEAKING PRACTICE

I. Ms. Chandra is talking to a male friend shortly before the end of the year.

チャンドラ：もうすぐおしょうがつね。仕事(しごと)はいつまでなの？

友人(ゆうじん)（男(おとこ)）：２８日(にち)。年末(ねんまつ)はいつもいそがしくていやなんだよね。ねんがじょうも書(か)かなくちゃいけないし。

VOCABULARY

せいじんのひ	Coming-of-age Day (second Monday of January)	たなばた	Star Festival
せつぶん	*setsubun* (a day in early February for performing various rituals such as throwing beans to drive away bad luck and bring in good)	おおみそか	New Year's Eve
		（お）そうしき	funeral
ひなまつり	Girl's Day, Doll Festival	～なくちゃいけない	have to —— (colloquial for ～なくてはいけません; see p. 216)
こどものひ	Children's Day		

チャンドラ：おしょうがつはどっか行(い)くの？

友人(ゆうじん)（男(おとこ)）：じっかに帰(かえ)るつもり。まだひこうき予約(よやく)してないけど。

チャンドラ：(*before parting*) じゃ、よいお年(とし)を。

友人(ゆうじん)（男(おとこ)）：よいお年(とし)を。

Chandra: It's almost New Year's, isn't it. Till when do you have work?
friend: The 28th. I always dislike the end of the year because it's so busy. On top of everything else, I have to write my New Year's cards, too.
Chandra: Are you going anyplace for New Year's?
friend: I'm planning on going back to see family. I haven't reserved a flight yet, though.
Chandra: (*before parting*) Well, have a nice New Year.
friend: Have a nice New Year.

II. An exchange student is walking around inside a shopping mall with Emi Morita during the first part of February.

留学生(りゅうがくせい)：あのチョコレートのお店(みせ)、ずいぶん人(ひと)がならんでるわね。いつもはあんなにならんでないのに。

森田(もりた)エミ：もうすぐバレンタインデーだからですよ。

留学生(りゅうがくせい)：ああ。日本(にほん)ではバレンタインデーに女性(じょせい)が男性(だんせい)にチョコレートをあげるのよね。

森田(もりた)エミ：ええ。ギリチョコは知(し)ってると思(おも)いますけど、今(いま)は女友(おんなとも)だちにもあげたりするんですよ。

留学生(りゅうがくせい)：そうなの。

森田(もりた)エミ：がんばってる自分(じぶん)へのプレゼントに買(か)う女性(じょせい)もいるみたいですよ。

留学生(りゅうがくせい)：ふうん。私(わたし)も友(とも)だちと自分(じぶん)に買(か)おうかな。

student: That chocolate shop over there has an awful lot of people lined up in front, doesn't it? There's usually not that many people in line.
Emi Morita: It's because it's almost Valentine's Day.
student: Oh yes. In Japan women give men chocolates on Valentine's Day, isn't that right?
Emi Morita: Yes. I'm sure you're aware of "obligatory chocolates," but nowadays people do things like give chocolates to female friends, too.
student: Is that right?
Emi Morita: It seems there are also some women who buy chocolates as rewards for themselves for always working so hard.
student: Hmm. Maybe I'll buy some for myself and my friends, too.

VOCABULARY

どっか	somewhere, anywhere (contraction of どこか)
じっか	parents' house
よいおとしを	have a nice New Year (customary greeting exchanged toward the end of the year to give people good wishes for the coming year)
あんなに	that many, so much

III. It is Valentine's Day, and Mr. Mills's desk is piled high with chocolates.

同僚(どうりょう)（男(おとこ)）：ジョン、チョコたくさんもらったんだね。ホワイトデーのおかえしがたいへんだね。

ミルズ：　ホワイトデーって、何(なに)？

同僚(どうりょう)（男(おとこ)）：バレンタインにチョコをもらった人(ひと)が、おかえしをする日(ひ)だよ。ちょうど１か月後(いっかげつご)の３月１４日(さんがつじゅうよっか)。

ミルズ：　えっ、そんなこと知(し)らなかった。

同僚(どうりょう)（男(おとこ)）：つぎは男(おとこ)の番(ばん)なんだよ。ははは。

male colleague: You got a lot of chocolates, didn't you, John? You're going to have to make an awful lot of returns on White Day.

Mills: White Day? What's that?

male colleague: It's a day when people who received chocolates on Valentine's Day give gifts in return. It's on March 14, exactly one month from now.

Mills: What? I didn't know anything about that.

male colleague: It's the man's turn next. Ha ha ha.

IV. Ms. Martin asks a male friend about what she should give for a wedding present.

マルタン：　日本(にほん)ではけっこんのおいわいに何(なに)をおくるの？

友人(ゆうじん)（男(おとこ)）：ひろうえんに行(い)く場合(ばあい)は、ふつうげんきんだよ。そうじゃなければ、とけいとかしょっきとか。

マルタン：　げんきんをおくるの？

友人(ゆうじん)（男(おとこ)）：うん。特別(とくべつ)なふくろに入(い)れておくるんだよ。

マルタン：　どんなふくろ？　じつは、今度(こんど)友(とも)だちのひろうえんに行(い)くんだけど。

友人(ゆうじん)（男(おとこ)）：うーん。説明(せつめい)するのがむずかしいから、買(か)うなら、いっしょに行(い)こうか。

マルタン：　うん、ありがとう。

Martin: What do people give as wedding gifts in Japan?

friend: Usually cash, if you're attending the reception. If you're not attending the reception, then clocks or tableware or other such items.

Martin: You give cash?

friend: That's right. You give it to them enclosed in a special envelope.

Martin: What sort of envelope? I'm going to a friend's reception soon, actually.

friend: Let me see . . . it's a little hard to explain, so shall I go with you, if you're going to buy one?

Martin: I'd like that, thanks.

VOCABULARY

ホワイトデー	White Day (March 14)	ひろうえん	reception
おかえし	return (for a gift or favor)	しょっき	tableware
ばん	turn	ふくろ	bag, envelope
（お）いわい	celebration		

PRACTICE 3 Talking to Close Friends or Colleagues

PHRASE POWER

I. Upon meeting someone you haven't seen in a while:

① ひさしぶり。げんき？
It's been a while. Are you well?

② 最近(さいきん)、仕事(しごと)はどう？
How's work recently?

II. Talking about how something went:

① プロジェクト、うまくいった？
Did the project go well?

② まあまあうまくいったよ。／まあまあうまくいったわよ。 (used by women)
It went more or less okay.

③ しけん、どうだった？
How was the exam?

④ あんまりできなかったから、だめだと思(おも)う。
I wasn't able to do very well, so I think I failed.

⑤ 思(おも)ったよりできたから、うかるかも。
I did better than I expected, so maybe I'll pass.

III. Showing concern:

① あたまいたいの？
Do you have a headache?

② かおいろ悪(わる)いけど、だいじょうぶ？
You look pale. Are you all right?

③ 気分悪(きぶんわる)そうだけど、だいじょうぶ？
You look like you're not feeling well. Are you all right?

④ ちょっと休(やす)んだら？
Why don't you take a little rest?

⑤ げんきないね。何(なに)かあったの？
You look down. Is something the matter?

VOCABULARY

うまくいく	go well
まあまあ	so-so, more or less
あんまり	not much (colloquial for あまり)
やすんだら？	why don't you take a rest? (colloquial for やすんだらどうですか)

IV. Giving consolation:

① しょうがないよ。
There's nothing you can do about it.

② よくあることだよ。／よくあることよ。(used by women)
It happens all the time.

③ あんまり考えすぎないほうがいいよ。
You shouldn't fret about it too much.

V. Asking about a rumor:

① (*directly to that person*) 犬山さん、てんしょくするんだって？
Is it true you're going to switch jobs, Mr. Inuyama?

② (*to someone else*) 中村さん、会社やめるんだって？
Is it true that Ms. Nakamura is going to quit?

SPEAKING PRACTICE

I. Mr. Mills meets a male friend he hasn't seen in a long time.

ミルズ：　ひさしぶり。げんき？
友人（男）：うん。ジョンもげんきそうだね。
ミルズ：　最近、仕事はどう？
友人（男）：あいかわらずいそがしいよ。ジョンは？
ミルズ：　ぼくも今、会社のパーティーのじゅんびでたいへんなんだ。

Mills: It's been a while. Are you well?
friend: Yes. You look well, too, John.
Mills: How's work recently?
friend: Busy, same as always. And you?
Mills: Right now I'm swamped, too, with preparing for a company party.

II. Ms. Nakamura sees a male colleague holding a hand to his head.

中村：　かおいろ悪いけど、だいじょうぶ？　あたまいたいの？
同僚（男）：うん。でも、たいしたことないから、だいじょうぶ。
中村：　無理しないほうがいいよ。ちょっと休んだら？
同僚（男）：そうだね。ありがとう。

VOCABULARY

しょうがない	there is nothing one can do about it
あいかわらず	same as always
たいしたことない	nothing serious

Nakamura:	You look pale. Are you all right? Do you have a headache?
colleague:	Yes. But it's nothing serious, so no problem.
Nakamura:	You shouldn't push yourself. Why don't you take a little rest?
colleague:	That might be good. Thanks.

III. It is seven in the evening, and Mr. Suzuki is sighing at his desk.

同僚(どうりょう)（男(おとこ)）：げんきないね。何(なに)かあったの？
鈴木(すずき)：　ちょっとミスしちゃって……。もうかいけつしたんだけど。
同僚(どうりょう)（男(おとこ)）：じゃ、あんまり気(き)にするなよ。気(き)ばらしに飲(の)みに行(い)かない？
鈴木(すずき)：　いいね。
同僚(どうりょう)（男(おとこ)）：ぼくは仕事(しごと)だいたい終(お)わったんだけど、何時(なんじ)に出(で)れる？
鈴木(すずき)：　あと３０分(さんじゅっぷん)ぐらいで終(お)わるから、ちょっと待(ま)っててくれる？
同僚(どうりょう)（男(おとこ)）：いいよ。

male colleague:	You look down. Is something the matter?
Suzuki:	I messed up. But anyhow, the matter has been solved.
male colleague:	Well then, don't let it bother you too much. Shall we go out to drink for a change of pace?
Suzuki:	Sounds good.
male colleague:	I'm pretty much done with work, but what time can you go?
Suzuki:	I'll be done in about thirty more minutes, so could you wait for me a bit?
male colleague:	Sure.

IV. Ms. Chandra approaches Ms. Martin after learning that Ms. Nakamura is getting married.

チャンドラ：中村(なかむら)さん、けっこんするんだって？
マルタン：　うん。スミスさんとね。
チャンドラ：仕事(しごと)やめるって聞(き)いたけど。
マルタン：　スミスさんがアメリカにてんきんになったから、いっしょに行(い)くんだって。
チャンドラ：そうなんだ。さびしくなるね。

Chandra:	Is it true that Ms. Nakamura is going to get married?
Martin:	Yes, to Mr. Smith.
Chandra:	I heard she was going to quit her job.
Martin:	Mr. Smith is getting transferred to the United States, so she says she's going to go with him.
Chandra:	Oh. We're going to miss her. [lit., "It's going to be lonely (without her)."]

VOCABULARY

ミスする	mess up, make a mistake
かいけつする	be solved
きばらし	diversion, change of pace
だいたい	largely, pretty much
でれる	be able to go (colloquial way of saying でられる; the ら of the potential forms of Regular II verbs and くる are sometimes omitted in conversational speech)
さびしい	lonely

KANJI PRACTICE

性

男性 (だんせい)
女性 (じょせい)

sex
quality

慣

慣れる (な)
習慣 (しゅうかん)

be accustomed to

洋

洋服 (ようふく)
洋食 (ようしょく)

ocean
occidental

割

割れる (わ)
～割 (わり)

divide
cut

増

増える (ふ)

increase

兄	兄（あに） お兄さん（にい） 兄弟（きょうだい）
elder brother	

姉	姉（あね） お姉さん（ねえ）
elder sister	

弟	弟（おとうと） 兄弟（きょうだい）
younger brother	

妹	妹（いもうと）
younger sister	

曜	日曜日（にちようび）
day of the week	

Quiz 4 Unit 4 (Lessons 10–12)

I Fill in the blanks with the appropriate particle.

1) ＡＢＣフーズのミルズ（　　　）もうします。
2) またこちらからお電話(でんわ)する（　　　）お伝(つた)えください。
3) 先日(せんじつ)（　　　）きちょうなお時間(じかん)をいただき、ありがとうございました。
4) 中村(なかむら)さん、鈴木(すずき)さん（　　　）あした８時(じ)に来(く)るように伝(つた)えてください。
5) 私(わたし)が会社(かいしゃ)をやめたのは、自分(じぶん)の会社(かいしゃ)を始(はじ)めたかった（　　　）です。

II Choose the most appropriate word from among the alternatives (1–4) given.

1) （　　　）いらっしゃってくださったのに、あいにく加藤(かとう)が外出(がいしゅつ)しておりまして、もうしわけありません。
   1. しっかり　　2. せっかく　　3. そろそろ　　4. ずっと

2) グリーンが（　　　）お目(め)にかかりたいと言(い)っておりました。
   1. ぜひ　　2. たいへん　　3. たぶん　　4. きっと

3) （　　　）お電話(でんわ)した加藤(かとう)ですが、高橋(たかはし)さんはいらっしゃいますか。
   1. お先(さき)に　　2. ちょうど　　3. 最近(さいきん)　　4. 先(さき)ほど

4) 母(はは)：あそんでいないで、（　　　）しゅくだいをしなさい。
   1. ぜひ　　2. だいたい　　3. ちゃんと　　4. たびたび

5) Ａ：最近(さいきん)、仕事(しごと)はどう？
   Ｂ：（　　　）いそがしいよ。
   1. まるで　　2. できるだけ　　3. あいかわらず　　4. ほかに

III Change the form of the word given in parentheses to complete the sentence in a way that makes sense. Use honorific or imperative forms.

1) もしもし、中野(なかの)さんは（　　　　　）か。（います）
2) 加藤(かとう)はすぐ（　　　　　）ので、少々(しょうしょう)お待(ま)ちください。（来(き)ます）
3) 私(わたし)からご説明(せつめい)（　　　　　）。（します）
4) 部長(ぶちょう)、パーティーのスケジュールはもう（　　　　　）か。（知(し)っています）
5) 部長(ぶちょう)にあしたまでにしょるいを（　　　　　）と言(い)われました。（作(つく)ります）

IV Choose the most appropriate word or phrase from among the alternatives (1–4) given.

1) 先日(せんじつ)はありがとうございました。(　　　) よろしくおねがいいたします。
　1. 今後(こんご)とも　2. ちょうど　3. 今(いま)から　4. 今(いま)ごろ

2) A：本日(ほんじつ)はお時間(じかん)をいただきましてありがとうございました。
　B：(　　　)、ありがとうございました。
　1. そちらこそ　2. あなたこそ　3. こちらこそ　4. あちらこそ

3) A：おくさまはおげんきでいらっしゃいますか。
　B：(　　　)、げんきです。
　1. こちらこそ　2. そういえば　3. なるほど　4. おかげさまで

4) A：たいへんです！　新幹線(しんかんせん)が雪(ゆき)でとまっているそうです。
　B：それは（　　　）ね。大阪(おおさか)の会議(かいぎ)に間(ま)に合(あ)わないよ。
　1. まずい　2. くやしい　3. にがい　4. さむい

5) 友(とも)だちのけっこんの（　　　）にワイングラスを買(か)いました。
　1. お見(み)まい　2. おいわい　3. あいさつ　4. おかえし

V Fill in the blanks with the correct reading of each kanji.

1) 音楽を　聞きながら、お茶を　飲みました。
　(　　　)　　　　　(　　　)

2) 姉は　医者で、弟は　かいけいしです。
　(　　　)(　　　)(　　　)

3) かいがいではたらくために、英語を習う女性が　増えています。
　(　　　)(　　　)(　　　)

4) ＡＢＣ銀行から 連絡があったら、教えてください。
　(　　　)(　　　)

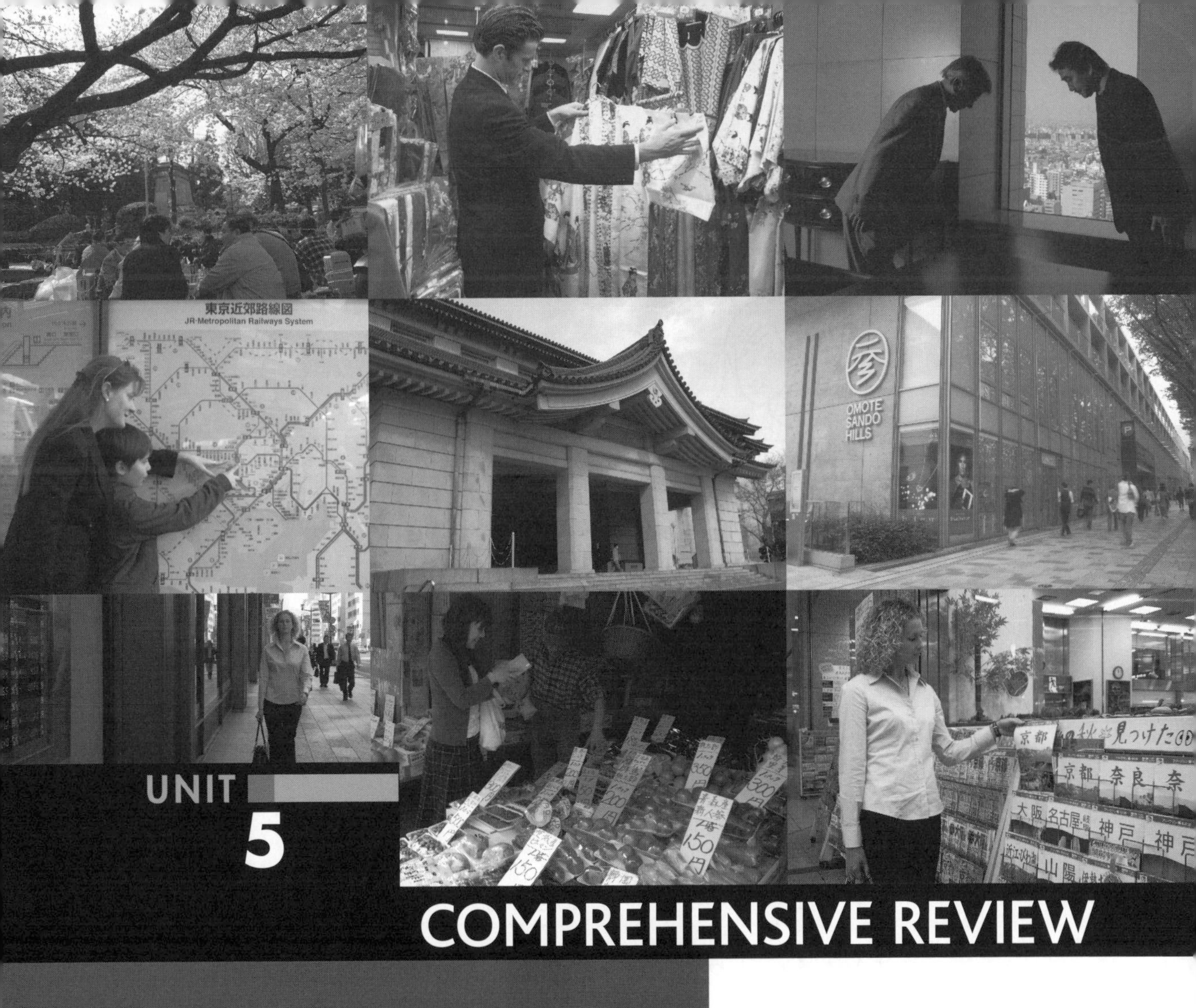

UNIT 5

COMPREHENSIVE REVIEW

Following a final check in Lesson 13 of whether you are able to handle talking about a slightly complicated problem, this unit wraps up your study of intermediate Japanese with scenes from a party. Parties are excellent chances to get to know others and to expand your world. The lessons cover expressive patterns commonly found in invitations, RSVPs, speeches, and other such party-related aspects. While making a speech or engaging in party talk in a foreign language may seem daunting at first, once you know these patterns you will find it easy to gracefully initiate and conclude exchanges. Try conducting conversations that draw on all the Japanese you have learned so far, and freely enjoy yourself.

LESSON 13

A CALL FROM THE HEALTH OFFICE

TARGET DIALOGUE

Mr. Suzuki informs Ms. Sasaki of an unexpected message from the health office.

鈴木(すずき)：　部長(ぶちょう)、たいへんです。

佐々木(ささき)：　どうしたんですか、そんなにあわてて。

鈴木(すずき)：　今(いま)、ほけん所(じょ)から電話(でんわ)があって、さくらまちのなつまつりで、おかしを食(た)べてふくつうを起(お)こした人(ひと)が何人(なんにん)も出(で)ていると言(い)うんです。うちのせいひんがげんいんじゃないかって言(い)うんですが。

佐々木(ささき)：　何(なん)ですって？

鈴木(すずき)：　すぐほけん所(じょ)に行(い)って、くわしい話(はなし)を聞(き)いてきます。

佐々木(ささき)：　おねがいします。マリーさん、しゅざいや問(と)い合(あ)わせの電話(でんわ)があっても、じょうきょうがはっきりするまでは、ていねいにおことわりしてください。

マルタン：わかりました。

The phone rings.

マルタン：はい、ＡＢＣフーズでございます。

新聞記者(しんぶんきしゃ)：あすか新聞(しんぶん)の者(もの)ですが、さくらまちのなつまつりの件(けん)で、せきにん者(しゃ)の方(かた)にお話(はなし)をうかがいたいんですが。

マルタン：その件(けん)は、ただ今(いま)ちょうさ中(ちゅう)でございます。わかりしだい記者会見(きしゃかいけん)をいたしますので、お待(ま)ちください。

佐々木(ささき)：もう新聞社(しんぶんしゃ)から電話(でんわ)がきたんですか。早(はや)いですね。今(いま)ほけん所(じょ)からうちに連絡(れんらく)があったばかりなのに……。

マルタン：来週(らいしゅう)、支社(ししゃ)の記念(きねん)パーティーがあるのに、たいへんな問題(もんだい)が起(お)きてしまいましたね。

The phone rings, and Ms. Sasaki answers. It's a call from Mr. Suzuki at the health office.

鈴木(すずき)：部長(ぶちょう)ですか。ご安心(あんしん)ください。まちがいでした。うちのせいひんじゃなくて、ＡＢＯ食品(しょくひん)のせいひんがげんいんでした。

佐々木(ささき)：えっ、まちがいだったんですか。よかった。でも、いったいどういうわけで、うちのせいひんがうたがわれたんですか。

鈴木(すずき)：パッケージがにていたので、ほけん所(じょ)にとどけた人(ひと)がまちがえたらしいんです。

佐々木(ささき)：わかりました。ほけん所(じょ)で、ふくつうのげんいんについて、くわしく聞(き)いてきてください。

鈴木(すずき)：わかりました。今(いま)ちょうど、説明(せつめい)が始(はじ)まるところです。

佐々木(ささき)：じゃ、よろしく。

Suzuki: Manager, there's a problem.
Sasaki: What's the matter? Why are you so flustered?
Suzuki: There was a phone call just now from the health office, and they told me that a large number of people have gotten stomachaches from eating snacks at the Sakura-machi summer festival. They say that our product may be the cause.
Sasaki: What?
Suzuki: I'll go to the health office right away and get details.
Sasaki: Please do. Marie, even if we get calls for interviews or inquiries, please politely turn them away until we know clearly what this is all about.
Martin: I understand.

Martin: Yes, this is ABC Foods.

reporter: I'm with Asuka Newspapers, and I'd like to have some comments from the person responsible regarding the matter of the Sakura-machi summer festival.

Martin: That matter is currently under investigation. We will hold a press conference as soon as we know anything, so please wait . . .

. . . . . .

Sasaki: Did a call come in from a newspaper company already? That was quick. It was only just now that we ourselves were contacted by the health office.

Martin: What an awful problem has come up, when next week we have that reception commemorating the five-year anniversary of the opening of our branch offices.

Suzuki: Manager? Please be reassured. It was a mistake. The cause wasn't our product, but one from ABO Foods.

Sasaki: What, a mistake? That's a relief. But for what reason was our product ever suspected?

Suzuki: Apparently the person who made the report to the health office made a mistake because the packages were similar.

Sasaki: I see. Please get details at the health office about the cause of the stomachaches.

Suzuki: I will. They're just about to begin explaining things now.

Sasaki: Well then, please take care of it for us.

VOCABULARY

ほけん所(じょ)	health office
さくらまち	Sakura-machi (fictitious neighborhood)
なつまつり	summer festival
ふくつうを起(お)こす	get a stomachache
ふくつう	stomachache
起(お)こす	get (a physical symptom)
何人(なんにん)も	many people
しゅざい	interview, news coverage
問(と)い合(あ)わせ	inquiry
はっきりする	become clear
ていねい(な)	polite
ことわる	refuse, turn away
あすか新聞(しんぶん)の者(もの)	someone with Asuka Newspapers (way of identifying one's own affiliation without giving one's name)
者(もの)	person, someone (humble)
せきにん者(しゃ)の方(かた)	person responsible (While せきにん者(しゃ) by itself already means "person responsible," adding の方(かた) makes it sound more polite.)
せきにん者(しゃ)	person responsible
わかりしだい	as soon as (one) knows
記者会見(きしゃかいけん)	press conference
新聞社(しんぶんしゃ)	newspaper company
～たばかり	only just —— (see Note 7 below)
記念(きねん)	commemoration
ABO 食品(しょくひん)	ABO Foods (fictitious food company name)
どういうわけで	for what reason
どういう	what, what kind of
わけ	reason
うたがう	suspect

NOTES

1. どうしたんですか、そんなにあわてて

This sentence is an inversion of そんなにあわてて、どうしたんですか. Sometimes in conversation, speakers will give what they most want to say first.

行くんですか、あしたのパーティー（に）。
Are you going to tomorrow's party?

よかったね、今日のコンサート。
Today's concert was good, wasn't it?

2. 何人も

The pattern "何 + counter + も" conveys that a number, while not specified, is nonetheless significant. The も adds emphasis.

かんじを何回も書いておぼえました。
I memorized the kanji by writing them over and over.

イベントにおきゃくさんが何百人も来ました。
Many hundreds of attendees came to the event.

3. 出ている

The verb 出る, which possesses a wide variety of meanings, is used here in the sense of victims or damage "emerging" from some negative occurrence (in this case, a stomachache). Although the damage has already taken place, Mr. Suzuki uses 出ている instead of the past form 出た because he regards the effects of the damage as ongoing and influencing matters he is dealing with at present.

4. うちのせいひんがげんいんじゃないかって言うんですが

〜じゃないか is a more colloquial way of saying 〜ではないか, which is the plain form of 〜ではありませんか. Here Mr. Suzuki uses it to indirectly quote the health office's conjecture that a product from ABC Foods may be the cause of the stomachaches.

5. ちょうさ中

The pattern "activity + 中" indicates that a certain activity, in this case an investigation, is ongoing. Other often-seen examples include 会議中, "in a meeting," 仕事中, "engaged in work," and 電話中, "in the midst of a phone call."

When 中 follows a spatial expression, then it means "all throughout" that place. 中 may also appear with certain words indicating periods of time to mean "all throughout" that time, e.g., 一日中, "all day," 一年中, "all year."

Finally, a temporal expression + 中 に indicates that an action is to take place or be performed within that period, e.g., 今日中に, "within today."

今、部長は会議中です。
The department manager is in a meeting right now.

たいしょくしたら、世界中(せかいじゅう)を旅行(りょこう)したいです。
When I retire, I want to travel all around the world.

一晩中(ひとばんじゅう)雨(あめ)がふっていました。
It rained all night.

今週中(こんしゅうちゅう)にレポートを出(だ)してください。
Please submit your report within the week.

6. わかりしだい

The *-masu* stem of a verb + しだい is an expression meaning "as soon as . . ." It tends to be used more commonly in business and other formal situations than in everyday conversation.

7. 連絡(れんらく)があったばかりなのに……。

The pattern "*-ta* form of a verb + ばかりだ" expresses that only a very short time has elapsed since the action or event described by the clause modifying ばかり took place. Here, "short" means short for the speaker, not necessarily according to some objective standard.

日本(にほん)に来(き)たばかりなので、まだ日本(にほん)のせいかつに慣(な)れていません。
I've only just come to Japan, so I'm not used to living here yet.

中村(なかむら)さんは、ゴルフを始(はじ)めたばかりなのに、とても上手(じょうず)です。
Ms. Nakamura is very good at golf, even though she has only just started.

8. うちのせいひんじゃなくて

Aじゃなくて is the conjunctive form of the clause Aじゃない（です）.

9. どういうわけで、うちのせいひんがうたがわれたんですか

There are two points to be made about this sentence:

(1) While どういう is similar to どんな in that they both mean "what kind of," どういう implies expectation of a more fully detailed answer going beyond simple appearances or obvious qualities.

(2) わけ, meaning "reason," also carries the connotation of being not just any reason but one that provides thorough justification for a matter, including all the circumstances and background behind it. わけ is a noun and so words preceding it take plain forms in the noun-modifying pattern, as all noun modifiers do.

A question asking どういうわけで, "for what reason," gives the feeling that the speaker is demanding a fully satisfying explanation and thus will often come off as rather strong.

わけ may also be used in the sense of "no wonder" or "so that's why" when you come across a satisfying answer to something you have been puzzling about, as in the following dialogue, which takes place on a train to work at about 8:30 in the morning in mid-August.

ミルズ：(*looking around puzzledly*) 今日(きょう)はすいてますね。どうしてこんなにすいているんでしょうか。

鈴木(すずき)　：今日(きょう)は8月(がつ)15日(にち)で、おぼんだからですよ。

ミルズ：おぼんって何(なん)ですか。

鈴木(すずき)：　おぼんというのは日本(にほん)の行事(ぎょうじ)なんです。このじきは休(やす)みになる会社(かいしゃ)が多(おお)いので、みんなじっかに帰(かえ)ったり、旅行(りょこう)したりするんです。

ミルズ：それで、こんなにすいているわけですね。

Mills: (*looking around puzzledly*) It's empty today, isn't it? Why are there so few people, I wonder.

Suzuki: That's because today is August 15, so it's Obon.

Mills: What's Obon?

Suzuki: Obon is a Japanese festival. A lot of companies shut down during this period, so everyone takes trips to see family back home or to go on vacation.

Mills: So that's why the train is so empty.

10. 今(いま)ちょうど、説明(せつめい)が始(はじ)まるところです。

ところ means "place." The pattern "plain form of a verb + ところだ" serves to focus on the individual "points" or "stages" in an action, almost as if the speaker were presenting snapshots of that action taking place.

今(いま)から夕食(ゆうしょく)を食(た)べるところです。
I am just about to eat dinner. (i.e., I am at the point where I will start eating dinner.)

今夕食(いまゆうしょく)を食(た)べているところです。
I am right now eating dinner.

今夕食(いまゆうしょく)を食(た)べたところです。
I have just now finished eating dinner.

ところ thus is used when wishing to emphasize what stage or phase a certain process is in at that moment.

佐々木：　コンサートはもう始まってしまいましたか。
マルタン：いいえ。今始まるところです。
Sasaki: Has the concert begun already?
Martin: No, it's just about to start.

加藤：　会議のしりょうはもうできましたか。
中村：　今コピーしているところです。
Kato: Are the materials for the meeting done already?
Nakamura: I'm just now making copies.

On a cell phone:

鈴木：　ミルズさん、今どちらですか。
ミルズ：　今駅に着いたところです。
Suzuki: Where are you now, Mr. Mills?
Mills: I've just now arrived at the station.

PRACTICE 1 Making Complaints

WORD POWER

こわれている be broken
割(わ)れている be cracked
やぶれている be torn
足(た)りない not enough, insufficient

クレーム complaint, objection
ふりょう品(ひん) defective product
ほしょう書(しょ) warranty
ほしょうきかん term of warranty

たんとう者(しゃ) person in charge
せきにん者(しゃ) person responsible
店長(てんちょう) store manager

PHRASE POWER

I. Calling to make a complaint:

① とどいた品物(しなもの)が割(わ)れていたんですけど……。
The item I received was broken.

② ちゅうもんとちがう品物(しなもの)がとどいたんですけど……。
I received an item different from what I ordered.

③ 三(みっ)つちゅうもんしたはずなのに、二(ふた)つしか入(はい)っていなかったんですけど……。
There were only two, when I'm sure I ordered three.

④ そちらで買(か)ったケーキを食(た)べたら、子(こ)どもがふくつうを起(お)こしたんですけど……。
My child got a stomachache after eating the cake that I bought at your place.

II. Complaining at a store or restaurant:

① これ、こちらで買(か)ったばかりなのに、もうこわれてしまったんですけど……。
I just bought this here and it's already broken.

② ちゅうもんしてから、もう３０分(さんじゅっぷん)も待(ま)っているんですけど……。
It's been half an hour since I placed my order . . .

VOCABULARY しなもの goods

SPEAKING PRACTICE

TRACK 48

I. A customer is talking to a clerk at the watch section of a department store.

客(きゃく)： このとけい、先週(せんしゅう)こちらで買(か)ったばかりなのに、もうこわれてしまったみたいなんですけど……。

店員(てんいん)： そうですか。ちょっとはいけんしてもよろしいでしょうか。

客(きゃく)： ええ。(*hands over the watch*) でんちも、新(あたら)しいのを入(い)れたばかりなんですけど、ぜんぜん動(うご)かないんです。

店員(てんいん)： (*looking it over*) もうしわけございません。おあずかりして、おしらべいたします。

customer: I bought this watch here only just last week, but it already seems to be broken.
salesperson: Is that so? May I be allowed to take a look?
customer: Yes. (*hands over the watch*) I just put in new batteries, too, but it still won't move at all.
salesperson: (*looking it over*) I'm sorry. I'll take it for a while and see what the matter is.

II. Ms. Nakamura is waiting at a restaurant for her lunch, which is taking a long time to arrive.

中村(なかむら)： すみません。まだでしょうか、Aランチ。もう20分(にじゅっぷん)も待(ま)ってるんですけど……。

店員(てんいん)： あ、もうしわけございません。Aランチでございますか。

中村(なかむら)： ええ。となりのテーブルの人(ひと)は、さっきちゅうもんしたばかりなのに、もう料理(りょうり)が来(き)てるみたいですけど……。

店員(てんいん)： たいへん失礼(しつれい)いたしました。すぐお持(も)ちいたします。

中村(なかむら)： すみませんが、早(はや)くしてもらえますか。あまり時間(じかん)がないんです。

………………

The manager comes over to Ms. Nakamura with her dish.

店長(てんちょう)： おきゃくさま、お待(ま)たせして、もうしわけございませんでした。

Nakamura: Excuse me. Isn't my A lunch ready yet? I've been waiting for twenty minutes already.
waiter: Oh, I'm sorry. The A lunch, did you say?
Nakamura: Yes. The person at the next table seems to have her food already, even though she just ordered.
waiter: Please excuse the error. I'll bring it to you right away.
Nakamura: I'm sorry, but will you make it quick? I don't have much time.
……
manager: Please accept our apologies for making you wait.

VOCABULARY

Aランチ	A lunch (name of a lunch special)
はやくする	hurry, make it quick

PRACTICE 2 Making and Responding to Apologies

SPEAKING PRACTICE

I. The phone rings in the midst of a party at the Kato residence.

加藤（かとう）（妻（つま））：はい、加藤（かとう）です。あ、鈴木（すずき）さん、今（いま）どちらですか。
鈴木（すずき）：今（いま）タクシーでそちらにむかっているところです。あと１０分（じゅっぷん）ぐらいで着（つ）くと思（おも）います。おそくなってすみません。
加藤（かとう）（妻（つま））：いいえ、だいじょうぶですよ。じゃ、お待（ま）ちしてます。

Mrs. Kato: Hello, this is Kato. Oh, Mr. Suzuki, where are you now?
Suzuki: I'm on my way over right now in a taxi. I think I'll get there in about ten more minutes. I'm sorry I'm late.
Mrs. Kato: Oh, no problem. Well then, we'll be expecting you.

II. Mr. Kato asks Ms. Martin to prepare some materials for him one morning at the office.

加藤（かとう）：このしりょうを今日中（きょうじゅう）に作（つく）ってもらえますか。あしたていしゅつするきかく書（しょ）に、このしりょうがひつようなんです。
マルタン：わかりました。

....

That afternoon at about four o'clock:

加藤（かとう）：けさおねがいしたしりょう、もうできましたか。
マルタン：すみません。今（いま）作（つく）っているところです。もうすぐできますので、できしだいてんぷで送（おく）ります。
加藤（かとう）：ありがとう。急（いそ）がせて、悪（わる）いね。

Kato: Will you prepare these materials for me sometime today? I need them for the proposal I'm submitting tomorrow.
Martin: I understand.

......

Kato: Are you done with the materials I asked you to prepare this morning?
Martin: I'm sorry. I'm preparing them now. They'll be done soon, so I'll send them to you by e-mail attachment as soon as they're finished.
Kato: Thanks. Sorry to rush you.

VOCABULARY

ていしゅつする	submit
きかくしょ	written proposal

III. Mr. Mills arrives late for a date to see a movie with a female friend.

ミルズ：　おそくなって、ごめん。
友人（女）：私も今来たところだから、だいじょうぶ。
ミルズ：　映画、もう始まっちゃった？
友人（女）：ううん、今始まるところ。早く中に入ろう。

Mills: Sorry I'm late.
friend: I just came myself, so no problem.
Mills: Has the movie already started?
friend: No, it's just about to. Let's hurry up and go in.

VOCABULARY
ううん　no (colloquial for いいえ)

PRACTICE 3 Asking For and Responding to Explanations

SPEAKING PRACTICE

TRACK 50

I. Mr. Mills and Ms. Sasaki are talking during lunch about their colleague, Mr. Yamamoto.

ミルズ：この間(あいだ)、山本(やまもと)さんがフランス語(ご)を話(はな)しているのを聞(き)いたんですが、ネイティブみたいにペラペラで、おどろきました。
佐々木(ささき)：山本(やまもと)さんは子(こ)どものころ、ずっとフランスに住(す)んでいたんですよ。
ミルズ：そうだったんですか。うまいわけですね。

Mills: The other day I heard Mr. Yamamoto talking in French, and I was amazed that he spoke so fluently, like a native speaker.
Sasaki: Mr. Yamamoto used to live in France for a long time when he was a child, you see.
Mills: Was that so? No wonder he's so good.

II. Ms. Martin gives Mr. Suzuki a message from a client.

マルタン：鈴木(すずき)さん、さっきのぞみデパートの高橋(たかはし)さんから電話(でんわ)があって、ちゅうもんとちがう商品(しょうひん)がとどいたと言(い)っていましたが。
鈴木(すずき)：ほんとうですか。すぐ連絡(れんらく)します。
………………

Mr. Suzuki reports his mistake to the department manager.

鈴木(すずき)：部長(ぶちょう)、もうしわけありません。私(わたし)のミスで、ちがう商品(しょうひん)がまざっていました。
佐々木(ささき)：どういうわけで、こんなことが起(お)きたんですか。
鈴木(すずき)：私(わたし)がよくかくにんしなかったためだと思(おも)います。もうしわけございません。
佐々木(ささき)：これからは気(き)をつけてください。

Martin: Mr. Suzuki, there was a phone call just now from Mr. Takahashi of Nozomi Department Store, and he said that they received merchandise different from what they ordered.
Suzuki: Really? I'll contact him right away.
……
Suzuki: Manager, I'm sorry. There were some other merchandise mixed in [with the order] due to my mistake.
Sasaki: How did such a thing come to happen?
Suzuki: I think it's because I didn't double-check. I'm sorry.
Sasaki: Please be careful from now on.

VOCABULARY

ネイティブ	native speaker
ペラペラ	fluent (mimetic word for describing fluent speech, especially in a foreign language; often written in katakana)
まざる	get mixed in
ためだ	be because (used in formal situations to state causes or reasons)

PRACTICE 4 Reading about the Reasons behind Customs

READING PRACTICE

写真①
しゅうぎぶくろ

写真②
しゅうぎぶくろ

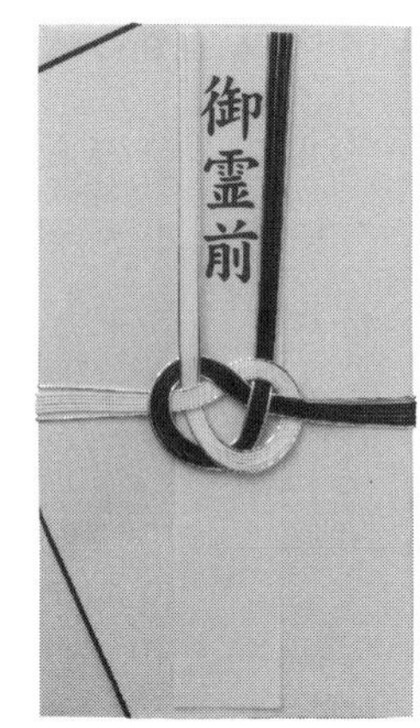

写真③
ぶしゅうぎぶくろ

日本は、けっこんしきやそうしき、赤ちゃんが生まれたときなどに、特別なふくろにお金を入れておくる習慣がある。このふくろは、いろいろなしゅるいがあり、いつ、どんなふくろを使うかきまっている。

まず、ふくろによって、使われている色がちがう。おいわいに使うしゅうぎぶくろ（写真①②）は、きほんてきには赤と白だが、最近はそれ以外のカラフルな色のふくろも多い。ぶしゅうぎぶくろ（写真③）に使われている色は、黒と白だ。

また、ふくろには、みずひきというひもがついており、二しゅるいのむすび方がある。一つはちょうむすびで、かんたんにほどけるので、何度でもむすぶことができる。けっこんしきやそうしき用のみずひきは、むすび方が特別で、一度むすんだらかんたんにはほどけない。つまり、けっこんしきやそうしきは一度だけで、くりかえさないようにしたいというわけだ。*

VOCABULARY

しゅうぎぶくろ	celebratory envelope (envelope used to give gifts of money for happy occasions)
きほんてきに	basically, fundamentally
いがい	other than, besides
カラフル（な）	colorful
ぶしゅうぎぶくろ	envelope for a mournful occasion (in which money is placed to give to someone who has lost a loved one)
くろ	black
みずひき	*mizuhiki* (colored paper cords)
ひも	string, cord
ついており	come with, is attached with (a conjunctive form of ついている that means the same as ついていて but that is used more frequently in formal writing)
むすびかた	way of tying, knot
ちょうむすび	bowknot
ほどく	undo
むすぶ	knot, tie
つまり	in other words, in short

In Japan, there is a custom of enclosing money in special envelopes to give to people for weddings, funerals, births, and other such occasions. These envelopes come in many different types, and there are set rules about which kinds are to be used for which occasions.

First of all, colors used on the envelopes vary according to envelope type. しゅうぎぶくろ (photos ①②) used for celebrations basically come in red and white, although nowadays there are also many colorful kinds in shades besides these two. Black and white are the colors used for ぶしゅうぎぶくろ [for use in unhappy occasions] (photo ③).

Each envelope also comes with cords called みずひき that are tied around it into a decorative knot in one of two ways. The first of these is the bowknot, which, being easy to undo, can be tied and untied any number of times. Cords for wedding and funeral envelopes are tied in a special way that cannot be easily undone once fashioned. In other words, they express the wish that weddings and funerals will only take place once and not be repeated.

> ＊ ～というわけだ can be used for summing up what one has just said or written, the sense being "in short."

KANJI PRACTICE

記
record
describe

記入(きにゅう)する
日記(にっき)
記事(きじ)
記者(きしゃ)

早
early

早(はや)い

心
heart

安心(あんしん)

重
heavy

重(おも)い

正
correct
right

正(ただ)しい
お正月(しょうがつ)

元

元気 げんき

origin
source

不

不便 ふべん

un-, in-, not

牛

牛肉 ぎゅうにく

cattle
cow

肉

肉 にく
牛肉 ぎゅうにく
肉屋 にくや

meat

飯

晩ご飯 ばんごはん
夕飯 ゆうはん

cooked rice
meal

LESSON
14
A FEW WORDS FROM THE HOST

TARGET DIALOGUE

Mr. Green is about to give a speech at the reception commemorating the five-year anniversary of the opening of ABC Foods Japan.

司会(しかい)：　みなさま、本日(ほんじつ)はご多忙(たぼう)の中(なか)、ＡＢＣフーズ日本支社(にほんししゃ)の開設(かいせつ)５周年記念(しゅうねんきねん)パーティーにご出席(しゅっせき)くださいまして、ありがとうございます。日本支社代表(にほんししゃだいひょう)、フランク・グリーンから、一言(ひとこと)ごあいさつをもうしあげます。

グリーン：グリーンでございます。みなさま、本日(ほんじつ)はお忙(いそが)しい中(なか)お集(あつ)まりくださいまして、ありがとうございます。

　このような席(せき)で日本語(にほんご)でお話(はな)しするのは初(はじ)めてですので、失礼(しつれい)がありましたら、おゆるしください。

　今年(ことし)ＡＢＣフーズ日本支社(にほんししゃ)は、おかげさまで開設(かいせつ)５周年(しゅうねん)をむかえました。今日(きょう)このように多(おお)くの方々(かたがた)におおいわいをしていただきまして、たいへんうれしく思(おも)っております。

　ショコラショコラは、世界中(せかいじゅう)で子(こ)どもからおとしよりまで、広(ひろ)い年代(ねんだい)のおきゃく様(さま)に親(した)しまれてきました。これからも、みなさまにあいされる商品(しょうひん)をていきょうしていきたいと思(おも)います。

　また、げんざい、海外(かいがい)むけの日本食(にほんしょく)や、ペット・フードの開発(かいはつ)にもとりくんでおります。社員一同(しゃいんいちどう)、これからもいっそうのどりょくをしてまいりますので、今後(こんご)とも、どうぞよろしくおねがいもうしあげます。

emcee: Ladies and gentlemen, thank you all today for taking the time in the midst of your busy schedules to attend this reception commemorating the five-year anniversary of the opening of the ABC Foods Japan offices. We will now have a few words from Frank Green, head of the Japan offices.

Green: I'm Green. Thank you all for kindly gathering here today in the midst of your busy schedules.

This is my first time speaking in Japanese at an occasion like this, so if I make any rude mistakes, please do excuse me.

This year, thanks to all of you, the ABC Foods Japan offices have reached their five-year anniversary. I am exceedingly happy that we have so many people here with us today to celebrate this occasion.

Chocolat-Chocolat has long been embraced around the world by consumers of all generations, from young to old. From now on, too, it is our wish to continue offering products that will be loved by everyone.

We are currently engaged in developing Japanese-style food for overseas markets and pet food, among other products. All of us at the company are prepared to pour ever more energy into our work, so please, everyone, continue to extend us your consideration now as always.

VOCABULARY

司会(しかい)	emcee
みなさま	ladies and gentlemen . . .
(ご) 多忙(たぼう)	busyness, busy schedule
中(なか)	in, in the midst of
開設(かいせつ)５周年(しゅうねん)記念(きねん)パーティー	fifth (grand) opening anniversary party
開設(かいせつ)	opening (of a business)
～周年(しゅうねん)	-th anniversary
一言(ひとこと)	a word, a few words
席(せき)	occasion
ゆるす	forgive, excuse
むかえる	reach (a certain time or stage), greet, welcome
方々(かたがた)	people (politer way of saying 人々(ひとびと))
親(した)しむ	love, be fond of
あいする	love
ていきょうする	offer
げんざい	(at) present
日本食(にほんしょく)	Japanese-style food
ペット・フード	pet food
とりくむ	undertake, engage in
一同(いちどう)	everyone, all
いっそうの	ever more, all the more

NOTES

1. パーティーにご出席くださいまして、ありがとうございます

This dialogue focuses on expressions commonly encountered in speeches made by hosts on formal occasions. Take note, in particular, of the honorific language used in both the emcee's introduction and Mr. Green's speech.

2. フランク・グリーンから、一言ごあいさつをもうしあげます

A typical way of introducing a speech given by the host of an event. The same pattern may also be used to introduce yourself before a speech when there is no emcee.

わたくし（ジョン・ミルズ）から、一言ごあいさつ（を）もうしあげます。
I (, John Mills,) would now like to say a few words.

3. ショコラショコラは、広い年代のおきゃく様に親しまれてきました。これからも、みなさまにあいされる商品をていきょうしていきたいと思います

～てくる here indicates that something has been continued from the past all the way up to the present, ～ていく that something will be continued from the present all the way into the future.

子どものときからピアニストになりたいと思ってピアノを習ってきました。これからは、しゅみとして、楽しんでいくつもりです。
Ever since I was a child, I have been taking piano lessons out of a desire to become a pianist. From now on I intend to continue enjoying piano as a hobby.

For more on the usage of ～ていく／～てくる, see p. 51.

4. 今後とも、どうぞよろしくおねがいもうしあげます

A set expression commonly used to conclude not only speeches but also letters.

READING PRACTICE 1 A Formal Invitation

The following is a formal invitation, sent out to clients, to attend a reception commemorating the five-year anniversary of the opening of the ABC Foods Japan offices. The letter is written in vertical text that reads from top to bottom and from right to left. Refer to the English translation and notes on the following pages to understand what the invitation says.

拝啓　盛夏の候、貴社ますますご清栄のこととお喜び申し上げます。さて、おかげさまで弊社は来る九月に開設五周年をむかえます。これも、みなさまからのご支援の賜物と深く感謝申し上げます。

　つきましては、左記のとおり心ばかりの記念パーティーをもよおしたいとぞんじます。ご多忙中まことにおそれいりますが、どうぞご出席くださいますようお願い申し上げます。

　まずは、略儀ながら書中をもってご案内申し上げます。

敬具

記

日時　九月七日（金曜日）午後四時〜午後六時

場所　ホテル東京「春秋の間」（別添の案内図をごらんください）

なお、まことに恐縮ながらご都合のほどを、八月十日までに同封のはがきにてお知らせくださいますようお願い申し上げます。

平成十九年七月

ABCフーズ

日本支社代表　フランク・グリーン

Dear ——: On this midsummer day we would like to express our gladness over the continuing prosperity of your company.

This coming September our company will, thanks to you, reach its five-year anniversary. We are deeply grateful to everyone's support for making this possible.

We would therefore like to host a commemorative reception as noted at left as a small token of our gratitude. We apologize for imposing upon you in the midst of your busy schedule, but we request that you please be kind enough to attend.

We present this informal letter to you as our invitation.

Yours,

Notes
Date & time: September 7 (Fri.) 4–6 p.m.
Place: Hotel Tokyo, Shunju Hall (see the location map)

We sincerely regret to impose upon you, but we further request that you kindly use the enclosed postcard to inform us regarding your attendance by August 10.

July 2007 [lit., "July of the 19th year of the Heisei era"]

President, ABC Foods Japan
Frank Green

VOCABULARY

記 (き)	notes (see Note 1 below)
日時 (にちじ)	date and time
春秋 (しゅんじゅう)	spring and autumn
間 (ま)	room, hall
別添 (べってん)	attached
なお	furthermore, in addition
まことに	truly, sincerely
恐縮 (きょうしゅく)	feeling of regret for imposing on someone
ながら	but, in spite of
～のほど	about ——, regarding —— (humble way of saying ～のこと, ～について)
同封の (どうふう)	enclosed
～にて	through ——, using ——
よう	so as to . . . (same as ように)
平成 (へいせい)	the Heisei era (1989–)

NOTES

1. 拝啓 and 敬具

   拝啓 and 敬具 are set phrases placed at the beginning and end of a formal letter, as "Dear" and "Yours" are done in English. Although several other expressions are also possible, a letter begun with 拝啓 will close with 敬具.

2. 盛夏の候

   盛夏の候 is an example of a seasonal greeting used to open a formal letter. The letter here is written in July and so employs a July greeting out of the different possibilities that exist for each of the twelve months.

3. 貴社ますますご清栄のこととお喜び申し上げます

   This is one conventional greeting phrase used to follow the seasonal greeting. It is appropriate for a letter addressed to a company.

4. さて

   さて is placed at the beginning of a sentence when wishing to introduce or change a topic.

5. (これも、)みなさまからのご支援の賜物と深く感謝申し上げます

   This is a conventional expression of gratitude used in business letters. It is similar in function to おかげさま, "thanks to you."

6. つきましては

   つきましては is used to mean "therefore" when going on to state the main purpose of your message.

7. まずは、略儀ながら書中をもってご案内申し上げます

   This is one conventional expression for ending a business letter.

8. 記

   This is a set indicator used in formal documents to show that details, for example about the time and place of an event, are to follow.

9. 同封のはがき

   An RSVP postcard will be printed with honorific expressions, for example ご出席, お名前, 貴社名, and ご芳名, used in respect of the recipient of the invitation. The proper way of replying is to write in the required information after first crossing out the honorific portions of each word (for the four words above, ご, お, 貴, and ご芳, respectively). See next page for an example.

   お名前 and ご芳名 both mean "name," with the distinction being that the former is heard more in speech while the latter tends to be used mostly in writing.

10. RESPONDING

    To respond with an RSVP postcard, cross out 行 and write in below it 御中 if the addressee is a company or other organization and 様 if it is an individual. See next page.

Back

ABCフーズ日本支社開設5周年記念(にほんししゃかいせつ しゅうねんきねん)
パーティー

~~ご~~出席(しゅっせき) いたします

~~ご欠席~~(けっせき)

~~ご~~住所(じゅうしょ) 中央区銀座(ちゅうおうくぎんざ)○-○-○

~~貴~~社名(きしゃめい) のぞみデパート

~~ご芳~~名(ほうめい) 高橋真吾(たかはししんご)

Front

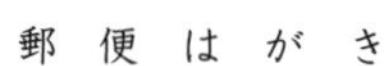

105-0001

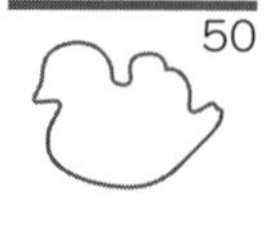

東京都港区虎ノ門(とうきょうとみなとくとらのもん)○-○-○

ABCフーズ日本支社~~行~~(にほんししゃいき)

御中(おんちゅう)

104-0061

READING PRACTICE 2 Casual Wedding Invitation

お元気(げんき)でおすごしのことと思(おも)います

とつぜんですが、私(わたし)たちけっこんすることになりました

私(わたし)たちの新(あたら)しい門出(かどで)をみなさまに見(み)まもっていただきたくささやかですがパーティーを開(ひら)きます

ぜひおこしくださいますよう、ごあんないもうしあげます

みなさまにお会(あ)いできるのを楽(たの)しみにしております

平成(へいせい)19年(ねん)6月吉日(がつきちじつ)

マイク・スミス　中村(なかむら)まゆみ

We trust that you are keeping well.

Please excuse the sudden notice, but we two are going to get married.

We are holding a modest party in the hopes of having all of you watch over us as we embark on our new life together.

We extend this invitation to ask for you to by all means kindly come.

We look forward to seeing all of you.

An auspicious day in June 2007

VOCABULARY

門出(かどで)	start (of a journey, new phase of life, etc.)
見(み)まもる	look upon, watch over
ささやか（な）	modest
おこしくださる	kindly come (honorific expression)
楽(たの)しみにする	look forward to
吉日(きちじつ)	auspicious day (a customary way of dating an invitation to a celebratory occasion)

NOTES

1. お元気(げんき)でおすごしのことと思(おも)います

This is a somewhat formal set greeting used to open a letter. Other common greetings include お元気(げんき)ですか, "Are you well?" and お元気(げんき)でおすごしですか, "Have you been keeping well?"

2. みなさまにお会(あ)いできるのを楽(たの)しみにしています

～（できる）のを楽(たの)しみにしています, "I look forward to . . . ," is a common and useful way of closing a letter.

READING PRACTICE 3 E-mail Invitation to a Home Party

送信者(そうしんしゃ)：マリー・マルタン
件名(けんめい)：おさそい

みなさま

お元気(げんき)ですか。マリーです。
早(はや)いもので、今回(こんかい)日本(にほん)に来(き)てから１年(ねん)がたちました。
いつも忙(いそが)しくて、なかなかみなさんにお会(あ)いできなかったのですが、仕事(しごと)もやっとおちついたので、うちでお花見(はなみ)パーティーをしようと思(おも)いつきました。かんたんな料理(りょうり)を用意(ようい)するつもりです。
さ来週(らいしゅう)の土曜日(どようび)の午後(ごご)を予定(よてい)していますが、ご都合(つごう)はいかがですか。
うちのマンションのとなりに大(おお)きい木(き)があって、去年(きょねん)きれいな花(はな)がさきました。今年(ことし)もつぼみがついているので、たぶん２週間後(しゅうかんご)にはさいていると思(おも)います。

では、みなさまにお会(あ)いできるのを楽(たの)しみにしています。
おへんじ、お待(ま)ちしています。

マリー・マルタン

From: Marie Martin
Subject: Invitation

Dear everyone,

How are you? This is Marie.
Time certainly goes by quickly, and a year has passed since I came to Japan this time around.
I was always so busy that I never had a chance to see all of you, but work has settled down at last and so I have come up with the idea of holding a cherry-viewing party at my place. I intend to prepare some simple dishes for your enjoyment.
I am planning on the afternoon of Saturday after next, but how would that look for you?
There is a big cherry tree next to my apartment that had beautiful flowers last year. It has buds on it this year, too, so I think it'll be in bloom by about two weeks from now.

Well then, I look forward to being able to see all of you.
I will be waiting for your replies.

Marie Martin

VOCABULARY

送信者(そうしんしゃ)	sender
件名(けんめい)	subject
早(はや)いもので	time flies, time passes quickly
今回(こんかい)	this time
たつ	pass, go by (of time)
おちつく	settle down
思(おも)いつく	think of, come up with
つぼみがつく	bud (v.)
つぼみ	bud (n.)

NOTES

1. 早いもので、今回日本に来てから１年がたちました。

The phrase 早いもので is often used before a sentence of the pattern "period of time + たちました" to remark on the rapid passage of time. It frequently shows up in letters. Marie says 今回, "this time," because this is her second time in Japan.

READING PRACTICE 4 Replies to a Party Invitation

I.

送信者：森田エミ
件名：Re：おさそい

マリーさま

お花見パーティーへのおさそい、ありがとうございます。
うれしいです。母といっしょにうかがいます。
母が、何か日本の家庭料理を作って持っていくと言っています。
リクエストがあったら、お知らせください。
それから、早めに行ってお手伝いしたいのですが、いいですか。
前にマリーさんが作ってくれた「おばあちゃんのタルト」がすごく
おいしかったので、母が今度レシピを教えてほしいって言ってます。
では、楽しみにしています。

エミ

From: Emi Morita
Subject: Re: Invitation

Dear Marie,

Thank you for the invitation to the cherry-viewing party.
I'm delighted [you thought of me]. My mother and I will both come.
My mother says that she will make some kind of homemade Japanese dish to bring.
If you have any requests, please let me know.
Also, I would like to go a little early to help you prepare, but would that be all right?
The "grandma's tart" that you once made for us was really good, so my mother is saying that she wants you to give her the recipe sometime.
Well then, I look forward to seeing you.

Emi

VOCABULARY

リクエスト	request	おばあちゃん	grandma
早めに	early, in advance	タルト	tart

II.

送信者：鈴木
件名：Re: おさそい

マリーさん

鈴木です。おさそい、ありがとうございます。
マリーさんの手料理、楽しみです。ワインは、赤でいいですか。
いつか飲もうと思って大切にとっておいたのがあるので、持っていきます。

From: Suzuki
Subject: Re: Invitation

Dear Marie,
This is SuzukI. Thank you for the invitation.
I look forward to tasting your cooking. Will red wine be all right [for me to bring]?
I have one that I was saving for a special occasion, so I'll bring that.

VOCABULARY

手料理	(someone's) own cooking
とっておく	keep, save

READING PRACTICE 5 Plans for a Surprise Party

送信者：ヒロ
件名：さっちゃんのたんじょう日

ヒロです。
来週１４日って、さっちゃんのたんじょう日だよね。
最近、みんな忙しそうだけど、さっちゃんのたんじょう日に何か楽しいことしない？
さっちゃんにはないしょで、みんな集めてサプライズ・パーティーするのはどう？
ちょうど日曜日だから、みんなで朝からうちに集まって料理作ってもいいし、忙しかったら、持ちよりでもいいし。
さっちゃんには３時ごろうちに来いって言っとくから、みんなでびっくりさせようよ。
じゃ、へんじ、待ってます。

From: Hiro
Subject: Sat-chan's birthday

This is Hiro.
The 14th next week is Sat-chan's birthday, right?

I know everyone seems to be busy recently, but why don't we do something fun for Sat-chan's birthday?
How about if we get everyone together, without telling Sat-chan, to have a surprise party?
As it just so happens, the 14th is going to be on a Sunday, so we can all get together at my place from the morning to make some food, or if everyone is busy, we can just make it potluck.
I'll tell Sat-chan to come to my house at around three, so let's all surprise her.
Well then, I'll be waiting to hear back from all of you.

VOCABULARY

ないしょ	secret
サプライズ・パーティー	surprise party
ちょうど	just, conveniently, as it happens
持ちより	potluck

NOTES

1. みんなで朝からうちに集まって料理作ってもいいし、忙しかったら、持ちよりでもいいし

The pattern ～て（で）もいいし、～て（で）もいいし is used to indicate that any of several options would be acceptable.

妻：　晩ご飯、何がいい？
夫：　そうだねえ。わしょくでもいいし、イタリアンでもいいし。きみにまかせるよ。
wife:　What do you want to have for dinner?
husband:　Hmm. Japanese or Italian, I'll leave it up to you.

READING PRACTICE 6　Reply to Plans for a Surprise Party

送信者：中村まゆみ
件名：Re: さっちゃんのたんじょう日

おそくなってごめんなさい。今、帰ったところ。
さっちゃんのサプライズ・パーティー、いいね！　楽しそう。学生時代を思い出すね。
今日は、部長にはきかく書を書きなおせって言われるし、帰りに電車に乗ろうとしたら、おりてきた人におされてころびそうになってヒールがとれちゃうし、最悪な一日だったんだけど、ヒロからのメール読んで元気になった。ありがとう。
私は、１４日朝から行けます。ほかに知らせたほうがいい人がいたら、私から連絡しとくから、言ってね。

じゃ、はっきりきまったら、また、知(し)らせて。

まゆみ

From: Mayumi Nakamura
Subject: Re: Sat-chan's birthday

Sorry this is late. I just got home.
A surprise party for Sat-chan—sounds good! Sounds like it'll be fun. Doesn't this remind you of our college days?
I had the worst possible day today, what with being told by the department manager to rewrite my proposal and having the heel come off my shoe on my way home after almost tripping from being pushed by the people coming off the train right as I was about to get on, but I feel better after reading your e-mail. Thank you.
I can go from the morning on the 14th. If there's anyone else we should let know about this, I'll contact them, so please tell me.
Well then, let me know again when things are definitely decided.

Mayumi

VOCABULARY

書(か)きなおす	rewrite
ヒール	heel (of shoe)
最悪(さいあく)（な）	abysmal, worst possible
はっきり	definitely, clearly

NOTES

1. おそくなってごめんなさい
   ごめんなさい is often used by women to make apologies. It is not appropriate for use in business or other formal situations (see also Note 5, p. 124).

2. POLITENESS LEVEL
   Note that even in letters or e-mails to those to whom one is close, some degree of politeness should be maintained at the beginning and end. Here, Mayumi uses ごめんなさい, not ごめん. Similarly, Hiro in Reading Practice 5 (p. 258) uses ヒロです, not ヒロだよ, and へんじ、待(ま)ってます, not へんじ、待(ま)ってる.

KANJI PRACTICE

忙
忙しい (いそが)
多忙 (たぼう)
busy

表
代表 (だいひょう)
予定表 (よていひょう)
express
table

集
集める (あつ)
集まる (あつ)
collect
gather

海
海 (うみ)
海外 (かいがい)
北海道 (ほっかいどう)
sea

漢
漢字 (かんじ)
Chinese

文	
letter writing	文化（ぶんか） 文学（ぶんがく） 文字（もじ） 注文（ちゅうもん）

字	
character	文字（もじ） 漢字（かんじ）

紙	
paper	紙（かみ） 手紙（てがみ）

計	
measure	時計（とけい） 計画（けいかく）

町	
town	町（まち）

LESSON **15**

AT A RECEPTION

TARGET DIALOGUE

Mr. Mills is approached by Mr. Nakano while at the five-year anniversary reception.

中野(なかの)：　ミルズさんは日本語(にほんご)がお上手(じょうず)ですね。

ミルズ：いえいえ、まだまだわからないことばかりです。

中野(なかの)：　日本(にほん)に来(こ)られて、何年(なんねん)ですか。

ミルズ：来月(らいげつ)で、まる３年(ねん)になります。

中野(なかの)：　３年(ねん)でそんなに上手(じょうず)に？

ミルズ：いえ。大学生(だいがくせい)のとき、友(とも)だちに日本(にほん)からの留学生(りゅうがくせい)がいたんです。かれから少(すこ)し教(おし)えてもらったのが最初(さいしょ)です。

中野(なかの)：　そうなんですか。

ミルズ：ええ。でも、そのときは、ぜんぜん話(はな)せなかったんですよ。話(はな)せるようになったのは、日本(にほん)に来(き)て仕事(しごと)で毎日(まいにち)使(つか)うようになってからですね。

中野(なかの)：　外国語(がいこくご)は「習(なら)うより慣(な)れろ」って言(い)いますからね。

ミルズ：すみません。何(なん)ですか、習(なら)うより……？

中野(なかの)：　……慣(な)れろ。日本(にほん)のことわざで、「人(ひと)に教(おし)えてもらうより、じっさいに使(つか)ったほうが早(はや)く上手(じょうず)になる」っていうことかな。

ミルズ：ああ、私(わたし)もそう思(おも)います。

Nakano: You speak very good Japanese, Mr. Mills.

Mills: Oh no, there are still lots of things I don't understand.

Nakano: How many years has it been since you came to Japan?

Mills: It'll be a full three years next month.

Nakano: You've gotten so good in just three years?

Mills: No. When I was in college there was an exchange student from Japan among my friends. My first experience with Japanese was when I had him teach me a little of it.

Nakano: Is that right?

Mills: Yes. But at that time I couldn't speak at all. It was only after I came to Japan and started using Japanese every day at work that I became able to speak it.

Nakano: You know what they say about foreign languages: 習(なら)うより慣(な)れろ.

Mills: I'm sorry, what was that, 習(なら)うより . . . ?

Nakano: . . . 慣(な)れろ. It's a Japanese saying, and I guess it means something like "you get better faster by actually putting a skill to practice than by having someone else teach you about it."

Mills: Ah, I agree.

VOCABULARY

慣(な)れる	get used to, accustom oneself to
ことわざ	saying
じっさいに	actually

NOTES

1. いえいえ、まだまだわからないことばかりです

When people in Japanese society receive positive comments about themselves or about family and other members of their in-group, generally the custom is for them to demur rather than to immediately accept the compliment. Thus Mr. Mills modestly brushes off Mr. Nakano's compliment about his Japanese by saying いえいえ instead of straightforwardly responding with something like ありがとうございます. Nowadays this custom is changing, however, so that especially in casual settings people will often simply say "thank you" right away.

SPEAKING PRACTICE 1 Thanking Someone for a Prior Encounter

マルタン：	あ、中野(なかの)さん！　お忙(いそが)しいのにいらしてくださって、ありがとうございます。先日(せんじつ)はたいへんお世話(せわ)になりました。
中野(なかの)：	いえいえ、おまねきいただいて、ありがとうございます。
マルタン：	中野(なかの)さんからうかがった無農薬野菜(むのうやくやさい)のお話(はなし)、ほんとうに勉強(べんきょう)になりました。あれ以来(いらい)、私(わたし)もできるだけ体(からだ)にいいものを食(た)べるようにしているんですよ。
中野(なかの)：	そうですか。そう言(い)ってもらえるとうれしいですよ。
マルタン：	中野(なかの)さんのところでいただいた野菜(やさい)、ほんとうにおいしかったです。今度(こんど)うちの課(か)のみんなで、またうかがわせてください。
中野(なかの)：	ぜひ。お待(ま)ちしていますよ。

Martin:	Oh, Mr. Nakano! Thank you for being kind enough to come when you're so busy. I'm grateful for all the assistance you gave me the other day.
Nakano:	Oh no, thank *you* for inviting me.
Martin:	What you told me about pesticide-free vegetables was really very enlightening. Since then I've been trying as much as possible to eat things that are good for me, too.
Nakano:	Is that right? It makes me happy to have you say so.
Martin:	The vegetables you gave me from your farm were truly delicious. Please allow me to visit you again, this time with everyone from my section.
Nakano:	By all means. I'll be looking forward to it.

VOCABULARY

いらして	(short for いらっしゃって)
以来(いらい)	since

NOTES

1. 先日(せんじつ)はたいへんお世話(せわ)になりました

Both in business as well as in other social settings, it is considered proper manners to begin a conversation by first giving thanks about the time you last met. Especially if you happened to receive any gifts or services from the other person, failing to acknowledge them may result in the person thinking you rude.

2. いえいえ、おまねきいただいてありがとうございます

Upon being thanked by Ms. Martin, Mr. Nakano demurs by saying いえいえ. This is another instance of the practice of showing modesty that was covered in the Note to the Target Dialogue.

SPEAKING PRACTICE 2 Apologizing for a Prior Misstep

TRACK 54

加藤：　高橋さん、今日はどうもありがとうございます。
高橋：　ああ、加藤さん。本日はおめでとうございます。
加藤：　ありがとうございます。のぞみデパートさんには先日のフェアでも、たいへんお世話になりました。
高橋：　ああ、あの時は場所の件で、手ちがいがあり、もうしわけありませんでした。
加藤：　とんでもない。今後ともよろしくおねがいいたします。
高橋：　こちらこそ。

Kato: Thank you for [coming] today, Mr. Takahashi.
Takahashi: Oh, Mr. Kato. Congratulations on today.
Kato: Thank you. I'm grateful for all the assistance your company gave us during the fair the other day.
Takahashi: Oh, I apologize that there was a mix-up that time on the matter of your space.
Kato: Not at all. Please continue to extend us your consideration now as always.
Takahashi: We ask the same of you.

VOCABULARY

手ちがい	mistake, mix-up
とんでもない	not at all

NOTE

1. のぞみデパートさん

In business conversations, people occasionally add ～さん to the names of companies beside their own. This is generally not done in other settings, however.

SPEAKING PRACTICE 3 Giving Introductions

TRACK 55

マルタン：あ、中野さん、うちの部長の佐々木にはもう会われましたか。
中野：　いえ、まだ……。
マルタン：今、そこにおりますので、ごしょうかいさせてください。

Ms. Martin introduces Ms. Sasaki to Mr. Nakano.

マルタン：中野さん、部長の佐々木です。
佐々木：　佐々木でございます。

マルタン：こちら、先日しゅざいさせていただいた中野さんです。
中野：　本日はおまねきありがとうございます。
佐々木：　ああ。そのせつはたいへんお世話になりました。
中野：　こちらこそ。

Martin: Oh, Mr. Nakano, have you met our department manager Sasaki yet?
Nakano: No, not yet.
Martin: She's right over there now, so please allow me to introduce her to you.
. . . . . .
Martin: Mr. Nakano, this is Sasaki, our department manager.
Sasaki: I'm Sasaki.
Martin: This is Mr. Nakano, whom I had the pleasure of interviewing the other day.
Nakano: Thank you for inviting me today.
Sasaki: Oh, no. I'm grateful for all the assistance you gave us at the time.
Nakano: And I for yours.

VOCABULARY

おまねき　invitation
せつ　time, occasion (そのせつは = at the time)

SPEAKING PRACTICE 4 Asking After an Acquaintance

来客：　ミルズさん、おひさしぶりです。お元気そうですね。
ミルズ：ああ、山口さん。ごぶさたしております。本日はおいでいただき、ありがとうございます。
来客：　こちらこそ、おまねき、ありがとうございます。５周年、おめでとうございます。
ミルズ：ありがとうございます。
来客：　今日は、チャンさんはいらっしゃっていないようですが。
ミルズ：じつはチャンは先月シンガポールにてんきんになったんですよ。
来客：　シンガポールに？　それは知りませんでした。あちらでもお元気でいらっしゃいますか。
ミルズ：ええ。てんきんしたばかりでたいへんなようですが、元気でやっています。
来客：　そうですか。よろしくお伝えください。*(seeing someone, and nodding toward Mr. Mills)* すみませんが、ちょっと失礼します。
ミルズ：*(nodding his head lightly)* また後ほど。

guest: Mr. Mills, it's been a while. You look well.

Mills: Ah, Mr. Yamaguchi. Excuse me for not keeping in touch. Thank you today for coming.

guest: Oh no, thank you for inviting me. Congratulations on your fifth anniversary.

Mills: Thank you.

guest: Ms. Chan doesn't seem to be here today, does she?

Mills: Actually, Chan was transferred last month to Singapore.

guest: To Singapore? I had no idea. Is she keeping well over there?

Mills: Yes. Things seem to be hectic given that she's only just transferred there, but she's well and carrying on.

guest: Is that so? Please give her my regards. (*seeing someone, and nodding toward Mr. Mills*) I'm sorry, but please excuse me a bit.

Mills: (*nodding his head lightly*) Perhaps again at a later time, then.

VOCABULARY

来客(らいきゃく) guest

山口(やまぐち) Yamaguchi (surname)

NOTE

1. (*seeing someone, and nodding toward Mr. Mills*) すみませんが、ちょっと失礼(しつれい)します。
(*nodding his head lightly*) また後(のち)ほど。

When taking leave of someone, it will often be appropriate to nod your head lightly toward that person even without going so far as to take a complete bow. Such characteristic nonverbal signs, too, are an important part of communicating in Japanese.

SPEAKING PRACTICE 5 Winding Up after a Reception

TRACK 57

グリーン：みなさん、今日(きょう)はおつかれさまでした。
みなさんのおかげで、とてもいいパーティーになりました。
これからもみんなでがんばりましょう。かんぱい！

みんな： かんぱい！

Later, when Mr. Green is not present:

加藤(かとう)： (*to Ms. Sasaki*) 支社長(ししゃちょう)のスピーチ、よかったですね。

佐々木(ささき)： ええ、発音(はつおん)がはっきりしていて、わかりやすかったですね。やっぱり日本語(にほんご)でスピーチをすると、気持(きも)ちが伝(つた)わりますよね。そういえば、今日(きょう)何人(なんにん)ものおきゃく様(さま)がマリーさんとミルズさんのことをほめていましたよ。日本語(にほんご)が上手(じょうず)になったって。

マルタン：そうですか。うれしいです。でも、日本語(にほんご)は勉強(べんきょう)すればするほどむずかしくなります。

ミルズ：　うん、むずかしいけど、ぼくには日本語(にほんご)の勉強(べんきょう)は最初(さいしょ)に思(おも)っていたほどむずかしくなかったです。

鈴木(すずき)：　みんな、二人(ふたり)が日本語(にほんご)を話(はな)せると知(し)って、安心(あんしん)するようですよ。ことばが話(はな)せるって、大切(たいせつ)ですね。ぼくも、外国語(がいこくご)、がんばろう。

マルタン：おたがいにがんばりましょう。

Green: Good work today, everyone. Thanks to all of you, we had a very good party. Let's keep on working hard together from now on. Cheers!

everyone: Cheers!

. . . . . .

Kato: (*to Ms. Sasaki*) The president's speech was good, wasn't it?

Sasaki: Yes, his enunciation was clear and easy to understand. Giving a speech in Japanese really does make your feelings come across, don't you think? Which reminds me, a great many guests were complimenting you today, Marie and Mr. Mills. They were saying that both of you have gotten very good at Japanese.

Martin: Is that so? I'm flattered. But the more I study Japanese, the more difficult it gets.

Mills: Well yes, studying Japanese is hard, but to me it didn't turn out to be as difficult as I thought it would be at first.

Suzuki: Everyone seems to feel reassured when they find out you two can speak Japanese. It's important to be able to speak the language, don't you think? I'm going to work hard on my foreign languages, too.

Martin: You and me both.

VOCABULARY

おつかれさまでした	good work (set phrase for showing appreciation toward others' work)
伝(つた)わる	spread, go across, come through
～ば～ほど	the more (something is the case) the more . . .
～ほど～ない	not so . . . as . . .
（お）たがいに	each other

NOTES

1. 支社長(ししゃちょう)のスピーチ、よかったですね

Mr. Kato does not compliment Mr. Green on his speech face to face, since directly giving one's opinions of someone of higher status (however favorable) could end up being rude.

2. やっぱり日本語(にほんご)でスピーチをすると、気持(きも)ちが伝(つた)わりますよね

やっぱり（やはり）, which variously means "also," "too," "still," "as expected," or "after all," is sometimes used without a specific meaning purely for the sake of emphasis. Here, Ms. Sasaki is saying that by speaking in Japanese, Mr. Green was able to impress upon the audience how hard he is working in Japan and to give them a better sense of his sincerity and dedication.

3. 日本語(にほんご)は勉強(べんきょう)すればするほどむずかしくなります。

The pattern "conditional form of a verb/-*i* adjective + ば + the dictionary form of the same word + ほど" means "the more (something is the case), the more . . ."

マリーさんのことを知(し)れば知(し)るほどすきになります。
The more I get to know about Marie, the more I like her.

アパートは広(ひろ)ければ広(ひろ)いほどいいです。
The bigger the apartment, the better.

やちんは高(たか)くなければ高(たか)くないほどいいです。
The less expensive the rent, the better.

For -*na* adjectives, the pattern is:

アパートはしずかならしずかなほどいいです。
The quieter the apartment, the better.

4. ぼくには日本語(にほんご)の勉強(べんきょう)は最初(さいしょ)に思(おも)っていたほどむずかしくなかったです。

The pattern "AはBほど + negative form of a verb/adjective" means "A is not so . . . as B." In this case, Mr. Mills is saying that while studying Japanese certainly is difficult, it did not prove to be as difficult as he imagined it might be at first.

KANJI PRACTICE

留
留学する (りゅうがく)
留学生 (りゅうがくせい)
stay

止
止まる (と)
止む (や)
中止 (ちゅうし)
stop

試
試験 (しけん)
試合 (しあい)
試着室 (しちゃくしつ)
try
test

験
試験 (しけん)
proof
examine

答
答える (こた)
answer

堂

食堂 しょくどう

hall
temple

春

春 はる

spring

夏

夏 なつ
夏休み なつやすみ

summer

秋

秋 あき

autumn

冬

冬 ふゆ

winter

Quiz 5 Unit 5 (Lessons 13–15)

I Fill in the blanks with the appropriate particle.

1) すみません、まだでしょうか。注文(ちゅうもん)してから３０分(さんじゅっぷん)（　　　）待(ま)っているんですが。

2) 何回聞(なんかいき)かれても、はっきりする（　　　）何(なに)も話(はな)せません。

3) このエレベーターの中(なか)でさいふをすられた人(ひと)が何人(なんにん)（　　　）出(で)ています。

4) みなさまにお会(あ)いできるの（　　　）楽(たの)しみにしています。

5) この食品(しょくひん)は無農薬(むのうやく)なので、子(こ)どもからおとしより（　　　）安心(あんしん)してめしあがっていただけます。

II Choose the most appropriate word from among the alternatives (1–4) given.

1) むかし（　　　）ところにおうじさまが住(す)んでいました。

１．あの　　２．あちらの　　３．あそこの　　４．ある

2) どうしたんですか。（　　　）あわてて。

１．こんなに　　２．こんな　　３．そんなに　　４．そんな

3) 忙(いそが)しくて、（　　　）友(とも)だちに会(あ)えません。

１．わざわざ　　２．なかなか　　３．やっと　　４．そっと

4) （　　　）どういうわけで、うたがわれたんですか。

１．いつか　　２．たしかに　　３．いったい　　４．だれか

5) あ、鈴木(すずき)さん、（　　　）よかった。ちょっと手伝(てつだ)って。

１．ちょうど　　２．ちょっと　　３．やっと　　４．じっと

III Change the form of the word given in parentheses to complete the sentences in a way that makes sense.

1) 子(こ)どもが（　　　）ばかりなので、毎日忙(まいにちいそが)しくすごしています。（生(う)まれます）

2) 今日(きょう)（　　　）はずのにもつがまだとどいていません。（着(つ)きます）

3) A：もしもし、鈴木(すずき)ですが、今(いま)、お話(はな)ししてもよろしいですか。

B：すみません。今(いま)、料理(りょうり)を（　　　）ところなので、すぐ後(あと)でこちらからお電話(でんわ)してもいいですか。（します）

4) A：マリーさんは子(こ)どものころからチェロを習(なら)っていたそうですよ。
B：それで、あんなに（　　　）わけですね。（上手(じょうず)です）

5) これからも地球(ちきゅう)の温度(おんど)は（　　　）いくんでしょうか。（上(あ)がります）

IV Choose the most appropriate word or phrase from among the alternatives (1–4) given.

1) あれ、このシャツ、（　　　）。
1. こわれてる　　2. やぶれてる　　3. 割(わ)れてる　　4. おれてる

2) みなさま、本日(ほんじつ)はお忙(いそが)しい（　　　）ご出席(しゅっせき)くださいまして、ありがとうございます。
1. うち　　2. 中(なか)　　3. 間(あいだ)　　4. とき

3) （　　　）ですが、私(わたし)たちけっこんすることになりました。
1. 急(きゅう)に　　2. 早(はや)く　　3. とつぜん　　4. 急(いそ)いで

4) その件(けん)は、げんざい、（　　　）です。
1. 電話中(でんわちゅう)　　2. ちょうさ中(ちゅう)　　3. 仕事中(しごとちゅう)　　4. 工事中(こうじちゅう)

5) その（　　　）はたいへんお世話(せわ)になりました。
1. とき　　2. せつ　　3. ところ　　4. ころ

V Fill in the blanks with the correct reading of each kanji.

1) 来年のお正月は　海外ですごすつもりです。
（　　　）（　　　）

2) 雨で野球の試合が　中止になりました。
（　　　）（　　　）

3) 留学生が　増えたという記事を新聞で読みました。
（　　　）　（　　　）

4) 春と　秋に世界の代表が　集まる　会議があります。
（　　　）（　　　）（　　　）（　　　）

APPENDIX

List of Transitive and Intransitive Verbs

TRANSITIVE			INTRANSITIVE		
Reg. I	Reg. II	Meaning	Reg. I	Reg. II	Meaning
	開ける	open	開く		open
	上げる	lift, raise	上がる		rise, go up
	集める	gather, collect	集まる		come together
	入れる	put in	入る		enter, come in
	終える（終わる）	finish, end	終わる		finish, end
	変える	change	変わる		change
	決める	decide on	決まる		be decided
	下げる	lower	下がる		go down
	閉める	close	閉まる		close
	助ける	help, save	助かる		be saved, be helped
	つかまえる	catch	つかまる		be caught
	つける	attach to	つく		attach to
	続ける	continue with	続く		continue
	届ける	deliver	届く		be delivered
	止める	stop	止まる		stop
	並べる	line up	並ぶ		line up
	始める	begin, start	始まる		begin, start
	見つける	find	見つかる		be found
動かす		move	動く		move
移す		move	移る		move
写す		copy	写る		come out
起こす		cause	起こる		happen
治す		cure	治る		be cured
直す		fix	直る		be fixed
残す		leave behind	残る		be left behind
折る		bend, break		折れる	be bent/broken
切る		cut		切れる	cut
消す		extinguish, turn off		消える	go out, disappear
壊す		break		壊れる	break
出す		send out		出る	come out
溶かす		melt		溶ける	melt
なくす		lose		なくなる	become lost
増やす		increase		増える	increase
減らす		decrease		減る	decrease
焼く		burn		焼ける	burn

ANSWERS TO EXERCISES AND QUIZZES

UNIT 1

Lesson 1

Grammar & Pattern Practice

I. **1** 1) 便利(べんり)でしょう。
2) しらないでしょう。
3) 少(すく)ないでしょう
4) かかるでしょう。

2 1) だれでしょうか。
2) きけんでしょうか。
3) 入(はい)っているんでしょうか。

II. **1** 1) いるよう／いるみたい
2) 終(お)わっていないよう／終(お)わっていないみたい
3) るすのよう／るすみたい
4) にがてなよう／にがてみたい
5) ねたよう／ねたみたい
6) おこっているよう／おこっているみたい
7) いいよう／いいみたい

2 1) 薬(くすり)のような／薬(くすり)みたいな
2) おちたような／おちたみたいな
3) うそのような／うそみたいな

3 1) はるのように／はるみたいに
2) べんごしのように／べんごしみたいに
3) きかいのように／きかいみたいに

4 1) I have a mountain of work to do, so I have it rough.
2) The new computer game sold so well, copies seemed to be flying off the shelves.
3) Apparently extremely tired, my husband slept as if he were dead.

III. **1** 1) ひいたそう
2) あるそう
3) 大(だい)すきだそう
4) ちゅうしだそう

5) わるいそう

2 1) According to the weather forecast, the wind is going to get stronger tonight.

2) According to the announcement at the station, there has been a train-car breakdown and the trains have stopped running.

3) To hear Marie tell it, Japanese anime is popular even in France.

IV. 1) ひやしておき

2) あたためておき

3) ならべておいて

4) とうろくしておき

Lesson 2

Grammar & Pattern Practice

I. **1**

Nakamura: Mr. Mills is late, isn't he? He may have forgotten about our appointment.
Suzuki: He should remember, since I talked to him on the phone just this morning.
Nakamura: Then maybe he doesn't know where this place is?
Suzuki: He should know, since I came here with him once before.
Nakamura: Then I wonder what the matter is.

2

Suzuki: My keys are missing. My keys are missing. I'm sure I put them in my pocket . . .
Nakamura: Did you look closely? Didn't you maybe put them in a different pocket?
Suzuki: No, it definitely was this pocket. Oh, there's a hole in it.

II.

Nakamura: Mr. Kato, there's a problem. Just now there was a phone call from the Kyoto branch office. I've been told Mr. Yamamoto, the branch president, won't be on time for the reception at six.
Kato: What, is something the matter?
Nakamura: I understand the Shinkansen that the president is on is running late.
Mills: Oh, there's supposed to have been an accident someplace around Nagoya.
Nakamura: President Yamamoto's speech is going to be from around 6:30, but I've been told he's probably going to arrive here around seven.
Kato: This is certainly a problem, isn't it? Inform the department manager right away.
Nakamura: Yes.

III. 1) 高(たか)そう

2) おもしろそうな

3) きもちがよさそう

4) じょうぶそうに

5) きえそう

IV. **1** 1) あったのに

2) しているのに

3) 買(か)ったのに

4) 日曜日(にちようび)なのに

5) 上手(じょうず)なのに、

6) まちだったのに

7) 高(たか)いのに

2 Suzuki: (*sighs*)

Mills: Is something the matter?

Suzuki: I had plans for a date with my girlfriend yesterday, but she didn't show up. I waited two hours, but she didn't show up. I've called several times today, but she doesn't answer. I've sent her many e-mails, but she hasn't replied.

Mills: Something might be wrong. You should go to her apartment immediately to check on her.

Lesson 3

Grammar & Pattern Practice

I.

A: I read an article about how our lifestyles have greatly changed because of cell phones becoming widespread.

B: That's true. I feel very reassured because thanks to my cell phone, I always know how work is going.

A: Is that so? I'm fed up since, all because of my cell phone, I get calls from the office even while I'm on vacation.

II. **1** 1) 食(た)べられるように

2) あるけるように

3) 読(よ)めるように

4) おくれなく

5) はけなく

2 1) けんかをするように

2) 着(き)なく

3) 書(か)かなく

III. 1) ふえていく

2) へっていく

3) 上(あ)がっていく

4) へんかしていき

5) かわっていき

QUIZ 1

I. 1) に 2) が 3) に 4) と 5) の

II. 1) 4 2) 2 3) 2 4) 1 5) 1

III. 1) 休(やす)みだ 2) 終(お)わっていない 3) 高(たか) 4) かぜな 5) 読(よ)める

IV. 1) 3 2) 3 3) 2 4) 4 5) 1

V. 1) かぞく どうぶつびょういん
2) ひく からだ しょくひん かいはつ
3) さいきん じゅうしょ
4) にわ ようす

UNIT 2

Lesson 4

Grammar & Pattern Practice

I. 1) こと 2) こと 3) の 4) こと 5) の

II. 1) 入(い)れて
2) 入(い)れないで／入(い)れずに
3) ならんで
4) 飲(の)まないで／飲(の)まずに
5) そうだんしないで／そうだんせずに

III. 1) おいて
2) あらって
3) かけて
4) はって
5) きって

IV. 1) We installed security lighting so thieves wouldn't get in.
2) I started taking dance lessons so my figure would improve.
3) We provided a quiet lounge so the staff would be able to get some rest.
4) I left home early so I wouldn't be late for the meeting.
5) I wrote in big letters so it would be easy to read.
6) We built a big parking lot so there would be space to park a lot of cars.

Lesson 5

Grammar & Pattern Practice

I. 1) 教(おし)えています。教(おし)えていました。

2) けっこんしていました。けっこんしていませんでした。

3) ねていました。

4) 始(はじ)まっていました。

5) 終(お)わっている

II. 1) あかるくしてください。

2) シンプルにしてください。

3) 少(すく)なくしてください。

4) かんたんにしてください。

5) きびしくしてください。

III. 1) 開発(かいはつ)するために

2) ならうために

3) むかえに行(い)くために

4) とるために

5) ちょうせんするために

IV. 1) はたらきながら

2) 聞(き)きながら

3) ながめながら

4) たのしみながら

Lesson 6

Grammar & Pattern Practice

I. 1) 食(た)べても

2) しらべても

3) ふべんでも

4) きびしくても

5) 仕事(しごと)でも

II. 1) You won't have to go to a store if you buy things on the Internet.

2) In Tokyo you don't have to buy a car, since public transportation is convenient.

3) In the town that I used to live in, I had to separate burnables from nonburnables when I put the trash out. I don't have to separate the trash where I live now. I hear they have a machine for doing that.

III. 1) ガーデニングをしたり、バーベキューをしたり

2) ミュージカルを見(み)たり、買(か)い物(もの)をしたり

3) 毎朝(まいあさ)ジョギングをしたり、にくを食(た)べるのをやめたり

IV. 1) A: I'm thinking of buying a new computer.
B: If you're going to buy a new computer, I recommend Nozomi Electronics. The staff is very friendly.

2) A: I want to make reservations for a hotel in Osaka.
B: If you're going to make hotel reservations, it'll be easy if you do it on the Internet.

3) A: I want to work in information technology once I graduate from college.
B: If you want to work in information technology, I'll introduce you to a friend who has an IT job.

QUIZ 2

I. 1) か 2) も 3) が 4) に 5) で

II. 1) 3 2) 1 3) 1 4) 2 5) 1

III. 1) ある 2) 悪く(わる) 3) わかる 4) なる 5) あるき

IV. 1) 3 2) 4 3) 2 4) 3 5) 1

V. 1) ひろ とち
2) せかいじゅう やさい りょうり
3) きって おし
4) きおん いじょう もんだい

UNIT 3

Lesson 7

Grammar & Pattern Practice

I. **1** 1) もらいました
2) くれました
3) あげました

2 1) When I was little, I often had my parents take me to the zoo.

2) A nice person once told me the reading for some kanji when I was at a loss, unable to figure out how the characters were supposed to be read.

3) A: That's a lovely coat, isn't it?
B: I had my father buy it for me.

4) A: Didn't you have a lot of work preparing for the party?
B: My friends helped me out, so I got it done in no time at all.

II. 1) A: What is your resolution for this year?
B: To pass my Japanese-language exam. I intend to memorize five new kanji every day.

2) I have always wanted to live in the countryside. Once I retire, I intend to move to the country and take up farming.

3) Martin: What will you take to the barbecue on Sunday?
Suzuki: Mr. Mills said he was going to provide the meat and vegetables, so I'm planning on taking drinks.
Martin: I guess I'll take some fruit, then.

4) I planned on not eating the sweets, but they looked so delicious, I just ate them up.

Lesson 8

Grammar & Pattern Practice

I. **1** 1) 使(つか)われる
2) すすめられる
3) 作(つく)られる
4) えらばれる
5) まちがえられる
6) しょうたいされる

2 1) 父(ちち)になぐられました。
2) 先生(せんせい)にほめられました。
3) スミスさんに映画(えいが)にさそわれました。
4) 女(おんな)の人(ひと)に足(あし)をふまれました。

3 1) よばれて
2) ゆにゅうされて
3) ゆしゅつされた
4) ほうそうされた
5) 行(おこな)われた

II. **1** 1) タクシーに乗(の)ろうとしたとき
2) 家(いえ)を出(で)ようとしたとき
3) 電車(でんしゃ)に乗(の)ろうとしたとき

2 1) にもつをはこぼうとしましたが
2) 勉強(べんきょう)しようとしましたが

III. 1) 入院(にゅういん)している
2) 買(か)い物(もの)をしている
3) 出(で)かけている
4) 旅行(りょこう)している
5) なつ休(やす)みの

Lesson 9

Grammar & Pattern Practice

I. 1) 習(なら)わせ

2) 持(も)ってこさせ
3) しらべさせ
4) こたえさせ
5) とらせる
6) あそばせ
7) 勉強(べんきょう)させる
8) わらわせ
9) 言(い)わせて
10) おぼえさせ
11) 行(い)かせ
12) 行(い)かせ

QUIZ 3

I. 1) に 2) に 3) に 4) を 5) に

II. 1) 3, 2 2) 1 3) 4 4) 1

III. 1) 代(か)わって 2) 行(い)く 3) 出(で)よう 4) 持(も)たせ 5) こわされ

IV. 1) 2 2) 2 3) 4 4) 4 5) 4

V. 1) せつめい いけん
2) ねんだい た しゃしん
3) みち ある かんが
4) じてんしゃ かよ

UNIT 4

Lesson 10

Grammar & Pattern Practice

I. 1) でいらっしゃいます でございます。
2) いらっしゃいました まいりました。
3) おっしゃいます もうします。
4) めしあがります いただきます。

II. **1** 1) お出(で)かけになります
2) お読(よ)みになります

3) お会(あ)いになります

2 1) お貸(か)ししましょう

2) お送(おく)りしましょう

3) ごしょうかいしましょう

III. **1** 1) Neutral: I got a book from my younger brother.
Polite: I received a book from my teacher.

2) Neutral: I will give my friend a book.
Polite: (on an advertisement) We will give you a free catalog.

3) Neutral: My father and mother gave me a book.
Polite: My teacher gave me a book.

2 1) 1. A 2. B

2) 1. A 2. B

Lesson 11

Grammar & Pattern Practice

I. **1** 1) また後(あと)で電話(でんわ)する

2) 送(おく)っていただいたにもつがとどいた

3) なるべくはやくおへんじをいただきたい

2 1) すぐ会社(かいしゃ)にもどる

2) 鈴木(すずき)さんに連絡(れんらく)する

3) 会議(かいぎ)におくれない

II. 1) 言(い)え　言(い)うな

2) 話(はな)せ　話(はな)すな

3) 買(か)え　買(か)うな

4) まがれ　まがるな

5) 開(あ)けろ　開(あ)けるな

6) 見(み)せろ　見(み)せるな

7) かたづけろ、かたづけるな

8) やめろ、やめるな

9) 持(も)ってこい　持(も)ってくるな

10) 勉強(べんきょう)しろ　勉強(べんきょう)するな

III. reporter: Excuse me, may I ask you a few questions? Where are you going today?
traveler: Italy.
reporter: About how many days will you stay there?
traveler: Two weeks.
reporter: Is that so. Take care.

Lesson 12

Grammar & Pattern Practice

I. 1) 悪(わる)いですから　2) 知(し)っていますから
3) どりょくしたからです　4) 終(お)わりますから

II. 1) です。　2) でしょうか。　3) のです。　4) でした。

III. 1) 書(か)かなければなりません。　2) 入(はい)ってはいけません。
3) わすれてしまいました。　4) ならべておいてください。

QUIZ 4

I. 1) と　2) と　3) は　4) に　5) から

II. 1) 2　2) 1　3) 4　4) 3　5) 3

III. 1) いらっしゃいます　2) まいります　3) いたします
4) ごぞんじです　5) 作(つく)れ

IV. 1) 1　2) 3　3) 4　4) 1　5) 2

V. 1) おんがく　ちゃ
2) あね　いしゃ　おとうと
3) えいご　じょせい　ふ
4) ぎんこう　れんらく

UNIT 5

QUIZ 5

I. 1) も　2) まで　3) も／か　4) を　5) まで

II. 1) 4　2) 3　3) 2　4) 3　5) 1

III. 1) 生(う)まれた　2) 着(つ)く　3) している　4) 上手(じょうず)な　5) 上(あ)がって

IV. 1) 2　2) 2　3) 3　4) 2　5) 2

V. 1) しょうがつ　かいがい
2) しあい　ちゅうし
3) りゅうがくせい　きじ
4) はる　あき　だいひょう　あつ

Japanese-English Glossary

Note: This list contains nearly all of the vocabulary introduced in the text, with page numbers given for first appearances. Omitted are words introduced in Books I and II (which can be found in the glossaries of those texts), certain idiomatic phrases, and certain particles and proper nouns. Verbs are given in their dictionary forms, with the exception of certain honorific and polite expressions.

The following abbreviations are used:

intr.	intransitive (verb)
R2	Regular II verb
tr.	transitive (verb)

ああ: yes, 22
あいうえおじゅん／あいうえお順: *a-i-u-e-o* order, 14
あいかわらず／相変わらず: same as always, 224
あいことば／合い言葉: slogan, catchphrase, 155
あいさつ／挨拶: address, speech, 33
あいする／愛する: love, 249
あいだ／間: while, 140; ～のあいだに／～の間に between, 123
あいにく: unfortunately, contrary to what one would like, 187
あう／合う: fit, go well with, 78
あう／遭う: meet, 72
あかワイン／赤ワイン: red wine, 179
あけましておめでとうございます／明けましておめでとうございます: happy New Year, 219
あさばん／朝晩: morning and evening, 53
あじ／味: taste, 10
あしおと／足音: footstep, 17
あす／明日: tomorrow, 140
あたためる／暖める: (R2) warm up, 14
あちこち: here and there, all throughout, 81
あとかたづけ／後片付け: putting things away, clearing up after, 160
あな／穴: hole, 32; あながあく／穴があく a hole opens up, 32
アナウンス: announcement, 13
あなた: Dear (said by a wife to her husband), 184
アニメ: anime, animation, 13
あまい／甘い: easy, lax, 161
あまる／余る: be left over, 102
あら: oh, 78
あらし／嵐: storm, 108
あるからだ: be because there is . . . , 210
アルバイト: part-time job, 90
あわてる／慌てる: (R2) move hastily, become flustered, 149
あんしん(な)／安心(な): reassuring, safe, 49
あんないず／案内図: guide map, 79
あんなに: that many, so much, 221
あんまり: COLLOQUIAL not much, 223

いえ: COLLOQUIAL no, 96
いか: squid, 155
いがい／以外: other than, besides, 244
いかす／生かす: put to use, take advantage of, 94
いきかえり／行き帰り: going to and returning from, 155
いけん／意見: opinion, 74
いし／医師: doctor, 94
いじめる: (R2) bully, pick on, 146
いただきます／頂きます: HUMBLE receive 179
いちどう／一同: everyone, all, 249
いちにんまえ／一人前: order (of food) for one person, 38
いっしゅ／一種: a kind (of), a type (of), 3
いっそう: ever more, all the more, 249
いったい／一体: what- (how-, when-, etc.) ever, 140
いっぱい: full, 86
いっぱいで: at the end of, 135
いつものように: as usual, like always, 39
いどうする／移動する: move, transfer, 194
いのる／祈る: pray, 218
いま／居間: living room, 72
いまごろ／今ごろ: now, at this point, 194
いみ／意味: meaning, 155
イメージ: image, 186
いや(な)／嫌(な): unpleasant, 17
いらい／以来: since, 265
イラスト: illustration, 22
いる／要る: need, 55
いろんな／色んな: COLLOQUIAL various, all kinds (of), 53
いわい／祝い: celebration, 222; いわう／祝う celebrate, 218
インド: India, 12
インドネシア: Indonesia, 12

うーん: hmm, let's see, 42
ううん: COLLOQUIAL no, 242
ウェイター: waiter, 189
うえる／植える: (R2) plant, 86
うかがう／伺う: HUMBLE ask, 73; うかがいたいこと／伺いたいこと HUMBLE something I want to ask, 73
うかる／受かる: pass (an exam), 94
うけとる／受け取る: receive, 123
うそ／嘘: lie, falsehood, 11
うたがう／疑う: suspect, 234
うまい: COLLOQUIAL delicious, 40; good at, skilled, 31; うまくいく go well, 223
うみだす／生み出す: give rise to, engender, 210
ウメ／梅: plum, 110
うりば／売り場: selling space, store/booth space, 194
うんざりです: be sick (of), be fed up, 49

えいきょう／影響: effect, influence, 101
えだ／枝: branch, 41
えつらん／閲覧: viewing, perusal, 80
えつらんしつ／閲覧室: reading room, 79
えと: Oriental zodiac (twelve-year cycle in which each year is named after a different animal), 219
エネルギー: energy, 114
えび: shrimp, 189
エピソード: episode, story, 47
える／得る: (R2) gain, earn, 94
えんきする／延期する: postpone, 43

おいしそうに: as if finding something delicious, 27
おいでいただく: HONORIFIC/HUMBLE come (to where one is), 174
おいわい／お祝い: celebration, 222
おうえん／応援: cheering, 109
おうじ／王子: prince, 22
おうぼしゃ／応募者: applicant, 95
おおきな／大きな: big, 19
おおくの／多くの: many, 210
おおごえ／大声: loud voice, 155
オーブン: oven, 78
おおみそか／大晦日: New Year's Eve, 220

サイト: website, 110
サイレン: siren, 20
サイン: sign, signboard. 50
サインかい／サイン会: autograph session, 13
さかん（な）／盛ん（な）: thriving, 47
〜さき／〜先: destination, receiving end, 39
さぎ／詐欺: scam, swindle, 147; さぎにあう／詐欺にあう be deceived in a scam, 147
さきつづける／咲き続ける: continue to bloom, 101
さきほど／先程: a little while ago, 194
さく／咲く: bloom, flower, 41
ささやか（な）: modest, 255
さしあげます／差し上げます: (R2) HUMBLE give (to someone else), 179
〜させていただく: HUMBLE be allowed to do, 173
さっか／作家: author, 13
さっそく／早速: right away, 66; さっそくですが／早速ですが to begin right away, without further ado, 66
さばく／砂漠: desert, 3
さびしい／寂しい: lonely, 225
サプライズ・パーティー: surprise party, 259
サポーター: supporter, fan, 109
サラリーマン: businessman, 54
サル／猿: monkey, 35
さわぐ／騒ぐ: make noise, cause a commotion, 157
さんぎょう／産業: industry, 113

じ／字: handwriting, character, print, 73
しあわせ（な）／幸せ（な）: happy, blissful, 40
しおからい／塩辛い: salty, 18
しか／歯科: dentist's office, 131
しかい／司会: emcee, 249
しかる: scold, 146
じき／時期: time, period, 210
しげん／資源: (natural) resource, 111
じけん／事件: incident, crime, 148
ししゃちょう／支社長: branch president, 33
ししょ／司書: librarian, 94
じじょう／事情: situation, circumstance, 140
システムアナリスト: systems analyst, 94
システムエンジニア: systems engineer, 94
しぜんのうほう／自然農法: organic agriculture, 86
したしい／親しい: close, on familiar terms (with), 93
したしむ／親しむ: love, be fond of, 249
しっ: shh!, 3
じっか／実家: parents' house, 221
しっかり: diligently, 204
じっかん／実感: feeling of reality, 101; じっかんがわく／実感がわく seem real, 101
じっさいに／実際に: actually, 264
じっと: patiently, quietly, 23
しつもんする／質問する: ask a question, 66
しつれいですが／失礼ですが: excuse me, but . . . , 177
しないと: must do, need to do, 114
しなもの／品物: goods, merchandise, 239
じはんき／自販機: vending machine, 54
しま／島: island, 112
しまった（あ、しまった！）: oh no, oops! how stupid of me!, 203
シミュレーションする: run a simulation, 110
しめくくる／締めくくる: wrap up, end, 219
〜しゃ／〜者: -er, -or, -ant (person who performs a certain job), 94
しゃかい／社会: society, 102
ジャケット: jacket, 70
しゃしんか／写真家: photographer, 97
ジャズ・バー: jazz bar, 203
シャトー: chateau, 20
じゃない？: isn't it . . . ?, 3
しゃないメール／社内メール: employee mailing list, 93
じゃまする／邪魔する: hinder, get in the way (of), 144
しゃりょう／車両: train car, 13
しゃりょうこしょう／車両故障: train-car breakdown, 13
しゅうかん／習慣: custom, practice, 210
しゅうぎぶくろ／祝儀袋: celebratory envelope, 244
しゅうしごう／修士号: master's degree, 94
シュートする: shoot (a ball), 198
しゅうにゅう／収入: income, 94
〜しゅうねん／〜周年: -th anniversary, 249
じゅうばこ／重箱: stacked boxes, 218
じゅうぶん（な）／十分（な）／充分（な）: sufficient, enough, 102
しゅうりする／修理する: repair, 130
しゅざい／取材: interview, news coverage, 234
〜しゅっしん／〜出身: from ——, 110
しゅっせきする／出席する: attend, 128
しゅっちょうさき／出張先: destination of a business trip, 39
しゅっちょうちゅう／出張中: on a business trip, 12
しゅっちょうになる／出張になる: have a business trip coming up, 39
しゅってんする／出店する: put out a store/booth, exhibit, 173
しゅりゅう／主流: mainstream, 219
〜じゅん／〜順: order of ——, 14
しゅんじゅう／春秋: spring and autumn, 252
しょうが: ginger, 18
しょうがくせい／小学生: elementary school kid, 76
しょうがない: there is nothing one can do about it, 224
じょうきょう／状況: situation, circumstance, 149
しょうけんアナリスト／証券アナリスト: investment analyst, 94
しょうたいする／招待する: invite, 143
じょうだん／冗談: joke, 158
しょうひりょう／消費量: amount of consumption, 210
じょうぶ（な）／丈夫（な）: sturdy, strong, 35
じょうむ／常務: managing director, 173
しょうわ／昭和: the Showa era (1926–1989), 97
しょくにん／職人: craftsperson, 75
しょくひん／食品: food product, 27
しょくぶつ／植物: plant, 72
じょげん／助言: advice, 190
しょぞくさき／所属先: affiliation, 80
しょっき／食器: tableware, 222
ショッピングセンター: shopping center, 140
しんこく（な）／深刻（な）: serious, grave, 101
しんさつ／診察: medical examination, 130
しんじる／信じる: (R2) believe, 92
しんせいひん／新製品: new product, 11
しんねん／新年: New Year, 218
しんぱいする／心配する: worry, 157
しんぶんしゃ／新聞社: newspaper company, 234

すうねん／数年: number of years, 56
スカート: skirt, 51
すぎ／過ぎ: too, 57; すぎる／過ぎる do too much, 204
スキーじょう／スキー場: ski resort, 110
すこしして／少しして: after a little while, 4
ずじょう／頭上: overhead, 205
すすむ／進む: progress, proceed, 51
すすめる／勧める: (R2) offer, urge, 27
スタイル: style, 49
スタッフ: staff, 73
すっかり: entirely, completely, 86

English-Japanese Glossary

Note: This glossary includes only words and expressions introduced in this text. For the Japanese equivalents of words introduced in Books I and II, refer to the glossaries in those volumes. For the sake of simplicity, honorific and humble Japanese expressions have been omitted, as have a number of idiomatic expressions, proper nouns, and so on that do not fit well anywhere in an A to Z list.

The following abbreviations are used:

intr.	intransitive (verb)
n.	noun
tr.	transitive (verb)
v.	verb

110: (emergency phone number) １１０ばん／１１０番, 148

ability: ちから／力, 86
ability: のうりょく／能力, 94
able: be able to go でれる／出れる, 225; become able to ようになる, 47, 50
abysmal: さいあく(な)／最悪(な), 260
according to ——: 〜によると, 12
accustom oneself to: なれる／慣れる, 264
acquaintance: ちじん／知人, 187
actually: じっさいに／実際に, 264
addition, in: なお, 252
address: あいさつ, 33
advance, in: はやめに／早めに, 257
advertisement: こうこく／広告, 210
advertising: せんでん／宣伝, 210
advice: じょげん／助言, 190
affiliation: しょぞくさき／所属先, 80
after: after a little while すこしして／少しして, 4; after all けっきょく／結局, 150; after that そのご／その後, 210
age: としをとる／年を取る, 51
agriculture: のうぎょう／農業, 129
air: たいき／大気, 111
all: (everyone) いちどう／一同, 249; all the more いっそう, 249; all throughout あちこち, 81
alligator: ワニ, 21
allowed to do, be: 〜させていただく, 173
also: また／又, 102
always: かならず／必ず, 114
amazing: ふしぎ(な)／不思議(な), 19
animation: アニメ, 13
announcement: アナウンス, 13
annoying: めいわく(な)／迷惑(な), 55
annual: ねんかん／年間, 210
answer: こたえる／答える, 158
-ant: (person who performs a certain job) 〜しゃ／〜者, 94
any case, in: とにかく, 148
anything: なんでも／何でも, 53
anyway: とにかく, 148
anywhere: どっか, 221
apart, be: はなれる／離れる, 218
apparently: らしい, 27, 32
apple orchard: りんごえん／りんご園, 66
applicant: おうぼしゃ／応募者, 95
appointment: まちあわせ／待ち合わせ, 47
approach: ちかづく／近づく, 109
architect: けんちくし／建築士, 94
arise: わく, 101
arrange: (neatly in a row) ならべる／並べる, 14
arrangement to meet: まちあわせ／待ち合わせ, 47
article: きじ／記事, 49
as: (in the capacity of ——) 〜として, 47; (as some process takes place) 〜につれて, 51; as . . . as possible なるべく, 197; as is このまま, 112; as much as possible できるだけ／出来るだけ, 66; as usual いつものように, 39
ask: たずねる／尋ねる, 80; ask for directions みちをきく／道を聞く, 155; ask too much むりをいう／無理を言う, 132; please ask おたずねください／お尋ねください, 80
at all: まったく／全く, 66
at this point: いまごろ／今ごろ, 194
atmosphere: たいき／大気, 111
attachment: べってん／別添, 252
attend: (school) かよう／通う, 90; (a meeting, etc.) しゅっせきする／出席する, 128
auspicious day: きちじつ／吉日, 255
author: さっか／作家, 13
autograph session: サインかい／サイン会, 13
average: へいきん／平均, 101

babysitter: ベビーシッター, 161
bad: まずい, 151; bad at へた(な)／下手(な), 146
bag: ふくろ／袋, 222
baked apple: やきりんご／焼きりんご, 78
barkeeper: マスター, 96
basically: きほんてきに／基本的に, 244
bass: ベース, 203
battery: でんち／電池, 37
be able to: ことができる, 80
bean: まめ／豆, 218
bear: クマ／熊, 15
beautician: びようし／美容師, 94
because: all because of —— 〜のせいで, 49; be because —— 〜からだ, 210, ためだ, 243; just because —— 〜からって, 21
beginnings: はじまり／始まり, 210
believe: しんじる／信じる, 92
besides: いがい／以外, 244; ほかに, 218
between: 〜のあいだに／〜の間に, 123
big: おおきな／大きな, 19
bill: せいきゅうしょ／請求書, 151
bird: とり／鳥, 3
bite: かむ, 146
bitter: にがい／苦い, 18
black: くろ／黒, 244; (of coffee) ブラック, 77
blissful: しあわせ(な)／幸せ(な), 40
bloom: さく／咲く, 41; continue to bloom さきつづける／咲き続ける, 101
booth space: うりば／売り場, 194
boring: たいくつ(な)／退屈(な), 145
bowknot: ちょうむすび／蝶結び, 244
boyfriend: ボーイフレンド, 135
brake: ブレーキ, 149
branch: えだ／枝, 41
branch president: ししゃちょう／支社長, 33
break: (tr.) (ruin) こわす／壊す, 9; (intr.) (of bone, branch) おれる／折れる, 41, (tr.) (bone, branch) おる／折る, 188 [*see also* smash, snap]

breakdown: こしょう／故障, 13
bring: もっていく／持って行く, 129
broadcast: ほうそうする／放送する, 143
bud: (n.) つぼみ, 256; (v.) つぼみがつく, 256
build: たてる／建てる, 142
bully: いじめる, 146
bump (into): ぶつける, 147, (from behind) ついとつする／追突する, 149
burn: (of food) こげる／焦げる, 17
business trip: be on a business trip しゅっちょうちゅう／出張中, 12; business trip destination しゅっちょうさき／出張先, 39; have a business trip coming up しゅっちょうになる／出張になる, 39
businessman: サラリーマン, 54
busyness: (ご) たぼう／(ご) 多忙, 249
but: ながら, 252
buzzer: ブザー, 155
by ——: ～によって, 142
by the way: ところで, 3

cage: ケージ, 4
called ——: ～という／～と言う, 47
call out (to): こえをかける／声をかける, 155
calorie: カロリー, 27
campaign: キャンペーン, 210
can: ことができる, 80
cancellation: キャンセル, 49
candle: キャンドル, 35
canned food: かんづめ／缶詰, 56
capital: みやこ／都, 143
capture: つかまえる／捕まえる, 4
carbon dioxide: にさんかたんそ／二酸化炭素, 111
carry: はこぶ／運ぶ, 127
carry out: おこなう／行う, 143
cat: ネコ／猫, 3; cat food: キャットフード, 4
catchphrase: あいことば／合い言葉, 155
cause: げんいん／原因, 111
caution: ちゅういする／注意する, 161
celebrate: いわう／祝う, 218; celebration (お) いわい／(お) 祝い, 222; celebratory envelope しゅうぎぶくろ／祝儀袋, 244
cellular phone: けいたいでんわ／携帯電話, 155
centimeter: センチ, 112
certainly: きっと, 7
chance: チャンス, 206
change: (batteries, etc.) とりかえる／取り替える／取り換える, 37; change of pace: きばらし／気晴らし, 225
character: (letter) じ／字, 73; もじ／文字, 129
chateau: シャトー, 20
cheat: だます, 146
check out: (of a hotel) チェックアウトする, 140
cheering: おうえん／応援, 109
chestnut,: くり／栗218
chew: かむ, 146
chocolate: チョコ, 210
circulation: (in a library, etc.) かしだし／貸し出し, 79
circumstance: じじょう／事情, 140; じょうきょう／状況, 149
city: とし／都市, 115
class: きょうしつ／教室, 160; classroom きょうしつ／教室, 9
cleaning: かたづけ／片付け, 132
clear: become clear (of facts) はっきりする, 234; clearing up after あとかたづけ／後片付け, 160
clearly: はっきり, 260
climate: きこう／気候, 111
close: (on familiar terms) したしい／親しい, 93
cloudy: くもり／曇り, 108; become cloudy, cloud up くもる／曇る, 108
coffee shop: きっさてん／喫茶店, 145
collapse: たおれる／倒れる, 41
college years: がくせいじだい／学生時代, 95
colorful: カラフル (な), 244
combine: くみあわせる／組み合わせる, 78
come across: みかける／見かける, 47
come into existence: できる／出来る, 123
come into one's possession: てにはいる／手に入る, 123
come off: とれる／取れる, 41
come through: (be communicated) つたわる／伝わる, 269
come to think of it: そういえば, 22
come up: できる／出来る, 123
come up with: おもいつく／思い付く, 256
comic book: まんが／漫画, 54
commemoration: きねん／記念, 234
commotion, cause a: さわぐ／騒ぐ, 157
commute (to): かよう／通う, 161
complaint: ぐち／愚痴, 165
completely: すっかり, 86
computer catalog: けんさくようパソコン／検索用パソコン, 79
computer game: コンピューターゲーム, 11
concentrate: せんねんする／専念する, 95
concern: なやみ／悩み, 164; be concerned (about) かんしんがある／関心がある, 74
condition: (physical) ぐあい／具合, 157
confirm: かくにんする／確認する, 190
conserve: せつやくする／節約する, 102
consider: けんとうする／検討する, 173
considerably: かなり, 9
construction: こうじ／工事, 49; under construction こうじちゅう／工事中, 49
consumption, amount of: しょうひりょう／消費量, 210
content: ないよう／内容, 127
contest: コンテスト, 75
continue to ——: ～ていく, 47, 51
contrary to what one would like: あいにく, 187
conversation, sound of: はなしごえ／話し声, 17
cook: (licensed cook) ちょうりし／調理師, 94
cooking, someone's own: てりょうり／手料理, 258
cool down: ひやす／冷やす, 14
cord: ひも, 244
correct: ただしい／正しい, 53; that's correct そのとおり／その通り, 66
cost: コスト, 9; cost performance コストパフォーマンス, 102
countermeasure: たいさく／対策, 111
cover for: かわる／代わる, 123
craftsperson: しょくにん／職人, 75
crime: (accident, incident) じけん／事件, 148; (criminal act) はんざい／犯罪, 155
crocodile: ワニ, 21
crumble: くずれる／崩れる, 41
cry: (of animal) なく／鳴く, 3; (of person) なく／泣く, 17; sound of crying なきごえ／泣き声, 17
curator: がくげいいん／学芸員, 94
curry: カレー, 19
custom: しゅうかん／習慣, 210

damage: わるくする／悪くする, 85
dangerous: きけん (な)／危険 (な), 9
date and time: にちじ／日時, 252
Dear: あなた, 184
decade: ～ねんだい／～年代, 55
deceive: だます, 146
decrease: へらす／減らす, 114
definitely: きっと, 7; はっきり, 260
degrees Celsius: ～どC／～度C, 78
delicious: うまい, 40
dentist's office: しか／歯科, 131
deposit: (of money) ふりこみ／振り込み, 52
desert: さばく／砂漠, 3
destination: ～さき／～先, 39
detailed: くわしい／詳しい, 149
develop: はったつする／発達する, 113; developed country せんしんこく／先進国, 111; developing country とじょうこく／途上国, 111

-or: (person who performs a certain job) 〜しゃ／〜者, 94
order: (n.) (of food, for one person) いちにんまえ／一人前, 38; (v.) (place an order) ちゅうもんする／注文する, 78; in order to ために, 85, 90; order of —— 〜じゅん／〜順, 14
orderly: きそくただしい／規則正しい, 53
ordinarily: ふだん／普段, 210
organic agriculture: しぜんのうほう／自然農法, 86
other: ほか, 161, ほかに, 218; in other words つまり, 244; other than いがい／以外, 244; the other day このあいだ／この間, 55
ought to: はず, 27, 31
oven: オーブン, 78
overhead: ずじょう／頭上, 205
owner: (of a pet) かいぬし／飼い主, 4
oyster: かき, 189

paper: (thesis, essay) ろんぶん／論文, 201
parent: おや／親, 155; parents' house: じっか／実家, 221
parking violation: ちゅうしゃいはん／駐車違反, 147
partner: パートナー, 47
part-time job: アルバイト, 90
pass: (be successful in: an exam, etc.) うかる／受かる, 94; (elapse: of time) たつ／経つ, 256
pass away: なくなる／亡くなる, 47
pass out: (distribute) くばる／配る, 210
patiently: じっと, 23
pedestrian: ほこうしゃ／歩行者, 205
peel: (n.) (skin of fruit) かわ／皮, 78; (v.) むく, 78
people: かたがた／方々, 249
period: じき／時期, 210
person: person in charge かかりのひと／係の人, 80, たんとうしゃ／担当者, 194; person responsible せきにんしゃ（のかた）／責任者（の方）, 234; the person himself/herself ほんにん／本人, 76
perusal: えつらん／閲覧, 80
pesticide: のうやく／農薬, 66; pesticide-free むのうやくの／無農薬の), 66
pet food: ペット・フード, 249; pet-food development department ペットしょくひんかいはつぶ／ペット食品開発部, 27
photographer: しゃしんか／写真家, 97
pick on: いじめる, 146
pickpocket: (n.) すり, 147; (v.) する, 139; get pickpocketed すられる, 139
pile up: つもる／積もる, 108
place: ばしょ／場所, 31
plan: きかく／企画, 206; (intention) つもり, 123
plane ticket: こうくうけん／航空券, 139
plant: (n.) しょくぶつ／植物, 72, plants (appreciated primarily for their leaves) かんようしょくぶつ／観葉植物, 81; (v.) うえる／植える, 86
plenty (of): たっぷり, 77
plum: ウメ／梅, 110
police: けいさつ／警察, 4
policy: ほうしん／方針, 106
polite: ていねい（な）／丁寧（な）, 234
popular: にんきの／人気の, 32; become popular はやる, 54; popularity にんき／人気, 32
post: (put up) はる／貼る, 72
poster: ポスター, 155
postpone: えんきする／延期する, 43
potluck: もちより／持ち寄り, 259
pour: かける, 78
power: ちから／力, 86
practice: しゅうかん／習慣, 210
praise: ほめる／褒める, 143
pray: いのる／祈る, 218
premium: こうきゅう／高級, 210
present, at: げんざい／現在, 249
press conference: きしゃかいけん／記者会見, 234
prevent: ふせぐ／防ぐ, 102
price: ねだん／値段, 51; price rise: ねあがり／値上がり, 115
prince: おうじ／王子, 22
print: (characters on paper) じ／字, 73
private car: マイカー, 115
probably: たぶん, 3
proceed: すすむ／進む, 51
produce: せいさんする／生産する, 66
product: せいひん／製品, 11
program: (TV or radio) ばんぐみ／番組, 143
progress: (move forward) すすむ／進む, 51
pronunciation: はつおん／発音, 148
property: とち／土地, 51
proposal: きかく／企画, 206; written proposal: きかくしょ／企画書, 241
protect: まもる／守る, 155
public accountant, certified: こうにんかいけいし／公認会計士, 94
put: put effort (into) ちからをいれる／力を入れる, 155; put on sale はつばいする／発売する, 219; put to use いかす／生かす, 94; putting things away: あとかたづけ／後片付け, 160
put together: くみあわせる／組み合わせる, 78
put up: (post) はる／貼る, 72
qualification: のうりょく／能力, 94
question, ask a: しつもんする／質問する, 66
quietly: じっと, 23; そっと, 4
quite: なかなか, 133; (quite a lot of) けっこう, 21

race: レース, 96
rapidly: どんどん, 51
rare: めずらしい／珍しい, 3
rather: かなり, 9
reach: (a certain time or stage) むかえる／迎える, 249
reading room: えつらんしつ／閲覧室, 79
reality, feeling of: じっかん／実感, 101
rear-end: ついとつする／追突する, 149
reason: りゆう／理由, 212; わけ／訳, 234; for this/that reason ですから, 57; for what reason どういうわけで／どういう訳で, 234
reassuring: あんしん（な）／安心（な）, 49
receive: うけとる／受け取る, 123; receiving end 〜さき／〜先, 39
recent situation: きんきょう／近況, 219
reception: (desk) レセプション, 33; (party) ひろうえん／披露宴, 222
red wine: あかワイン／赤ワイン, 179
refuse: ことわる／断る, 234
regarding ——: 〜にかんする／〜に関する, 56
register: とうろくする／登録する, 14; registration fee にゅうかいきん／入会金, 151
regret, feeling of: (for imposing on someone) きょうしゅく／恐縮, 252
regular: きそくただしい／規則正しい, 53
regulate: きせいする／規制する, 111; regulation: きそく／規則, 53
rehabilitation: リハビリ, 50
relating to ——: 〜かんれん／〜関連, 47
release: かいじょする／解除する, 38
remain: のこる／残る, 97
remember: おもいだす／思い出す, 55
removed, be: はなれる／離れる, 218
repair: しゅうりする／修理する, 130
repeat: くりかえす／繰り返す, 11
replace: (batteries, etc.) とりかえる／取り替える／取り換える, 37
report: (v.) (complain about to police) とどける／届ける, 4; (n.) (statement) ほうこく／報告, 219; reporter: リポーター, 200
representative: だいひょう／代表, 93
reputation: ひょうばん／評判, 11
request: リクエスト, 257
research: けんきゅうする／研究する, 66

systems engineer: システムエンジニア, 94

tableware: しょっき／食器, 222
take: (bring) もっていく／持って行く, 129; (steal) とる, 139; take advantage of いかす／生かす, 94; take care きをつける／気を付ける, 72
take over: (work in someone else's place) かわる／代わる, 123
talk: talk (to) はなしかける／話しかける, 165; talk over はなしあう／話し合う, 155
tart: タルト, 257
taste: あじ／味, 10
tax accountant: ぜいりし／税理士, 94
teaching materials: きょうざい／教材, 91
tedious: たいくつ（な）／退屈（な）, 145
tell: (inform) つたえる／伝える, 33
temperature: きおん／気温, 101
ten percent: ～わり／～割, 56
-th anniversary: ～しゅうねん／～周年, 249
thank you for your time/assistance: おせわになります／お世話になります, 66
thanks to ——: ～のおかげで, 49
therefore: (therefore) だから, 109
thesis: ろんぶん／論文, 201
think of: おもいつく／思い付く, 256
this one: こっちの, 40
thriving: さかん（な）／盛ん（な）, 47
through ——: ～にて, 252
thunder: かみなり／雷, 17
tie: むすぶ／結ぶ, 244; way of tying: むすびかた／結び方, 244
time: ところ, 174; さい／際, 189; じき／時期, 210; せつ／節, 267; this time こんかい／今回, 256; time flies/passes quickly はやいもので／早いもので, 256
to: (in order to) ために, 85, 90; (for ——) ～にとって, 101, 102
today: ほんじつ／本日, 174
tomorrow: あす／明日, 140
tonight: こんや／今夜, 13
too: すぎ／過ぎ, 57; do too much すぎる／過ぎる, 204
traffic: つうこう／通行, 54; to-left traffic ひだりがわつうこう／左側通行, 54
train car: しゃりょう／車両, 13; train-car breakdown しゃりょうこしょう／車両故障, 13
transfer: (of money) ふりこみ／振り込み, 52; (move elsewhere) いどうする／移動する, 194
translate: やくす／訳す, 199; translator ほんやくしゃ／翻訳者, 94
trap: つかまえる／捕まえる, 4
traveler: りょこうしゃ／旅行者, 200
treat: (to a meal) ごちそうする, 123; get treated (to a meal) ごちそうになる, 163
trouble: (concern) なやみ／悩み, 164; cause/give (someone) trouble めいわくをかける／迷惑をかける, 187; take the trouble to do わざわざ～する, 132
truly: まことに／誠に, 252
truth be told . . . : ほんとうは／本当は, 123
tsunami: つなみ／津波, 12
turn: ばん／番, 222
twenty-first century: ２１せいき／２１世紀, 101
type (of), a: いっしゅ／一種, 3
typhoon: たいふう／台風, 108

understand, from what I: そう, 3, 12
undertake: とりくむ／取り組む, 249
undo: ほどく, 244
unfortunately: あいにく, 187
unintentionally: つい, 114
United States: べいこく／米国, 173
unpleasant: いや（な）／嫌（な）, 17
unskilled: へた（な）／下手（な）, 146
unusual: めずらしい／珍しい, 3
using ——: ～にて, 252
usually: ふだん／普段, 210; ふつう／普通, 3

valuable: きちょう（な）／貴重（な）, 185
various: いろんな／色んな, 53
vegetarian: ベジタリアン, 86
vending machine: じはんき／自販機, 54
very: とっても, 23
veterinary clinic: どうぶつびょういん／動物病院, 47
viewing: えつらん／閲覧, 80
visit: (to someone who is sick or injured) おみまい／お見舞い, 133

waiter: ウェイター, 189
want: (when speaking of someone else) ほしがる, 159; want to do (speaking of someone else) たがる, 159
warm up: あたためる／暖める, 14
warm winter: だんとう／暖冬, 110
warming: おんだんか／温暖化, 101
warn: ちゅういする／注意する, 161
waste: むだにする／無駄にする, 114
wasteful: もったいない, 114
watch over: みまもる／見守る, 255
way to do, go out of one's: わざわざ～する, 132
website: サイト, 110
welcome: むかえる／迎える, 249
Western sweets: ようがし／洋菓子, 210
what: what could it be? なんだろう／何だろう, 3; what kind of どういう, 234
whatever: いったい／一体, 140
while: (during the time that) あいだ／間, 140; (while someone does something . . .; at the same time that) ながら, 86, 91; a little while ago さきほど／先程, 194
whispers, in: ひそひそ, 19
whole, the: ぜんたい／全体, 56
why: なぜ, 85; that's why ですから, 57
widespread, become: ふきゅうする／普及する, 49
wind: かぜ／風, 13; wind blows かぜがふく／風が吹く, 108; wind starts to blow かぜがでる／風が出る, 109
windowpane: まどガラス／窓ガラス, 148
wine cellar: ワインセラー, 20
wish for: ねがう／願う, 218
with ——: ～との, 96
wither: かれる／枯れる, 145
without ——: (-free) む～／無～, 66; without fail かならず／必ず, 114; without further ado さっそくですが／早速ですが, 66
word: ことば／言葉, 11; a word (= a few words) ひとこと／一言, 249
worry: しんぱいする／心配する, 157
worst possible: さいあく（な）／最悪（な）, 260
wrap up: (a letter, etc.) しめくくる／締めくくる, 219
write in/down: きにゅうする／記入する, 80; please write in: ごきにゅうください／ご記入ください, 80

years: number of years すうねん／数年, 56; these past few years ここすうねん／ここ数年, 56
yes: ああ, 22
young: わかい／若い, 214

zodiac, Oriental: えと, 219
zoo: どうぶつえん／動物園, 127

Index

(改訂第3版)コミュニケーションのための日本語　第3巻　テキスト
JAPANESE FOR BUSY PEOPLE III: Revised 3rd Edition

2007年9月26日　第1刷発行

著　者　社団法人 国際日本語普及協会
挿　画　角 愼作
発行者　富田 充
発行所　講談社インターナショナル株式会社
〒112-8652 東京都文京区音羽 1-17-14
電話　03-3944-6493(編集部)
03-3944-6492(マーケティング部・業務部)
ホームページ　www.kodansha-intl.com
印刷・製本所　大日本印刷株式会社

落丁本・乱丁本は購入書店名を明記のうえ、講談社インターナショナル業務部宛にお送りください。送料小社負担にてお取替えします。なお、この本についてのお問い合わせは、編集部宛にお願いいたします。

定価はカバーに表示してあります。

Printed in Japan
ISBN 978-4-7700-3011-5